RAYMOND R̶O̶S̶E̶LIEP

MAN OF A̶R̶T̶ ̶W̶H̶O̶ ̶L̶O̶V̶E̶S̶ THE ROSE

Donna Bauerly

THE HAIKU FOUNDATION
2015

Raymond Roseliep: Man of Art Who Loves the Rose

© 2015 Donna Bauerly

Cover, book design, and typography by Charles Trumbull
Rose ornament by Cynthia Henderson

ISBN 978-0-9826951-1-1

Printed in the United States of America

THE HAIKU FOUNDATION
www.thehaikufoundation.org

CONTENTS

ACKNOWLEDGMENTS

Many thanks to the haiku community: Charles Trumbull, my outstanding editor, to whom I can never convey enough thanks; to the officers and members of the Haiku Society of America who have been so supportive over the years; to all at *Modern Haiku* who have offered assistance, starting with the current editor, Paul Miller, Modern Haiku Press editor Lee Gurga, and Webmaster Randy Brooks; to those at the Haiku Foundation, especially Jim Kacian, Dave Russo, and Billie Wilson; to the American Haiku Archives, especially Kevin Starr and Jerry Kilbride, founders of this inspired institution.

I owe special thanks to my community and colleagues at Loras College, who have given endless direction and ongoing assistance: Jim Collins, president; Joyce Meldrem, director of the Academic Resource Center and literary executor pro tempore for Raymond Roseliep; Robert Klein, Loras Library director, 1969–2004; Michael Gibson, College Archivist and Director of the Center for Dubuque History; Tim Olson, photographer who assists at the Center for Dubuque History; Cheryl Jacobsen, provost and academic dean; Kevin Koch, chair, Division of Language and Literature; and to all my colleagues in the Department of English; to the Rev. Daniel Rogers, literary executor for Roseliep from 1983 to 2015; to Msgr. Robert Vogl, final executor for Roseliep's estate; and to Rev. Loras Otting, former archivist for the Archdiocese of Dubuque.

Roseliep's friends and correspondents have been most generous in patiently answering my myriad questions and granting me permission to use their words in this biography. In this regard I would single out Elizabeth Searle Lamb, decades-long friend of Father Ray, and her daughter and literary executor Carolyn Lamb. Special friends and former students of Roseliep's include Thomas Reiter, Bill Pauly, David Rabe, Dennis Schmitz, Edward Rielly, Rev. Robert Beck, Vincent and Denise Heinrichs, Wanda Wallis, and David Locher; to Sr. Gracia Schmitt and other Franciscan sister poets and friends of Fr. Roseliep, and Msgr. Francis Friedl, his classmate and friend.

The editors and publishers who supported Raymond Roseliep and pushed him to ever greater accomplishments form a special category to be acknowledged. In particular I would like to thank Randy and Shirley Brooks of *High/Coo* and Brooks Books, David Dayton of Alembic Press, John Judson of Juniper Press, Nobuo Hirasawa of *Outch,* John McHale of Newman Press, photographers Cyril A. and Renée Travis Reilly, Hal Roth of *Wind Chimes,* Ernest and Cis Stefanik of Rook Press, Felix and Selma Stefanile of Sparrow Press, Ed Rayher of Swamp Press, and Robert Schuler of Uzzano Press.

Thanks also to those who helped with the history and background of our subject: Marcella Anderson Becker, Roseliep family historian, and her daughter Margy Becker; Farley, Iowa, historians Mary Palmer and Joanie Wilwert; and Will Roseliep, great-nephew and only surviving relative of Raymond whom we could interview. Special thanks to Becky Barnhart for her careful reading of the final manuscript. My gratitude also goes to my special friends and former students who provided a bedrock of hope and encouragement along the way.

Every effort has been made to contact each person quoted in this biography as well as the publishers and editors of Raymond Roseliep's work in order to obtain permissions to reuse materials. If we have overlooked anyone, please accept our apologies and our promise to rectify our oversight in any way possible.

for Charles Trumbull

RAYMOND ROSELIEP

MAN OF ART WHO LOVES THE ROSE

A Roseliep Chronology

1917, August 11	Born in Farley, Iowa, to John Albert Roseliep (1874–1939) and Anna Elizabeth Anderson (1884–1967).
1917, August 19	Christened Raymond Francis Roseliep, St. Joseph Church, Farley, Iowa.
1922	Age 5—Enters St. Joseph's Grade School, Farley, Iowa.
1923	Age 6—Moves to Dubuque, Iowa. Attends Sacred Heart School for one year.
1924	Age 7—Moves to 2709 Jackson St., Dubuque.
1926	Moves to 655 Clarke Drive. Attends St. Patrick's School from fourth to eighth grades.
1928	Age 11—First poem published, St. Patrick's School, honoring the arrival of the new archbishop, Francis Beckman.
1931	Graduates from eighth grade, St. Patrick's School.
1931	Enters Columbia Academy (later renamed Loras Academy).
1934	As a senior in high school, wins the three top prizes and all honorable mentions in a poetry contest.
1935	Graduates from Columbia Academy. Receives a one-year tuition scholarship to Columbia College (renamed Loras College in 1939).
1937	Writes words for "A Centennial Hymn" to music by Alphonse Dress.
1939	Receives Bachelor of Arts degree from Loras College.
1940, January 31	Roseliep's father dies.
1939–1943	Attends the Theological Seminary, Catholic University of America, Washington, D.C. He later does graduate work in English there and from Catholic University Extension, Loras College.
1943, June 12	Ordained as a priest for the Archdiocese of Dubuque by Archbishop Francis Beckman at St. Raphael's Cathedral.
1943, June 13	Celebrates first solemn Mass, St. Patrick's Church, Dubuque.

1

1943–1945	Serves as Associate Pastor under Rev. William Cremer, Immaculate Conception Church, Gilbertville, Iowa.
1945–1946	Managing Editor, *The Witness*.
1945–1948	Resident chaplain, St. Anthony's Home, Dubuque, Iowa.
1946–1966	Serves on the faculty of the Department of English, Loras College: 1946–1948, Instructor; 1948–1960, Assistant Professor; 1960–1966, Associate Professor.
1948	Receives Master of Arts in English from Catholic University of America.
1948–1950	Studies for Doctor of Philosophy at the University of Notre Dame, Notre Dame, Ind.
1950–1954	Serves as resident chaplain, Mount St. Francis, Dubuque; teaches religious studies. Finishes graduate studies at the University of Notre Dame and Loras College in absentia.
1952	Elected to membership in the Poetry Society of America.
1954, June	Receives Ph.D. in English Literature from University of Notre Dame with a dissertation titled *Some Letters of Lionel Johnson*.
1954	Resumes teaching at Loras College.
1955–65	Moderator of *The Spokesman*, the literary magazine of Loras College.
1959, April 14	Pictured with Robert Frost at a symposium in Iowa City, Iowa.
1960	Begins writing haiku.
1960, December	Begins correspondence with Katherine Anne Porter.
1961	*The Linen Bands* published by the Newman Press.
1963	Makes a sound recording of poems from *The Linen Bands* for the Library of Congress.
1963	*The Small Rain* published by the Newman Press.
1963–1966	In residence in Beckman Hall, Loras College.
1964, summer	Serves as poet-in-residence at Georgetown University, Washington, D.C.
1965	*Love Makes the Air Light* published by W. W. Norton and Co.
1965, August 10	Places himself in St. Mary's Hospital, Madison, Wis., for treatment of a nervous condition and severe problems with his speech.
1966, June	Upon his release from St. Mary's, appointed by Archbishop Byrne as chaplain at Holy Family Hall, Dubuque; additional duties at Dubuque Country Nursing Home. He remains in residence at Holy Family Hall until his death.

1967, December 6   Roseliep's mother dies.

1967   Meets W. H. Auden at a reading of Auden's poetry in Dubuque.

1968   Receives the Montgomery Poetry Award of the Society of Midland Authors.

1972, October   Visits the Mayo Clinic about his continuing voice difficulties; he is diagnosed as having "nervous tension."

1973   First publication of "Thoreauhaiku," *Thoreau Journal Quarterly.*

1974   *Voyage to the Inland Sea, IV. Essays and Poems,* edited by John Judson, published by the University of Wisconsin—La Crosse.

1976, summer   Begins correspondence with Elizabeth Searle Lamb.

1976   *Flute Over Walden,* his first all-haiku text, published by Vagrom Chap Books.

1976   *Walk in Love* published by Juniper Press.

1976   *Light Footsteps* published by Juniper Press.

1976   *A Beautiful Woman Moves with Grace* published by the Rook Press.

1976   Purchases a rosewood casket and keeps it in his spare room at Holy Family Hall to house his manuscripts.

1977   Wins First Prize in the Haiku Society of America's Harold G. Henderson Awards for best unpublished haiku.

1977   *Sun in His Belly* published by High/Coo Press.

1977   *Step on the Rain* published by the Rook Press.

1977   *Wake to the Bell* published by the Rook Press.

1978   *A Day in the Life of Sobi-Shi* published by the Rook Press.

1978   *Sailing Bones* published by the Rook Press.

1978   *Uzzano* 9/10 (spring–summer 1978) features "50 Haiku by Raymond Roseliep."

1978   Wins an honorable mention in the Yuki Teikei Society Haiku Contest.

1979   *Sky in My Legs* published by Juniper Press.

1979   *Firefly in My Eyecup* published by High/Coo Press.

1979   *The Still Point* published by Uzzano Press.

1979   Wins a third place and an honorable mention in the Yuki Teikei Society Haiku Contest.

1980   *A Roseliep Retrospective: Poems & Other Words By & About Raymond Roseliep,* published by Alembic Press.

1980	*Listen to Light* published by Alembic Press.
1980	Wins the Shugyō Takaha Award (grand prize) in the Yuki Teikei Society Haiku Contest.
1980	"In Praise of Roseliep," special section by Eric Amann, is published in *Cicada*.
1981	A haiku sequence of Roseliep's is selected for display on buses in New York.
1982	*Swish of Cow Tail* published by Swamp Press.
1982	Appointed Professor Emeritus, Loras College.
1982	Wins First Prize in the Haiku Society of America's Harold G. Henderson Awards for best unpublished haiku.
1983	*Rabbit in the Moon* published by Alembic Press.
1983, December 6	Dies at 3:00 A.M., Mercy Hospital, Dubuque, of an aneurysm.
1983, December 9	Buried near the new chapel, Regina Caeli, in Mount Calvary Cemetery, Dubuque.
1984	*The Earth We Swing On* published by Winston Press.
1984	*Wind Chimes* issue 12, "In Memoriam. Raymond Roseliep," is published.
1984	*Studia Mystica* issue 7:2, dedicated to Raymond Roseliep, is published.

Preface

> When our circumferences extend too far and
> our centers dissolve nearly to emptiness, the
> precise jewels of Roseliep's haiku are over and
> over again a happy find.
>
> — *A. R. Ammons* [1]

I met Rev. Raymond Roseliep for the first time in 1952 when I was seventeen years old, a postulant in the Dubuque Franciscans. While cleaning windows with another postulant, I was leaning against a rusty doorbell just to see if it worked.

Soon a voice boomed out, "Who's ringing my doorbell?" When I looked up to the top of the stairs to excuse myself, I saw a tall man in black pants and white tee shirt with bristling black eyebrows and a startling frown on his face. Imagine my consternation when that same person appeared in a few days as the priest-teacher of our religious life class. He looked around the room to find me—and ever since I have been finding him, or trying to.

The journey to discovery for *Raymond Roseliep: Man of Art Who Loves the Rose* has been long and complex. I began writing about his haiku around 1976 when Frank Lehner, editor of the *Delta Epsilon Sigma Journal* and chairperson of the Loras College Department of English, asked me to prepare a review of *Flute Over Walden*. In the almost twenty years before his death in 1983, Roseliep read, edited, and critiqued my reviews.

The first thought of writing this biography came in 1977, prompted by Roseliep's salutation to me on the cover page of *Step on the Rain*: "my loving Boswell." In February 1981, Roseliep wrote to Elizabeth Searle Lamb, "Donna Bauerly sent the first draft of her review of *Listen to*

---

1. A. R. Ammons to Raymond Roseliep, October 15, 1980. Printed in an advertisement for *A Roseliep Retrospective*. See the Bibliography for complete accounts of correspondence and interviews.

Light.... She reads creatively, and so has read a good deal of 'biography of seasons' or rather 'seasons of biography' along with the seasons as such. My arrangement tempted her to do this, and I have not touched her interpretations." Actual research and writing for this biography began in 2003.

I have long admired the style and precision of Susan Vreeland, so I chose her way of one-word chapter headings as she had done for *The Passion of Artemisia*. The words Son, Scholar, Priest, Poet, *Haijin, Sensei*, Raymundo, and Sobi-Shi are hallmarks of Roseliep's intense life and writings.

The central question for discovering Raymond Roseliep the man has always been simply "who is he"? When I taught American poetry and included Roseliep's haiku, I often wrote on the chalkboard: "Priest" overwritten with "Poet." One would have to erase both words to free up either one. Roseliep himself and a host of critics and readers have been asking the same question for years. By the time I wrote the Epilogue I was still asking that same question: just who is Raymond Roseliep?

You will always turn to his poetry, certainly his haiku, to attempt to unlock Roseliep's complexity. He once wrote that he wanted no biography of himself but rather to be found in his writings. So please hear him saying, "Just skip all but the poetry, reader."

Chapter One: Son

a son is a boy is an ocean of wine stored in
soils of his loving

— *"For a Seventy Fifth Birthday"*[1]

The details of ancestry, the "begat" chapters of most biographies, can be stultifying when they are chronicled in a kind of isolation. We do not know these people. We may not even care. They are usually far removed from the life at the biography's center, and we often skip those chapters. When we have an artist who revels in his past and often writes about that long-ago time, however, we can take a more personal approach.

Raymond Roseliep, the son, often mined this past—most often his boyhood and particularly his love for his mother. The commemoration in the quotation at the beginning of this chapter, "For a Seventy Fifth Birthday," was written to honor his mother, Anna Anderson Roseliep, who would have celebrated her 75th birthday in 1959, two years before this poem and the year before the poet's first hardbound volume was published. The poem is a touchstone for Roseliep's life and his ardent devotion to his mother, a powerful inciting presence in many of his poems.

> Against the night my world will feather-
> shake when the last breath of you has dropped
> its syllable on me, my mother,
> and you will be younger than I hoped,
>
> I come running with berry buckets
> damp from woodgrass and the passed meadow,
> a pocketful of active crickets,

---

1. Raymond Roseliep, "For a Seventy Fifth Birthday," *The Linen Bands* (Westminster, Md.: The Newman Press, 1961), 58.

and a myth about them to read you:
a son is a boy is an ocean
of wine stored in soils of his loving;
a manchild is the child in motion
faster than a field song caught and sung.

I come leaping against the structure
of Novembers shortening the years,
at your table become a fixture
where candles in a diamond pierce.

The opening three words of this poem, at his direction, are carved on his gravestone in Mount Calvary Cemetery, Dubuque, Iowa.

"For a Seventy Fifth Birthday" gains emphasis from his direct address to her: "my mother." He seems to conjure her death in referring to her "last breath," but he also returns to a time when she was "younger than he hoped." Recalling his boyhood, he runs to his mother "with berry buckets" and "a pocket full of active crickets." However, he also has a "myth" to tell her that can raise questions about its veracity other than story: "a son is a boy is an ocean / of wine / stored in the soils / of his loving." Is Roseliep, the everlasting boy-man, the "child in motion" who leaps "against the structures / of Novembers," ever remaining a "fixture," always returning as a boy to "your table … / where candles in a diamond pierce"?

The many haiku and longer poems he wrote for and about his mother often join his childhood with his love for her:

hanging from the eaves
little chimes
of my mother's earrings[2]

Anna Anderson (November 3, 1884 — December 17, 1967) married John Roseliep (May 2, 1874 — January 31, 1940), the only son of Roseliep's paternal grandparents and locally proclaimed pioneers, Susan and Zachary (Zachrias) Roseliep, residents of Bankston, Iowa.

Before her marriage, Anna (Annie) Anderson was a teacher at the one-room Tivoli schoolhouse, across from the Roselieps' farmhouse, which still stands near Bankston. The Tivoli schoolhouse is gone, and only an empty field and a trailer home mark the place. A teacher living

---

2. Raymond Roseliep, *Rabbit in the Moon* (Plainfield, Ind.: Alembic Press, 1983), 28.

with parents of local schoolchildren was common in those days. During her tenure as teacher, Annie resided with John Roseliep and his first wife, Anna May.[3] John and Anna May had three sons, Walter, Edwin, and Will. Will died of typhoid fever in 1913 when he was 17 years old.[4] Anna May died shortly after Will, on June 6, at the home of her parents in Dyersville, Iowa. She had been ill for four months and had traveled to Chicago for various treatments before returning home to be cared for by local physicians.

In time John Roseliep married again, to Anna Anderson. Marcella Anderson Becker, the family historian, remarked that there was some town gossip about such a young woman marrying an older man. John was ten and a half years older than Anna.[5]

John and Anna moved to the farming town of Farley, Iowa, where they began rearing their own sons Donald, Raymond, and Louis. Looking to expand their opportunities, Anna and John moved to Dubuque in 1923, where John took over management of a gas station near their home on 2709 Jackson Street. That gas station still exists, though the two pumps are dismantled and only the two Os of the IOCO brand name remain on the front. Pline Battery Station, an auto repair shop, now inoperative, still stands behind the abandoned gas station. Across the street, a former livery stable and a boarded-up blacksmith shop which figured prominently in one of Roseliep's poems, remain as remnants of horse-and-buggy days.

In addition to teaching, Anna Roseliep often baked cakes that were lauded throughout Dubuque and sold at neighborhood Hartig's

---

3. May was the birth name of John Roseliep's first wife.

4. Joanie Wilwert, a family researcher from Bankston, Iowa, discovered the existence of this third son in Will's obituary in the *Dyersville Commercial*, May 4, 1913, which read in part: "William Roseliep, son of Mr. and Mrs. John Roseliep of near Bankston, died at the family home at 5 o'clock Monday morning, of typhoid fever, with which he has been ill but ten days. In company with his brother several weeks ago, the young man was engaged at chopping wood in the woods on the farm when in the course of the day he took a drink of water from a spring." On June 13 the *Commercial* added a note about Anna: "She was summoned to the bedside of her son. She arrived Sunday night, just a few hours before the young man passed away."

Even Raymond seemed unaware of this half-brother. In "Inscribed Memories," the sign-in book for his mother's wake, Raymond recorded only Walter J. and Edwin J. "Inscribed Memories" as well as the wake book for John Roseliep are located in the Loras College Academic Resources Center, Dubuque, Iowa, Room 325, File D, Drawer 2. Hereafter materials from the Academic Resources Center are cited in this format: LCARC 325, D:2.

5. Interview with Marcella Anderson Becker, 2003.

Drug Stores, one located just across from their home on Jackson Street. When the Roselieps moved to 655 Clarke Drive, where John owned and operated a grocery store, Anna established her own bakery/eatery in an addition to the rear of the two-story building. This structure is now occupied by the Four Seasons Beauty Salon. Though the building has been covered by siding, its original architectural elements remain. One can still see a separate entrance at the back of what was once Anna's Tea Room.

Anna was known for her sense of humor. Marcella Becker tells of a time when Anna put John's cap and tie on their big dog Shep, who stood man-high on his hind legs, then burst into the room waltzing with the dog.

In recalling his mother, similar images, seemingly insignificant when they occurred but magnified over time in Roseliep's memory, give a glimpse of his mother's personality and surroundings:

> a spider crocheted
> in my mother's sewing den:
> both had precision[6]

> cicada clatter:
> my mother at our supper
> dishes long ago[7]

In later years Anna helped her husband manage the Dubuque Shooting Gallery on Sageville Road. After John passed away, she worked for a collection agency and moved later to Mary of the Angels Home, a residence downtown operated by the Sisters of St. Francis. Her last residence was the Mount St. Francis Home, located across from the former Xavier Hospital on Windsor Avenue. This was just a short walk down the hill from Holy Family Hall, where Raymond was chaplain for the aging and infirm Franciscan sisters.

In those last months of his mother's life, Roseliep needed only to walk out his back door, down the hill, and into her room to find his inspiration. His last haiku naming his mother, written in 1983, captures both his love and his loss:

---

6. Raymond Roseliep, *Step on the Rain: Haiku* (Derry, Pa.: Rook Press, 1977), 36.

7. Roseliep, *Step on the Rain*, 28.

night window
click of pine
    my mother's needle[8]

Roseliep's relationship with his father seems to have been more complex than the unqualified love he felt for his mother. Raymond memorialized his father through many early poems and surprisingly wrote more haiku about him than about his mother.

afterglow
in folds of hill
and my father's neck[9]

This haiku seems to recall a time when he was very young, carried across his father's shoulder. Memory unites Roseliep's love of red and sunset with folds of hills and the wrinkles of his father's neck into which he snuggles. Some simple movement can often, for this poet, bring back the past with a deep poignancy:

continuous peel:
I re-create
my father's apple[10]

Many remembered intimacies belie the recollections of a rather standoffish father, usually reticent in expressing love:

Father
hoeing beans for ever
in our snapshot[11]

firefly-hunting:
my father's world
younger than mine[12]

---

8. *Modern Haiku* 13:1 (Winter–Spring 1982), 6, and Roseliep, *Rabbit in the Moon*, 105.
9. Roseliep, *Rabbit in the Moon*, 46.
10. Raymond Roseliep, *Listen to Light* (Ithaca, N.Y.: Alembic Press, 1980), 84.
11. *Modern Haiku* 8:1 (Winter–Spring 1977), 13.
12. *Wind Chimes* 2 (1981), 32.

in the tool shed
my father explaining
my 'growing tool'[13]

my father's back
loaded with me
and other frogs[14]

While the father loved sunsets too, perhaps he did so in a more gentlemanly manner:

Father tying his tie
before going out
to watch the sun set[15]

Some of Roseliep's haiku unite his mother and father:

Mother, why is
Father dying on the cross
in our cornfield?[16]

her hourglass figure
in
my father's watch[17]

Many of Roseliep's haiku recall his father's last years and death

"Old man" I whispered,
arms around my father:
no leaf moved[18]

---

13. Roseliep, *Listen to Light*, 25.
14. *High/Coo* 5:18 (November 1980) and Roseliep, *Rabbit in the Moon*, 14.
15. *HSA Frogpond* 1:2 (May 1978), 6.
16. Roseliep, *Step on the Rain*, 25.
17. *Cicada* (Toronto) 5:3 (1981), 10, and Roseliep, *Rabbit in the Moon*, 28.
18. *Modern Haiku* 11:1 (Winter–Spring 1980), 50, and Roseliep, *Listen to Light*, 66.

at my father's death
opening the attic door
to bring the wind's breath[19]

at my father's grave
the mourning dove
speaks soft German[20]

and, again, connecting his mother and father:

my mother stock-still
before the balloon I put
on my father's grave[21]

Just across the page from "For a Seventy Fifth Birthday" in *The Lin-en Bands*, Roseliep placed the poem "The Day My Father Was Buried."

THE DAY MY FATHER WAS BURIED

My father died and I said part of me
is dead. I peeled some willow twigs. Until
I saw a tanager streaking our grass
with fire. And I wanted to shout indoors
and tell my mother all about it and
undo the darkness at our supper hour.
But death is quiet like the kitchen or
my mother's eyes, so I would not disturb
the still life of her house.
                        On the porch I
brooded, and lost my appetite. Until
I was again distracted ...
                        And I would
not mention at the table that I felt
all right — lest I upset my mother's sol-
itude or call attention to the lack

19. *HSA Frogpond* 2:2 (May 1979), 12.
20. *Modern Haiku* 11:3 (Autumn 1980), 32, and Roseliep, *Listen to Light*, 82.
21. Roseliep, *Listen to Light*, 83.

she must have known just then—

                    though I had seen
a bluejay with the sky upon his back.[22]

Raymond was twenty-three when John Roseliep died on January 31, 1940. The son was a seminarian at the Catholic University of America in Washington, D.C., and he was probably called to return to Dubuque for his father's last days and funeral. In the poem, however, when he recalls the day of the burial, he places himself in the time frame of his boyhood. He is, in memory, outside that Farley farm home, though by that time the family was probably living at the Shooting Gallery. He is caught up in nature, noting a "tanager streaking our grass/ with fire." He longs, as he usually did, to tell his mother all about it, "to shout indoors ... and undo the darkness at our supper hour." The boy "broods" outside and is once again distracted by "a bluejay with the sky upon his back." Though he is aware of his "mother's sol-/ itude" and "the lack/ she must have known just then," he remains more concerned with his own responses to nature, perhaps some consolation for his own loss—of father and his mother's usually focused attention.

"My Father's Trunk," a much deeper tribute to his father, opens Roseliep's third hardbound collection, *Love Makes the Air Light* (1965).[23] The poem ends with these words: "Slyboots of that giant of my childhood, built/ so long of limb and entangled in those dark/ lidded privacies, I was equidistant/ to 'love that makes the air light.' Chip of his strength."[24]

· · · · ·

Raymond Roseliep (August 19, 1917—December 6, 1983), the middle son from his father's second marriage, was born in Farley, Iowa, as Roseliep remarked, "in the shadow of the church."[25] He had two brothers, Donald and Louis, and three half-brothers from his father's first marriage.

---

22. Roseliep, "The Day My Father Died," *The Linen Bands*, 59.

23. See Chapter Four for a full critique.

24. "My Father's Trunk," Raymond Roseliep, *Love Makes the Air Light* (New York: W. W. Norton & Co., 1965), 15–16.

25. Dick Martin, "Professor at Loras College Leads Three Lives." *The Telegraph Herald* (Dubuque, Iowa). No date listed on the clipping.

Louis Roseliep is said to have had a combination of his mother and father's temperaments, Raymond favored his mother, and Donald was most like his father. Marcella Becker's recollections date back to her first visit to the Roseliep home in Farley when she was about eight years old and Raymond just a tyke. Her younger brother Edward and Raymond's older brother Donald were friends, "little devils," she recalled. They relished trouble. In the age of the Great Depression and meager provisions, they managed to knock over a 100-pound sack of sugar so the contents were unusable. The children all had to share one pedal car. She remembered that they took turns with it but insisted that her share time was much shorter than the boys'. Becker also remembered that Donald was a big tease and sometimes poked fun at Raymond who was artistic, sensitive, and creative. One family photo shows Donald in regular clothes while Raymond and Louis sport Little Lord Fauntleroy matching outfits. She also recalled a time when she sat between Edward and Donald in a pew in St. Patrick's Church in Dubuque. They were making guns of their fingers and shooting the saints in the stained glass windows! Raymond and his brothers attended St. Joseph's Elementary School in Farley until 1923, when the family moved to Dubuque, and their school days began at Holy Ghost School.

Raymond recalled his brothers in many haiku. Donald, the tease, was probably intended in

> no towel-snapping
> brother
> body of my brother[26]

Louis, who served in World War II, was most probably the brother in:

> you have come home,
> weak-eyed brother
> leaving the stars at war[27]

Louis survived, but Raymond seemed to memorialize him in the following haiku:

---

26. Roseliep, *Rabbit in the Moon*, 82.
27. Raymond Roseliep, *Sky in My Legs* (La Crosse, Wis.: Juniper Press, 1979).

A Japanese ran
up to my dead brother's trench
with a pale banner.[28]

And Raymond remembered caring for a sick brother:

bathing you,
sick brother ...
the fallow field[29]

Sick brother upstairs:
the creaking of a loose board —
Ma crossing his room[30]

Once more he mentioned the death of a brother:

still brother
I give your mouth organ
to the pine wind[31]

and, even after death:

against the night
he wears
his dead brother's coat[32]

When Roseliep eventually ventured into his ancestors' long ago past,
he conjured up an ancient relative he never knew personally:

the clock's stopped;
must be the tick-tock of your pulse,
great-grandmother[33]

28. Roseliep, *Love Makes the Air Light*, 77.
29. Roseliep, *Listen to Light*, 36.
30. *Modern Haiku* 6:3 (Autumn 1975), 28.
31. *Frogpond* 4:2 (1981), 7.
32. Roseliep, *Step on the Rain*, 16.
33. Roseliep, *Step on the Rain*, 32.

Roseliep's great-grandparents were all dead by the time he came into the world, and he was one year old when his last grandparent, Susan Roseliep (1835–1918) died. Nonetheless, he envisioned the life and times of his forebears in haiku, recalling stories, primitive furniture, homesteads, and their hardscrabble and abstemious lifestyle:

> heirloom rocker
> rocking grandma
> and older ghosts[34]

> homestead excavation
> grandpa's jaw latching,
> unlatching[35]

> land and light play:
> glasses
> grandparents share[36]

• • • • •

The Roseliep ancestry is deeply rooted in the small eastern Iowa towns not far from Dubuque, where Raymond spent most of his adult life.[37] Travel twenty-three miles west of Dubuque and you will arrive at Roseliep's birthplace, Farley. Nearby Holy Cross, Rickardsville, Bankston, and Dyersville were home to paternal and maternal ancestors,[38] dating as far back

---

34. *High/Coo* 5:17 (August 1980) and Roseliep, *Listen to Light*, 24.

35. *Modern Haiku* 11:3 (Autumn 1980), 39, and with second and third lines indented, Roseliep, *Listen to Light*, 24.

36. "'More Light' — Goethe" [sequence], *Wind Chimes* 3 (1981), 38, and Roseliep, *Rabbit in the Moon*, 106.

37. These small towns often preserve ancient traditions in their farms, homes, and businesses as well as through town historians, such as Mary Palmer from Farley and Joanie Wilwert from Bankston/Dyersville. These feisty women research by every means known: old plats, obituaries — some printed in long-gone newspapers — local lore, cemetery listings and actual visits to various sites through which they identify and confirm ancient records.

38. Taken from a variety of small-town obituaries, the following partial genealogy may be of interest: Ancestors of Raymond Roseliep (1917–1983). Dates are included when known. Maternal great grandparents: Joseph Crevier (1818–1909) and Rachel (Lavelle) Valley (11 children).

as 1818–1909 for Joseph Crevier, Raymond's maternal great-grandfather, who, according to Marcella Becker, "was born in the United States but reared in Canada near Three Rivers in the vicinity where there is a sign reading 'St. Pierre Les Becquets—Birthplace of Julien Dubuque, founder of Dubuque, Iowa.'" Becker wrote further:

> Joseph Crevier came to Dubuque in 1836, one of the early French-men who established a community in Dubuque and then spread out to found the present communities of Rickardsville and St. Donatus.[39] Family lore has it that Crevier originally farmed in the area where the Dubuque City Hall now stands,[40] then moved after only a few years to the present town of Rickardsville. He married Rachel Lavelle (Valley) shortly after his arrival in Dubuque. Joseph was a colorful pioneer, one of the thousands of Americans to participate in the California Gold Rush of '49 when word carried around the world that gold was discov-ered in California at Sutter's Mill. Crevier lead a party of Rickardsville residents over the mountains into California by an ox-drawn wagon train. It took them months to make the trip and the party stayed in the Gold Fields approximately three months. They found some gold but not enough to compensate for the high living costs. So they returned home that year. Potatoes were selling at $7.00 a pound at the time the Rickardsville party was in California.[41]

Crevier married twice after Rachel's death. He was known to be a stin-gy man who didn't give his wives much to spend. He might have been the kind of man who would insist on sharing eyeglasses. After his return from the goldfields, he settled in South Dakota, but upon his death his body was returned to Rickardsville and buried next to Rachel.

Joseph and Rachel Crevier had eleven children—curiously, elev-en is a number of offspring that recurs often among Roseliep's ances-tors. Daughter Emily Crevier (the mother of Anna Anderson Roseliep, the tenth of their eleven children) was born on February 6, 1847, and died at Holy Cross, Iowa, on September 24, 1908. She married Nicholas Anderson, who was born in 1838 in Strekholm, Sweden, and died at Holy Cross on May 2, 1911. He came to the United States to the small

---

Maternal grandparents: Nicholas Anderson (1838–1911) and Emily (Crevier) Anderson (1847–1908) (11 children). Parents: John Albert Roseliep (1874–1940) + Anna Elizabeth (Ander-son) Roseliep (1884–1967) … Anna was the 10th of the 11 children. (The three children by Anna Roseliep, 2nd wife of John Roseliep: Donald, Raymond (1917–1983) and Louis. The three children by first wife of John Roseliep, Anna May 1874–1913: Walter, Edwin and Will—1896–1913). Pa-ternal grandparents: Zachary (Zachrias) Roseliep (18??–1888) + Susan Roseliep (1835–1918).

39. Marcella Anderson Becker genealogy.
40. Marcella Anderson Becker genealogy.
41. Marcella Anderson Becker genealogy.

town of Pin Oak, near Holy Cross. All the Anderson children were born in Rickardsville, Iowa.

The ancestral farmhouse of Susan and Zacharias Roseliep still stands prominently atop a small hill near Bankston with some original farm buildings nearby. Scott and Theresa Ostwinkle now operate this farm. The original Roseliep estate boasted 160 acres recorded on the 1874 and 1892 plats with 40 acres of timber nearby.[42]

The Nicholas and Emily Crevier Anderson homestead has not fared as well. The old house near Holy Cross was still standing in 2005 but was abandoned and dilapidated, headed for demolition following the construction of a new brick house for the Kluesner family.

Nicholas and Emily Anderson are buried in Holy Cross Cemetery, but some other ancestors are apparently interred beneath a cornfield in an area once known as the Anderson Cemetery. Such family cemeteries were common in those days. The only remnant of the family plot is a cut in the cement from one of the side roads just five feet away from where the cornfield begins. However, Isaac McGee, another pioneer, is said to have found a number of tombstones lying in a ditch near this cemetery, six bearing the name Anderson. He re-erected these stones in St. Clement's Cemetery, Bankston, Iowa, just across the road from the Bethel-McGee Cemetery, the site of a former Methodist church.

A few hours more over back roads and one can visit the grave sites of Raymond Roseliep's maternal great-grandparents, Joseph and Rachel (Lavelle) Crevier, in St. Joseph's Cemetery, Rickardsville; of his maternal grandparents, Nicholas and Emily (Crevier) Anderson, in Holy Cross Cemetery; and of paternal grandparents, Susan and Zachary Roseliep, in St. Clement's Cemetery in Bankston. Raymond's parents, John Roseliep and Anna Anderson, as well as their sons, Donald, Raymond, and Louis are buried in Mount Calvary Cemetery in Dubuque.

The "soils of his loving" were circumscribed for Raymond Roseliep in small towns not far from Dubuque—the city that would soon nurture the growing boy. Parental and familial love would remain a touchstone all his life, the deepest center of his poetry and passion.

---

42. Copies of original plats can be found at the Loras College Center for Dubuque History.

Photo Gallery

Roseliep family gathering ca. 1930. Anna Roseliep is shown in the center of the photograph and her husband John is on the far right in the back row. Young Raymond is next to his father, with his hands on his knees. Photo provided by Marcella Anderson Becker.

The Roseliep residence on Clarke Drive, Dubuque. The entrance to Anna's Teahouse is in the rear. Photo taken in 2010 by Donna Bauerly.

Raymond Roseliep upon his ordination (1943) and as a professor at Loras College (ca. 1965). Professional photographers unknown.

monarch winded,
milkweed
in my beard

Ray

*Love to
Donn*

Father Ray with a Monarch butterfly near his rooms at Holy Family Hall. Photographer unknown.

Roseliep's gravestone in Mount Calvary Cemetery. Photo by Donna Bauerly.

Chapter Two: Scholar

Childhood is over, and we shove
ourselves to manhood, linking arm with those
who feign a forward motion, or we move
from shadow into shadow, not from love

— *"Some Men a Forward Motion Love"*[1]

If one were looking for insights into the inner life of the young and adolescent Raymond Roseliep, not much would be found because throughout his life he kept no personal journals or diaries, at least none that he saved. He wanted to be remembered through his writings, and we can find him there in remembrances of himself allied with those "who shove ourselves to manhood," or through what he attributed to his students and, perhaps, to himself groping toward that "forward motion."

His remembrances were also tempered by a stern admonition to himself in a short poem, "Travel," from *Sun in His Belly.* The opening lines read:

Soul, I said, it is
unworthy to spread
your disturbance
round.[2]

Though there are many dark poems in this slim chapbook, Roseliep throughout his writing career chose the way that Emily Dickinson pointed out in one of her own poems: "Tell all the truth

---

1. Raymond Roseliep, *The Linen Bands* (Westminster, Md.: The Newman Press, 1961), 38.

2. Raymond Roseliep, *Sun in His Belly* (West Lafayette: Ind.: High/Coo Press, 1977), 46.

but tell it slant." Direct facing of starlight at night is not as revelatory as what you see slant or through the rods in your eyes. Truth, she affirmed, "must dazzle gradually / Or every man be blind."[3]

Roseliep's *The Linen Bands* is full of poems of youth and adolescence. After the opening eponymous poem, addressing his priesthood ordination and its meaning, he proclaimed in "A Short Letter to Dr. Johnson"

> Sir:
> I love the young dogs of my age.

Roseliep goes on to comment on his bifurcated life, that of the priest-poet: "You see, I have the oddest role: a priest / who teaches in a school of liberal arts / and science, one who seldom preaches or / baptizes; still, I hear confessions in / and out of season too."[4]

He follows that poem with many others, ostensibly addressed to or about the adolescents who surround him in the classroom: "No Laughing Matter," "Picasso's Boy with a Pipe," "From His Study Window," and "Three Students, Bearing Gifts" as well as many other youth-centered poems. Roseliep's personal memories of his own early years are often inextricably mingled with those he is teaching and mentoring. Roseliep is not unusual in such mingled remembrances of watershed moments from long ago. Many depth-psychologists such as Sigmund Freud, Abraham Maslow, and Carl Jung, as well as poets such as William Wordsworth, tell us that "peak experiences" (powerful memories) often cluster in our youth, but it is only when we are mature and in reflective moments that we unlock the deeper meanings of our young lives in what is often termed "self-actualization."

We may well wonder what to make of Roseliep's conflict, much more directly faced, in "Where Roots Tangle," perhaps the most powerful poem of remembrance in *The Linen Bands*:

> Where roots tangle the ground before their plunge
> under, he hooks his heels. His backbone rests
> keenly again the oak as the sun sets,
> making his faded sweater more like orange.
> His face reaches for chinks of light between

---

3. Emily Dickinson, Poem 1129, *The Poems of Emily Dickinson*, edited by Thomas H. Johnson. Cambridge, Mass.: The Belknap Press of Harvard University Press, Copyright © 1951, 506–7.

4. Roseliep, *The Linen Bands*, 6.

the leaves so he can time the moment day
is an equation with his fires that die,
and substitute a colder twig of moon.

The boy of love is moping while that hill
becomes a shadowgraph. But he must turn
from his esthetic distances almost
as sharply as he taught them to his will
once he discovers roots lead down and burn.
And he will mark the night, this light-heeled ghost.[5]

That burning, the kind of passion that permeated Roseliep's celibate life, was an ever-present theme throughout his life and writings.

In 1979, when Roseliep was looking forward to the publication of *A Roseliep Retrospective*, he granted an interview to Sr. Mary Thomas Eulberg, a friend whom he also mentored. His opening remarks relate to how he felt about himself as a poet: "I've often reflected on the courage it takes to pin the spider threads of poems and hang them in plain view of just any passerby. Those threads are my guts." In turning to his earliest roots, he said: "I had a happy boyhood in a home with great parents and two lively brothers and with assorted and miscellaneous kids of the neighborhood." After a few examples of their boyish escapades, he added, "I loved all art work of the artsy-craftsy kind.... I had an inborn knowledge of color, line, and form that carried over into my passionate affection for everything in nature." He attested that he loved hiking "in the picturesque hilly countryside surrounding Dubuque and to living outdoors as much as possible." Then, he affirmed what many might have thought to be a Roseliep myth. The actual facts seemed rather preposterous, but—at least from Sr. Mary Thomas's article, "Poet of Finespun Filaments: Raymond Roseliep," written after her interview with him—we know that the scholar/prizewinning poet in Roseliep was evident early in his career.[6]

"As a senior [in high school] he entered a dozen poems in a contest, competing against the whole school.[7] He took the top three prizes

---

5. Roseliep, *The Linen Bands*, 31.

6. Sr. Mary Thomas Eulberg, "Poet of Finespun Filaments: Raymond Roseliep." Originally published in *Delta Epsilon Sigma Bulletin* 24:4 (December 1979); reprinted in David Dayton, ed., *A Roseliep Retrospective* (Ithaca, N.Y.: Alembic Press, 1980), 11–15.

7. Columbia Academy, renamed Loras Academy in March 1939.

and all the honorable mentions. Since this embarrassed the school administration, he was asked to relinquish all but the top place in order that a second judging might give other students recognition."

In fact Roseliep was successful as a poet even earlier, as a seventh-grade student at St. Patrick's School in Dubuque. His first published poem, honoring the installation of a new archbishop, was printed in *The Witness,* the local Catholic newspaper.[8]

What other facts we know of earlier years are less detailed. In 1922 Roseliep and his family moved from Farley, Iowa, where the young Ray had been enrolled in kindergarten at St. Joseph's Grade School. After moving to their first home in Dubuque, he attended Sacred Heart School for first grade in 1923. In 1924 the family moved to 2709 Jackson Street, and Ray began school at Holy Ghost. After one more move in 1926 to 655 Clarke Street, he attended and graduated in 1931 from St. Patrick's Grade School. While it was an easy walk for Ray down Seminary Hill, now named North Main Street, to St. Patrick's, going home was a different story, since North Main is one of the steepest grades in Dubuque, famous then and now for its bluffs and hilly streets.

Roseliep attended Columbia Academy on Loras Boulevard, and in his junior year he and Stan A. Sear were appointed coeditors of *The Cee-Ay.* Roseliep soon began making a name for himself through his various writings of essays, poems, and short stories, often winning top prizes in the academy. Roseliep's first high school poem was published by *The Cee-Ay:*

> The lily, pure and white,
> The violet, meek and small,
> The oak so great and mighty,
> The Lord, God, made them all.
> The stars so bright and shining,
> The sky both huge and blue;
> Our Father, God, in heaven,
> Made each of them for you."[9]

Roseliep also won honors in elocution and humorous essay contests. His presence on the academy honor roll was consistent, though he often placed near the bottom of the list, perhaps because his energies were

8. "Magic and the Magician," interview with Dennis Hayes, *Today* 19:1 (October 1963), 18.
9. "Poet's Corner," *The Cee-Ay* 11:9 (March 10, 1934), 18.

usually shared with other activities, as was the case in 1934, when he was director of the student drama club.

If the young Roseliep proved his academic acumen in both grade school and high school, he more than fulfilled the promise of a local scholar quite early in his years at Columbia College. The early issues of *The Lorian*[10] during Roseliep's academic years reveal a college well aware of the turmoil in Europe.

The opinions of many involved college students across the United States about the growing threat in Europe, however, were divided. An article reprinted in *The Lorian* from the Associated Collegiate Press, "College Survey Favors Pacifism," stated: "Today, more students than ever before are prepared to view with cynical skepticism the flag-waving jingoism and propaganda so successfully used to drive America into participation in the World War."[11] *The Lorian* staff, often reprinting articles from national services, kept their classmates attuned to the larger issues in these troubling years. Priest-scholars were very influential in these Loras College students' lives. Fr. Isidore Semper, chairman of the Department of English, traveled abroad, later sharing his insights into the world at war. The locally famous historian, Fr. M. M. Hoffmann, who had been a chaplain in World War I, serving with an active combat unit in the trenches and on the front lines, gave a talk on the war in Spain: "We cannot sleep while thunder rumbles over Europe."[12]

Though the United States teetered on the brink of entering World War II, Roseliep did not seem to concern himself with the great issues of the day, preferring instead to concentrate on his writing, especially his poetry. If involved in the war debate at all, Roseliep through his writings did not distinguish himself as being an active participant. The themes of his poetry — his "effusions," as he so aptly named them — were not clarion calls for peace or war but rather musings on nature and seasonal motifs.

In his junior year, he joined the staff of *The Spokesman* and was eventually elected as literary editor of *The Lorian* as well as coeditor of *The Spokesman*.

---

10. *The Lorian* began publication at Columbia College on November 24, 1924, retained the name when Columbia College became Loras College, and is still called *The Lorian* name. Preceding *The Lorian* were three issues of *The Spokesmanette* published from October 11–31, 1924.

11. *The Lorian* 12:2 (October 25, 1935), 1.

12. *The Lorian* 13:4 (November 13, 1936), 1.

During his senior year at Loras College, Roseliep continued his frequent publishing, chronicled and printed in both *The Lorian* and *The Spokesman* of which he was once again coeditor. Roseliep was pictured prominently on page 1 of *The Lorian*'s November 11, 1938 issue, sharing that front page with Fr. Semper, the moderator of *The Spokesman*. An opening article in *The Spokesman* in 1938 celebrated the centennial of the founding of Loras College by Bishop Loras in 1838. Roseliep contributed an article titled "Presidents of Columbia: Father Downey," the first of a series celebrating the original rectors.[13]

Roseliep continued his involvement in humorous dramatic presentations at the college. He enjoyed creating voices and personae, both male and female, since men played all parts in this all-male college. He was often teased by his classmates about both his literary aspirations as well as his striking physical appearance. One college friend, the executive editor of *The Lorian*, wrote: "We hear that so much of Roseliep's stuff goes into the wastebasket that he is getting fan mail from the janitors."[14] Another editorial friend wrote: "My dear Ray Roseliep, you can't imagine what a fine guy we think you are ... but tell us one thing—where did you get the retractable widow's peak?" Perhaps his deep black hair was one reason why, as Marcella Becker remembered, that Raymond called himself "The Black Martin," skinny and bird-like.[15]

On the quieter home front, in the final issue of Roseliep's senior year, he reviewed the new book, *The Story of Loras College* by M.M. Hoffmann.[16] The college was all abuzz with the renaming of Columbia College as Loras College and with the building of a new gymnasium. Money for a statue of Bishop Loras was rolling in, and the Duhawks football team was a "juggernaut."

Roseliep was reported, once again, as being "the year's most prolific contributor to *The Spokesman*." He went forth from his college years, winning first place in both the verse and the essay contests for the second consecutive year.[17] Writing "The Centennial Hymn" for the college and winning first place in a variety of contests as well as penning the full-page

---

13. *The Spokesman* 36:2 (1938–39).

14. "On the Gazoom, *The Lorian* 15:4 (November 11, 1938), 2.

15. Interviews with Marcella Anderson Becker.

16. "The Story of Loras College," *The Lorian* 15:15 (May 19, 1939), 5.

17. "Roseliep, Reilly Win Verse, Story Contests," *The Lorian* 15 (May 19, 1939), 1.

review of "The Story of Loras College," a confident Roseliep embarked on a new and very different road.

In a 1963 interview, a reporter from *The Telegraph Herald* rephrased Roseliep's assertion: "There are three boys in the family and when the [middle son] was born, Mrs. Roseliep took the baby to the church and prayed that he would become a priest. 'I guess she thought that would take care of it,' Rev. Roseliep smiled.... Rev. Roseliep first decided to be a priest at his First Communion, when he was about seven years old."[18]

18. "Raymond Roseliep, Priest, Poet and Teacher" (interview with an unnamed reporter). *Telegraph Herald*, February 24, 1963, 17 and 24.

Chapter Three: Priest

The priest unbolted strands of white, and bound
my thumbs and fingers, like an open wound.
Thus I was tied to Christ, or Christ to me.

— "The Linen Bands"[1]

For any biographer, the unvarnished voice of anyone—let alone the subject of the biography—is pure gold. One can scour file after file of Raymond Roseliep's and find very few "plain voices" of the boy, the man, the priest—or any of his multitude of personae. Almost all of his own expressions were carefully guarded, crafted—even in the most personal of his letters, of which he almost always kept copies on file. So the young Loras College graduate's sentiments recorded as he headed off, in September 1939, to the Theological Seminary in Washington, D.C., provide the researcher with marvelous insights.[2]

> Saturday Night—8pm—Aboard the "Liberty." Enroute to Washington, D.C. Whoopee. Dear Mother and Dad and Louis: Bill's typewriter is a handy device. This train shakes like a hula-hula dancer; even the keys skip on me. Our trip on the Zephyr was magnificent; arrived in Chicago at 3—then hopped onto the Liberty. We are not stopping at Pittsburg [sic] as planned. We have pillows for tonight. Had a big supper on the train—real stylish like (for 65 cents), which we consider a real extravagance. We are due in Washington at 8:30 am. We aren't going directly to the sem [seminary]; intend to see the city a bit first, then out to the sem in the eve, when we hope to see Art.—My rose-rosary is on the sewing machine; send it with my package this week. I wish we had a box of cookies as all the passengers seem well supplied with food, and we get awful hungry watching them eat. Hello to all, including Chris, Mookey, Philip, Don's [sic], Viola, etc. All agog. R.[3]

---

1. Raymond Roseliep, "The Linen Bands," *The Linen Bands* (Westminster, Md.: The Newman Press, 1961), 3.

2. Another seminarian, John Roskopf from Marshalltown, Iowa, accompanied him.

3. Roseliep Family and Sentimentalia, LCARC 325, D2:22:31.

He wrote again on Sunday of the next week,

> Dear Folks. Just arrived in Wash. At the station, staring like 2 farm-
> ers. It's a big place. Will go to the seminary after dinner. Love, Ray.
> [Note at bottom of the postcard:] 12 Noon—Mass at St. Joseph's.
> Met Fr. McAdams, my Fr. Ryan friend there. Just ate—at a ham-
> burger dive. We are in the shadow of the Capitol right now—a
> grand feeling.—Write. Kiss Mookey for me."[4]

A final postcard (of the Washington Monument) on Wednesday of that
week, probably saved by his mother:

> Hello Dad—This is the monument I was in—clear to the top. You
> can see all over the city from the windows—even to the other states.
> Classes started today. There is a lot of work in the seminary, but it is
> a great life. Raymond."[5]

Nothing else of a personal nature was saved by Roseliep from those
seminary years, although the archives of the archdiocesan chancery in
Dubuque provide some indications of what life was like for this particular seminarian. Young Raymond's grades were mediocre. He had not
always been at the top of his class in high school or college, and his marks
in the seminary were not much different. Roseliep was often criticized in
letters from the Sulpician Fathers[6] to Archbishop Beckman and to Msgr.
D. V. Foley, chancellor of the Archdiocese of Dubuque. In rather mild
words Rector A. Vieban and Vice-rector John J. Jepson wrote the first
criticism in 1941, when Roseliep was a candidate for tonsure and minor
orders.[7] That letter, while attesting that "he is kindly and obliging," ended by saying "perhaps inclined to scatter his energies." Some of his high
school and college professors probably would have nodded their heads.
At Loras, Raymond had wide interests and was involved in a number of
clubs and organizations.

Roseliep probably never saw these letters when he was a candidate
for subdiaconate[8] in May 1942 and diaconate in September. Concerns

---

4. Mookey was most probably a dog. Raymond's mother dressed up this dog, like their previous dog, old Shep, in her husband's coat and hat and waltzed with him.

5. Roseliep Family and Sentimentalia, LCARC 325, D:2:31.

6. The Sulpician Order was founded in 1641 in Paris and expanded to the United States in
1791. In 1940 the Sulpician Seminary in Washington became the Theological College of the Catholic University of America.

7. A sacred rite instituted by the Catholic Church by which a baptized and confirmed Christian is received into the clerical order.

8. The subdiaconate is the lowest of the sacred or major orders in the Latin Church.

such as those reported in the following letter, had they been shared with Roseliep, might have been a heads-up for the young seminarian:

> In appearance and manner he is somewhat lacking in manliness. He wastes some of his time visiting or receiving visits from fellow seminarians.... While the Fathers make no serious charge against his character, and while the majority recommends him for Sacred Orders, they do so however on condition that he be given a serious warning by the Rector.

An even more serious warning was sent to Msgr. Foley in May 1942: "Hence, the Faculty decided in Council by a vote of 6 to 1 to recall our recommendation for sub deaconship previously given by a vote of 5 to 3. Moreover, three out of seven said they would never recommend him for Orders." At this time, however, the Sulpician rector probably awaited a final faculty decision until he received a response letter from Archbishop Beckman.

What seems to be a rather petty letter arrived on May 12, the date of the previous letter. The rector reported,

> It is true that some of the Fathers suspected right along that Mr. Roseliep's disposition was such as would make him "difficult" in the priesthood. They had heard remarks about his cynical attitude and about his having a sharp tongue. But, lacking full evidence, we felt it might be unjust to the young man to mention to His Excellency what to us was then only a suspicion or a fear.
>
> I regret that I must now report an event which has made clear to us that those fears had a foundation in fact.[9]

What followed was a description of his preparation for a farewell entertainment for the deacons in which Ray, elected by his classmates, obviously did not follow "rules." He gave orders directly to the sisters in charge of the dining room "for a fantastic meal" without consultation with the father treasurer who later remonstrated with Roseliep, a correction the young Ray did not take well. Instead he showed "a good deal of resentment and insisted that his ideas should be carried out." The rector, it seems, could not resist a more damning blow: "I feel it would hardly be fair to turn a problem student to another Seminary for his fourth year. I hope that the words of His Excellency have helped Mr. Roseliep to realize that he can and must correct the fault that caused a refusal of recommendation for the sub diaconate."

---

9. Raymond Roseliep file, records of the Archdiocese of Dubuque, Iowa.

Nonetheless, letters (and perhaps an external change initiated by Roseliep himself), from Archbishop Beckman, not on file, must have encouraged the Sulpician Fathers to recommend Roseliep for priesthood at the end of 1943. A more positive letter from the rector and vice-rector arrived in the same year:

> His fidelity to his seminary duties has been this year beyond question. There has been no manifestation of uncontrolled temper or of willfulness, that last year caused us to withdraw our recommendation for promotion to sub diaconate. All the Fathers here admit that externally his conduct this year has been beyond reproach. In spite of this, the three members of the Faculty who last year said they would never recommend him for ordination maintain their position, because they are convinced that the change for the better is purely external. The other six members of the Faculty do recommend him for promotion to Sacred Orders. Mr. Roseliep has talent, personality, and zeal. Under an exemplary, kind and firm pastor the six of us who recommend him hope that he will give satisfaction and do good work."[10]

When a knowledgeable and wise priest was asked about the logic behind first assignments for young priests, he replied that usually no reasons were given. One accepts the appointment given by the archbishop. In Roseliep's case, however, one might speculate that Gilbertville, Iowa, under the tutelage of Fr. William Cremer, was an obvious place for the young Roseliep to develop a proper priestly demeanor. His appointment to this small, out-of-the-way farming community had its own inexorable logic. Fr. Cremer was known to be "an exemplary, kind and firm pastor."[11]

The rite of ordination is powerfully described in the signature poem of Roseliep's book, *The Linen Bands* (1961). He writes of "a chasuble as heavy as a cross"; pain mixed with beauty is a hallmark of much of Roseliep's poetry. Most revealing about his views of the priestly life is the final stanza:

> My hands are busy in a blessing way
> since then, and they absolve and they unite,
> and in our several sacraments, anoint;
> they pour a water that is life. Today
> I pause to wonder why they often shake
> when lifting bread so light within the Mass,

10. Raymond Roseliep file, records of the Archdiocese of Dubuque, Iowa.
11. Interview with Rev. Loras Otting, archdiocesan archivist, 2007.

or why, when sometimes touching other flesh
they want to yield: and yet they do not break.
Priest hands—ah there's the holy rub, as Will
might pun it—and I live to comprehend
the meaning underneath the stringy bond
that holds them to an unseen love, and hill.
Each time I watch a young man pray, then go,
my facile breath grows audible and tight,
and mind re-girds the will with strips of white
that have the burning quality of snow.[12]

"Strips of white" has moved from the literal to the metaphorical, but the binding is just as real and far more inwardly searing.

Roseliep recorded a number of brief biographical notes over the years. He wrote of his birth and his early schooling, but he did not deal with his problem years at Catholic University. For his time in seminary he wrote only: "seminary training, 1939–1943. While there took graduate work in English (and also at the C.U. extension, Loras College, during summers), in preparation for the MA degree, which was conferred in 1948."[13]

After spending just two years as an assistant pastor at Immaculate Conception Church in Gilbertville, in 1945 Roseliep was made managing editor of *The Witness,* the newspaper of the Archdiocese of Dubuque. After this one-year assignment he was appointed instructor at Loras College to teach religion and English.

Roseliep rounded out his brief account of his formal education with notes about his attendance at the University of Notre Dame in 1948–1950 "for further graduate work leading to the PhD in English." He received the degree in June 1954. His dissertation was titled "Some Letters of Lionel Johnson." A Victorian-era English poet and convert to Catholicism, Johnson had long been of scholarly interest to Roseliep and was the subject of an award-winning essay of his in 1939 at Loras College.[14]

In August 1954, Dr. Raymond Roseliep, now an assistant professor, started the new academic year mentoring and ministering to the Duhawks, as the Loras College men were called. Roseliep's poetry book *The Linen Bands* is filled with texts about the lives of students. Titles of

12. Roseliep, "The Linen Bands," lines 49–64.
13. Raymond Roseliep Biographia, LCARC 325, D:2:25.
14. Raymond Roseliep Biographia, LCARC 325, D:2:25.

poems mirror the variety of ways that Roseliep approached the classroom and the confessional: "From His Study Window," "Three Students Bearing Gifts," "The Unrepentant," "Room 201: Shakespeare," "Professor Nocturnal," "For a Young Man Out of Love," "Campus Orbit" — the list contains at least fifteen poems celebrating how, as Roseliep said in "A Short Letter to Dr. Johnson," "Sir: / I love the young dogs of my age."[15]

Not all of Roseliep's daily life was filled with teaching and mentoring. About the time of his appointment to Loras College he also served as chaplain at Mount St. Francis, a convent where young women trained to become Sisters of St. Francis. He taught religion to the postulants and novices and encouraged many of them to try out their own poetic voices.

Very little of the unvarnished, personal side of Raymond Roseliep can be found in the files at Loras College. With certain correspondents he might drop his mask for a short time, but almost always one or other of his various public personae reemerged. With editors, friends, acquaintances, and faculty, however, Roseliep was a careful protector of his image.

In the midst of what he thought of as his professorial life, Roseliep experienced personal difficulties from a variety of encounters and experiences. Consequently, he accepted the advice of a close friend and sought psychiatric help. He placed himself in St. Mary's Hospital in Madison, Wis., on August 10, 1965. He kept this fact confidential from almost everyone. Certainly his mother knew, since she wrote to him at the St. Mary's address.[16] Responding to a letter from an insurance company querying "What is the nature of your disability?" Roseliep simply wrote "Nervous illness."[17] The manifestation of his condition was the inability to speak above a harsh whisper. Over the years from 1967 to 1981, Archbishop James Byrne had questioned Roseliep's absence from yearly priest retreats. In a letter dated April 23, 1981, Roseliep replied: "In response to your letter regarding my sacerdotal retreat for 1980.... You and I discussed my inability, because of my breakdown, to attend public functions. That conversation took place here in my room early

---

15. Raymond Roseliep, "A Short Letter to Dr. Johnson," *The Linen Bands*, 6.

16. He saved just one card from his mother, dated January 20, 1966, giving him special wishes for the feast day of his namesake, St. Raymond of Penafort. Roseliep Family and Sentimentalia, LCARC 325, D:2:13.

17. Letter dated October 14, 1965, Chancery — RR Personal File, LCARC 325, E:3:2.

in 1968, and at that time, dear Archbishop, you did indeed graciously excuse me from making the usual priests' retreat."[18]

Although Roseliep chose not to write autobiographical details in the journals or notebooks that he kept for his poetry, a researcher can elicit some details of his external and internal life from the thousands of letters to and from friends and acquaintances, many of them prominent writers.[19] A relatively reliable account of the activities of this complex priest-poet can also be assembled though interviews with his associates, mostly his clerical and student friends in Dubuque, who had vivid memories of their conversations and correspondence with Father Ray.

Perhaps the best way to begin an exploration of the personal side of Raymond Roseliep would be with his physical appearance. The word "striking" is used often. His ordination picture (*see* page 22), a study in gray tones, features a rather somber-looking man whose neck is ringed by a starkly white clerical collar. His hair is a halo of black with a hint of a widow's peak, which had often been the object of teasing by his college classmates. His eyebrows are full above rimless glasses.[20] His eyes seem to track an onlooker who moves in various directions, a direct stiletto of a piercing engagement. The impression is softened a bit by a sensitive mouth with a slight hint of what might be a smile. To the right of Father Ray's ordination picture, which hangs now in the Academic Resource Center at Loras College, is a treasured photograph of his mother. Anna's photo shows all the features she passed on to Raymond, but her hair is lighter, her smile broader, and her eyes have a warmer glow.

Ray was often called "Fatty" by his brother Donald, but he was not fat beyond childhood. One of his nicknames (and he had many) was "Spider," referring to his lanky frame, long arms, and delicate hands and fingers. In a 1980 essay I described Father Ray as follows:

> The poet Roseliep is a spare man. I remember one December afternoon when a spot of red in the winter greyness drew my attention to

18. Chancery—RR Personal File, LCARC 325, E:3:2. Roseliep's "difficulty" was his inability to speak above a whisper. No physical cause was ever determined.

19. A total of 13,384 letters from Roseliep's files are recorded at the LCARC. His letters were typed on a manual typewriter with a clear first copy and onion-skin duplicates. Modern-day computer users would find it difficult even to imagine how he corrected typos! And he did correct them—he was meticulous about appearance in all things.

20. Later those glasses were replaced with a Buddy Holly–type frame that accentuated his heavy dark eyebrows. His last pair of glasses is kept in the LCARC.

a lean striding figure. The flying red was Roseliep's stocking cap, and
as I neared that "frosty Ichabod," I remembered an artist's adage — if
you introduce a color into a picture, be sure to repeat it somewhere.
Roseliep's stocking cap was echoed in his cheeks, and for all that grey
winter world, I could see nothing but red."[21]

A former student of Roseliep's, Rev. Robert Beck, remembered him
as "tall, with long slender fingers, wearing a black coat that flapped like a
robe."[22] One former Loras student described a Roseliep who would come
"flying in, a man who moved *fast* up the stairs to his residential rooms on
second floor. But the ever friendly Roseliep would still take the time to
look in and wave a greeting."[23]

Bill Pauly, a former student and long-time friend of Father Ray's, remembers their first encounter, when Bill was still in high school. He went
to a reading by Roseliep and noted the priest exhibited a "stately way, an
inimitable style, dramatic and serious. When he was at the podium in his
priestly garb, he was taller than life."[24]

Bill Pauly knew Roseliep as a mentor as well. Roseliep had high expectations, and often, Pauly knew, he fell short of them in his visits to
Holy Family Hall and in responding to Father Ray's letters in a timely
fashion. Pauly knew both the priest's strengths and weaknesses, noting
that he was generous and nurturing, but also could be demanding and
opinionated. On December 6, 1983, Pauly was working at the Writing
Lab at Loras when his wife came to tell him "Raymond's dead." Pauly
was one of Roseliep's pallbearers and brought roses for many mourners at
the funeral. Bill and Deb Pauly plant red flowers each year on Roseliep's
grave in Mount Calvary Cemetery.[25]

For Rev. Daniel Rogers, who later became Roseliep's literary executor,
the most impressive aspects of Roseliep were his sensitivity, his caring about
others — always wanting to know more about them — and his curiosity about
the world, nature, and literature. Rogers knew Roseliep was fussy, but as they
became good friends, they could both laugh about that quality.[26]

21. Donna Bauerly, "Raymond Roseliep: 'Where Are You Going? Where Have You Been?'"
David Dayton, ed., *A Roseliep Retrospective* (Ithaca, N.Y.: Alembic Press, 1980), 29.
    22. Interview with Rev. Robert Beck, September 22, 2009.
    23. Interview with David Locher, September 9, 2002.
    24. Interview with Bill Pauly, June 2003.
    25. Interview with Bill Pauly, June 2003.
    26. Rev. Daniel Rogers joined the faculty of Loras College in the fall of 1956.

Msgr. Francis Friedl, a classmate of Roseliep's at Loras Academy and College, recalls some of Roseliep's nicknames—"Rosy" and "Spider" among them. The two men wrote for *The Spokesman*, the Loras College literary magazine. Friedl remembers that "Ray had a good sense of humor and charisma, and he was a good mimic, but not mean-spirited." He knew that Roseliep could get angry and might sometimes hold a grudge. He also remembered that his friend never really learned to drive a car. He had been coached by his brother Louis but ran into a mailbox and never drove again, relying on Fr. Vogl to be his chauffeur.[27]

A distant admirer of Roseliep's, longtime California State Librarian Kevin Starr, could only surmise about Roseliep's personality insofar as he knew him through his writing, particularly his early poetry and some of his haiku. Starr believed Roseliep was a "complicated man, an American original—unique and independent."[28]

Jerry Kilbride, a poet who likened himself to a "roustabout," met Starr in San Francisco in 1995. At that time both men were involved with the Haiku Poets of Northern California and were interested in Roseliep's iconoclastic haiku. At first, Kilbride wrote, he resented the Iowan and wondered who was this guy who broke so many of the so-called haiku rules. Roseliep later wrote "This Haiku of Ours," a defense of his haiku wanderings,[29] by which time he and Kilbride had become writing friends.

Dennis Schmitz, an accomplished poet who had been a student of Roseliep's, lived near St. Francis Home, just a short walk down the hill from the priest's residence at Holy Family Hall. It was easy for him to be an altar boy for Fr. Roseliep's Masses. He recalls Roseliep smoking a cigar on his daily walks past the Schmitz house "appearing jovial, always joking, teasing, distancing, holding people at arm's length."[30] Looking back on his student encounters with Roseliep, Schmitz wished he had been able to see the priest's interactions with adult friends. Dennis remembered that he and his wife Loretta traveled from Milwaukee, where Dennis was teaching at the University of Wisconsin campus in that city, to visit Roseliep at

---

27. Interview with Msgr. Francis Friedl, summer 2007.

28. Interview with Kevin Starr, April 2003.

29. Dayton, ed., *A Roseliep Retrospective*, 19–22. "This Haiku of Ours" is discussed in Chapter Five below. Starr asked Kilbride if he knew the work of Roseliep, and later Kilbride, who learned that Starr was beginning the American Haiku Archive at the California State Library, joined him in his efforts. Interview with Jerry Kilbride, April 2003.

30. Interview with Dennis Schmitz, April 2003.

St. Mary's Hospital in Madison. They spent some time at the University campus in Madison and stopped by one of the lakes in the area. After their visit, they drove him back to St. Mary's. Roseliep, essentially crippled by not being able to speak at full voice, exhibited unusual confidence in such an outing with Dennis and Loretta, an occasion not soon forgotten since Roseliep seldom allowed friends and visitors to take him anywhere and rarely invited anyone to his private rooms. Schmitz remembers that after Roseliep left the hospital in June 1966, he led an almost hermitic existence as chaplain for the sisters at Holy Family Hall. Schmitz has read some of a still unpublished manuscript of Roseliep's work, "Tip the Earth,"[31] and holds that "the St. Mary's poems are less continuous, more broken."[32] Schmitz also believes that haiku became a kind of retreat for Roseliep when he was in residence at Holy Family Hall. "There, and through haiku, he staked out a territory for himself—a safe haven—and, for haiku, in a small enough duration." Later, Schmitz wrote, "His writing voice saved him."[33]

Some of the most touching and vivid memories come from Msgr. Robert Vogl, the financial executor of Roseliep's estate. He first met Roseliep during the summer of 1948, when he, Roseliep, and Fr. Anthony Lang were taking a German class from Fr. Bernard Friedman and lived together at Smyth Hall. Vogl recalls Roseliep's unique appearance. "He was a cigar smoker, had his hair slicked back, and he couldn't drive a car because he was too nervous." Vogl also remembers Roseliep as "effeminate, meticulous, neat and well-read." Vogl felt that he got to know a different side of Roseliep than the other priests; he knew that Roseliep was more tolerant of other people. Vogl had always admired masculine men, preferring their company, so his evolving friendship with Roseliep was a new experience for him.

During this summer of 1948 the trio of fathers, Lang, Vogl, and Roseliep, shared short day excursions, a slightly more adventurous aspect of Roseliep's personality. Roseliep and Lang were always the instigators of trips to Mud Lake or Eagle Point Park to see a sunrise. The monsignor

---

31. "Calico June" (86–87), "At My Mother's Grave" (90–91), "In the Dry Light" (92–94), "Walk in Woods" (95–96), and "On His Return" (97–99), a set of five poems intended for a book to be titled *Tip the Earth,* are printed in *A Roseliep Retrospective.*

32. Schmitz's favorite Roseliep poems included "My Father's Trunk" and "At My Mother's Grave." Roseliep's mother died in 1967.

33. E-mail from Dennis Schmitz. November 19, 2014.

has a unique description of Roseliep on one of their trips to Mud Lake when the trio decided to take Fr. Friedman for a ride in a rented rowboat. Msgr. Bob, the youngest, was appointed to be the rower. He remembers quite vividly, with a compelling demonstration, the frightened Roseliep hanging onto both gunwales with a stranglehold. Questioned about their high jinx and their relative freedom from college rules, Msgr. Vogl replied, "We were priests, not nuns!" Vogl also remembers feeling sorry for Roseliep that first summer, since he did not seem to have many friends among the priests. But Vogl learned to understand Roseliep and enjoy his company, particularly after his departure from Loras College and during his stay as chaplain at Holy Family Hall.[34]

In considering the interior landscape of Raymond Roseliep, the aspect mentioned most by all those interviewed is that of poet. Of course, his former students, English Department colleagues, and early writing mentors would likely recall the priest-poet, a description that appeared frequently in print and interviews.

John Logan, a poet friend who met Roseliep at Notre Dame, wrote in his preface to *The Linen Bands,* "There is a special heat between the priest and the poet when the poet in question is the priest himself." Logan also touted Roseliep's craftsmanship: "Indeed, this artist gives the impression that he can write well and competently in any form and idiom he chooses. His wide craftsmanship is fit friend to Father Roseliep's long field of subjects and his good human sky of values. He is a poet to savor and one for whose future we will keep vigil."[35]

Logan published most of this preface in a critical article titled "Priest and Poet: A Note on the Art of Raymond Roseliep," in which he reiterated:

> The heat between priest and poet in Father Roseliep is increased by the presence of the teacher in him. It is a difficult combination because the best priest prays most, the best poet sings loudest, and the best teacher tries to keep quiet; and because the priest can kiss closely with hands or with the breath of his mouth, the poet kisses with imagination, but the teacher can touch only with the remote idea.[36]

Dennis Hayes, a teacher from St. Ambrose College in Davenport, Iowa, interviewed Roseliep and asked, "How do you connect poetry with your priesthood?" Roseliep answered:

---

34. Interviews with Msgr. Robert Vogl, June 2004 and October 2007.
35. John Logan, "Preface," Roseliep, *The Linen Bands,* xii.
36. John Logan, "Priest and Poet." *Mutiny* 3:2 (spring 1961), 125–29.

Poetry is like the linen bands of ordination; it's one more way that I get "tied to Christ, or Christ to me." Let me see if I can make that clearer. If I were a Christian layman I'd have a sacramental and sacrificial habit of mind. As a priest dealing intimately every day with the supernatural realities of sacraments and sacrifice, I'm practically forced to deepen this sacramental and sacrificial view of the world. When I look into the mirror of visible creation I see the Invisible—the world is the overflow of God's mind—and however imperfectly, I make the things of earth and sky into poems. When I give back these gifts to Beauty's Self and Giver, you can say I'm offering sacrifice. The incarnation of the word, then, is the reincarnation of the Word.[37]

Msgr. Robert Vogl, who was perhaps less familiar with poetry than some of Roseliep's other associates, provided a rare ordinary perception of a most extraordinary man. Vogl recalled,

One winter night, Roseliep invited, to his rooms, me and Jimmy Boland from the south end of Dubuque who often served mass for him. After supper I was sitting at Roseliep's typewriter chair and fell asleep while Ray was reading poetry. Ray was my introduction to poetry but I often felt it was very obscure and I needed regular interpretations from him. I often felt I was "too German" to truly appreciate poetry.[38]

David Locher saw his first poem of Roseliep's, "Maiden Eyes" in *I Sing of a Maiden,* an anthology of Catholic poems, when he was a Loras College student.[39] When Locher was asked if he and Roseliep had discussed the poems, he replied, "No, he explained them to me." Locher always took a personal copy of *The Linen Bands* with him when he went to visit Roseliep in his college rooms. Each time, Roseliep would pencil in a few more comments or short explanations about poems of particular interest. Locher was never quite sure about the gender of various pronouns that Roseliep used, particularly in erotic poems that perplexed some readers, including Archbishop Byrne and other colleagues in the priesthood. Roseliep did not explain or comment about his profane love poems. Locher accepted them as they were: poems.

Rev. Robert Beck was aware of Roseliep the poet before he went to Loras in 1958 and took classes, notably creative writing, from him.

---

37. Dennis Hayes, "Magic and the Magician. A Conversation with Father Raymond Roseliep on the Poet, His Method and his Art," *Today* 19:1 (October 1963), 20.

38. Interviews with Msgr. Robert Vogl, June 2003 and October 2007.

39. Sr. Mary Therese Lentfoehr, ed., *I Sing of a Maiden: A Mary Book of Verse* (New York: Macmillan, 1947).

At one time he accompanied Roseliep to Chicago with two other students for a reading by E. E. Cummings. Beck said "I was introduced to a much larger world of poetry through Roseliep who was friends with such poets as John Logan." Roseliep also helped Beck publish some of his own poetry in various journals, a typical gesture of professional generosity. Beck believed that "haiku for Roseliep meant something pristine, an epiphany."[40] Beck was especially appreciative of the community of Loras men who served on the literary magazine *The Spokesman.* Later, when he was among the seminarians assigned a special dining room, Beck missed out on much of the camaraderie in "*The Spokesman* building." He was on the editorial board at the time that David Rabe was appointed editor by Moderator Roseliep. Though Beck was disappointed not to receive that honor himself, he understood the trajectory that was already apparent for Rabe, who became a prominent playwright.

Rabe was perhaps the student who most deeply probed Roseliep's complex interior. He had the ability to see the darker as well as the lighter side of humanity, as evidenced especially in his plays. Rabe realized the power of the priesthood that Roseliep embodied, even as he learned creativity from him. Rabe said Roseliep was the first truly creative person he had ever met, having encountered him in a creative writing class as a sophomore at Loras.

In a way, the Loras professors competed for the hearts and souls of their students. When trouble occurred at *The Spokesman* in 1962 over freedom of expression, Rabe learned how harshly superiors could react to any breach of what they saw as propriety. In contrast to Beck, who did not know of Roseliep's stay at St. Mary's Hospital, Rabe was aware of circumstances that stressed Roseliep so deeply that he could not speak normally, even to say Mass. After St. Mary's, Roseliep was never granted permission to return to Loras to teach but was assigned instead to be chaplain at Holy Family Hall, a retirement center for Franciscan sisters.

Rabe felt that he had enjoyed, in varying degrees, a deep friendship with Roseliep that arose out of Roseliep's inner life and his own, a form of deep male bonding not unlike what he knew in the army, only in this case the "coin" was art and its trials, hopes and ambitions.[41] To this day, Rabe has great difficulty breaking certain rules taught in Roseliep's creative writing class.

40. Interview with Rev. Robert Beck, September 22, 2009.
41. E-mail from Rabe, November 20, 2014.

Over the years, Rabe was privy to Roseliep's poetic expressiveness while at the same time he could recognize the vanity of the artist: the desire to be known and recognized by other artists, and more famous ones, to the point of pursuing artistic recognition and even adulation through letters and phone calls. Sometimes Rabe rebuffed Roseliep's queries about details of his life and relationships. Roseliep could be a demanding friend, one who expected frequent contact and positive feedback. Rabe, among other students who became his friends, could not always deliver. Roseliep had an enormous capacity of sensitivity to be hurt and, according to more than one friend, could be slow to bury a hatchet.[42]

Sr. Gracia Schmitt, who had first met Roseliep in 1952 when she was a postulant at Mount St. Francis, remembered how he could make everyone laugh, how he loved alliterations and gave everyone A's in his classes unless they really "goofed it up good." She returned to Holy Family Hall in 1977 and was one of the few persons, even among the Franciscan sisters, whom Roseliep truly trusted. She remembered him as being sad in those years, and once he told her "Well, I guess I have emerged from a lot." He often sat outside his rooms on the west side of Holy Family Hall, and Sr. Gracia would share with him what she saw on her walks around the grounds. Sometimes her own insights would emerge in a haiku of Roseliep's. Sr. Gracia knew that Sr. Marcellus, the head nurse on third floor at Holy Family Hall, was another trusted soul, someone he would allow into his rooms to clean for him and take care of his "stuff." Roseliep's tastes were "super elegant," and he wanted everything perfectly placed. He "could not handle things broken or cracked." According to Sr. Gracia, Roseliep was "not handy," and it took him weeks to hang the very special ornaments on his Christmas tree. She confided, "At this point, I liked everything about him, but he could make me so mad since he was fussy and very self-centered. His 'stuff' was extremely important. I think he liked me because I wasn't perfect." Sr. Gracia saw Father Ray the morning of his last day, before he went to the dentist and again that night in the intensive care unit after his aneurism. She claims that Sr. Marcellus, who also went to see Roseliep in the ICU, heard bells ringing just before midnight and had a vision of a sleigh going into the sky.[43]

---

42. Telephone interview with David Rabe, October 2005.
43. Interview with Sr. Gracia Schmitt, July 2002.

Fr. Daniel Rogers was among the few visitors Roseliep welcomed to his residence at Holy Family Hall. One of his closest friends, Rogers believed Roseliep enlarged his life through the use of various personae in his poetry. He felt that Roseliep purposefully slowed down after he went to Holy Family Hall, getting "the microscope" out, trying not to focus on everything at once but "catching the heart of something." While Fr. Rogers was instrumental in encouraging Roseliep to go to St. Mary's Hospital to "get away and get some extended rest, to have some doctor work with him on the problems he was having with his voice," he said he did not really know why Roseliep did not return to Loras College to teach.[44] Roseliep never talked about his reassignment, and the details of his new assignment by the archdiocesan officials remain unclear.

Studia Mystica, a quarterly from California State University, Sacramento, dedicated an issue as a memorial to Roseliep. That volume opened with this author's review of Roseliep's entire oeuvre,[45] a critique that closed with these words: *"Rabbit in the Moon* ends/begins with a bravery of assertion about Roseliep's own disappearance:

> what is
> in light
> is light

> I am
> all around
> me

Roseliep's own words appear in a text titled, "From a Haiku Diary." Roseliep chronicles each month of a full year, ending in his death month of December with these resonating words of light:

> ill blows the wind
> though shadow find
> light trembling good[46]

Faithful friends and appreciative critics, such as Elizabeth Searle Lamb, Thomas Reiter, Dennis Schmitz, and David Locher penned

44. Interview with Rev. Daniel Rogers, November 2007.

45. Donna Bauerly, "One More Roseliep," *Studia Mystica* 7:2 (Summer 1984), 121. The poem is from Roseliep, *Rabbit in the Moon*, 121.

46. Raymond Roseliep, "From a Haiku Diary," *Studia Mystica* 7:2 (Summer 1984), 14–15.

their recollection tributes in a variety of forms: poetry, prose and letter/
poem.[47] Issue number 12 of the haiku journal *Wind Chimes* was also
published as a memorial for Raymond Roseliep. Centered on the red
cover are three words:

> Priest
> Professor
> Poet

emphasizing his multiple personae.[48] Many of Roseliep's long-time friends
and critics submitted words of farewell and evaluation of his talent, particularly in haiku. The first text is the homily for Roseliep's funeral, composed
and delivered by Msgr. Vogl. He details how he met Ray in 1948 when
Vogl was "only a year old as a priest."[49] Vogl's words speak deeply of the
complexity of Father Ray, but the homily ends with the words of Roseliep
himself. Vogl asserts that "he had been a Franciscan at heart throughout his
priesthood, and, I suspect, before that." Roseliep wrote:

> For the finale of my Last Will and Testament, I can think of no
> summary more meaningful than these words of St. Francis, whose
> name was given to me by my beloved Father and Mother at my
> Baptism—Raymond Francis. This is the prayer I had printed on
> one of the souvenir cards at the time of my Ordination, a prayer I
> have tried however unsuccessfully to live: "Lord, make me an instru-
> ment of your peace.... And it is in dying that we are born to eternal
> life." Amen.

Roseliep kept Death as a nearby companion. Most of his papers were
stored in a coffin, hand-carved by James P. Fabricius, that Roseliep kept
in his rooms. He also directed the making and placing of his tombstone
with the inscription "Against the Night." Vogl quoted Roseliep's words
to his coffin maker:

> I live within a stone's throw of Mount Calvary Cemetery, and intend
> to take my friends to the spot, just inside the gates, to let them see
> my marker which will soon be there. I look at all this with joyful
> anticipation, almost merriment. Death is an alleluia, a long, long
> one at that.[50]

---

47. The tributes appear on these pages: Lamb, 16–19; Reiter, 20–21; Schmitz, 22–24;
Locher, 13.

48. *Wind Chimes* 12 (1984).

49. "Funeral Homily for Father Roseliep," reprinted in *Wind Chimes* 12 (1984), 2–4.

50. Letter to coffin craftsman, James P. Fabricius, May 21, 1976.

Many of the farewells in the *Wind Chimes* memorial issue are haiku. The one on the frontispiece is by Elizabeth Searle Lamb:

> before the Star was lit
> there was a light   that left
>   singing

Bill Pauly's sequence included this haiku:

> snow storm ...
> a longer walk
> against the night

Two reviews of *Rabbit in the Moon*, Roseliep's last volume of haiku, by LeRoy Gorman and Donna Bauerly, appeared on pages 8–15 in the *Wind Chimes* issue.[51] Sr. Mary Thomas Eulberg, a long-time friend and poet, mentored by Roseliep, wrote a tribute that ends: "For seven years I was gifted with the brilliant, stimulating coaching of that generous, extremely sensitive priest-poet-professor, Father Raymond Roseliep."[52]

Bernard Kennedy, OFM, opened his tribute to Roseliep in *Wind Chimes:*

> When the death notice arrived across the frozen miles of timeless memories I could not cry. Roseliep is dead, but yet is his hope full of immortality. The mystique of Father Roseliep haunts me just as much today as it did many years back when I first met him. In "pre-poetic" days, it was Roseliep the priest who intrigued me.

Among his musings about their rare but influential meetings, specifically about Kennedy's own forays into haiku, he wrote, "I dared to lay proud claim to him since he was a priest-poet from my side of the tracks.... An upstart in literary acumen, I had a too brief glimpse of the enigma that shall remain Father Raymond Roseliep."[53]

Edward J. Rielly, Roseliep's student at Loras and a long-time friend, provided a reflection of Roseliep that ended with the following haiku bearing witness to our man:

---

51. Bauerly's review first appeared in the *Delta Epsilon Sigma Journal*, March 1984.

52. Sr. Mary Thomas Eulberg, "Poet of Finespun Filaments: Raymond Roseliep," in *A Roseliep Retrospective*, 11–15. That essay ends: "for poet-priest Roseliep, love is the fire of his poetry consuming every five minutes of his whole life."

53. Bernard Kennedy, "The Nazareth Man," *Wind Chimes* 12 (1984), 30–31.

new year's:
ice melts
the poet-priest[54]

Tributes came from former students and friends who included David
Locher, Thomas Reiter, and Dennis Schmitz. Schmitz wrote in *Wind
Chimes,* "The Ray I want to hold in memory is the Ray holding the
Monarch. But I don't want to be sentimental about it.... Here, finally, is
a haiku he wrote on the photo of the Monarch:

from my hand
winghold
on the void"[55]

Elizabeth Searle Lamb's remembrance began:

> Strange and wonderful are the threads which draw people into one's
> life. It was a skein of colored silk labeled haiku which brought Ray-
> mond Roseliep into my world. We came to share in a communion
> of the spirit based outwardly on the written work. And while haiku
> remained central to our friendship, there was much else.[56]

Indeed, much else remains for all of us from Raymond Roseliep's multifaceted life and writings.

---

54. Edward J. Rielly, *Wind Chimes* 12 (1984), 46.

55. Dennis Schmitz. "Ray Roseliep," *Wind Chimes* 12 (1984), 22–24. The poem first
appeared in slightly different form in *Modern Haiku* 14:2 (Summer 1983), 6.

56. Elizabeth Searle Lamb, "Words for Raymond Roseliep," *Wind Chimes* 12 (1984), 16–17.

Chapter Four: Poet

I chose a lyre.

— "Variation on a Theme"[1]

Although Raymond Roseliep is internationally known as a writer of haiku, he did not begin his writing career with this Japanese verse form. Rather, from his earliest years, in grade school, high school, and college, he merely imitated the prevalent sentimental poems of the times. In an interview[2] Roseliep replied to a question about his beginnings, "My first published poem came out when I was in seventh grade. It welcomed a new Archbishop to Dubuque and was printed in our hometown Catholic weekly. It wasn't good at all, but I'm sure my intention was. The school publications during academy and college days printed my effusions. Looking back, I'm ashamed to admit that my own students today are writing poems far superior to those mannered and lush outpourings of mine."[3]

Roseliep maintained a poetic method during most of his writing life. One file drawer in the Roseliep Collection at Loras College is filled with his small notebooks, the first of which was dated February 27, 1967, to August 27, 1968. It contained short observations, word lists, and a multitude of haiku variations, but no personal musings. Later, he titled this little brown spiral notebook "Poetrie" and directed that it be kept in care of his "Lit. Executor."[4] He kept these small spiral notebooks until his death, but he used larger spiral notebooks as well (also to be kept by his literary executor) from 1976 onward. These notebooks contained very

---

1. Raymond Roseliep, *Sun in His Belly* (West Lafayette, Ind.: High/Coo Press, 1977), 27.

2. Dennis Hayes, "Conversation with a Poet: The Method and the Art of Father Ray Roseliep, the Famous Priest-Poet," *Acorns & Oaks* 5:2 (June 5, 1964), 4–12.

3. Hayes, 10.

4. Rev. Daniel Rogers, priest of the Archdiocese of Dubuque, personal friend of Roseliep's.

little personal commentary, so could not be considered journals.[5] After his death in 1983, his bedside table in Holy Family Hall held five spirals, so noted by Sr. Marcellus, who often cared for his rooms.[6]

Early Publication in Magazines and Journals

As an adult, his poetry much improved, Roseliep began publishing in journals and small-press magazines. He told his friend Dennis Hayes, "After ordination in 1943 I began sending things to the Catholic magazines." In the beginning these included titles such as *America, The Catholic World, The Christian Century,* and *Commonweal.* He continued, "As my writing improved I managed to get acceptances in quite a few secular journals too, like the *University of Kansas City Review, Modern Age, College English,* the *Beloit Poetry Journal,* to name a few of the early ones."[7]

Roseliep kept detailed files of his correspondence with editors and lists of the books and periodicals — some 200 sources in total[8] — in which his work appeared. These files — the major source of information for this biography — are now housed in the Roseliep File Room at the Loras College Academic Resources Center. The 152 folders are filed by periodical title, and correspondence in each folder is arranged chronologically. Accordingly, a researcher can get an idea of which journals Roseliep favored — and which favored him — by judging the thickness of the folders. By the same token, reading chronologically through the thicker folders, the researcher will often trace a deepening personal relationship between the poet and his editors. Among the thicker folders are those for *Alembic, Delta Epsilon Sigma Bulletin/Journal, Mutiny, Poetry, Studia Mystica, Thoreau Journal Quarterly,* and *Yankee.*

---

5. Roseliep, however, kept a small black "Permanent Record and Memorandum" book in which he kept odd information such as remembered lists of his grade school graduation class or "The Cathedral Gang." He originally directed his literary executor to destroy this book, then wrote on August 1, 1983, "Why?" and signed that note RR. At one point, he entered a rare personal comment: "3-19-62, +Byrne [Archbishop James Joseph of the Dubuque Archdiocese, 1962 to 1983] to Dubuque. — Alas!"

6. The dates and labels of these last notebooks are 20 October 20 (1983–); T. Reiter (hike); 16 November 83; 26 May 1982; Misc. personal notes (black). These so-called personal notes contain names and dates of a wide variety of people; the color of his drapes, his office furniture, his eighth grade class as St. Patrick's, and the like.

7. Hayes, 10.

8. Vita. LCARC 325, D:2:30. *See* Appendix.

As a college English professor, Roseliep had ready access to these periodicals, which often provided leads to places he could possibly publish. His faculty and library contacts were likely helpful in this regard as well. Most often, of course, Roseliep was the initiator of contact with an editor. By the time of his initial approach, Roseliep had familiarized himself with the publication, and those first letters were often filled with praise of the editor and the journal's content. Later, as he became better known, his work might be recommended by a poet or writer friend and draw an inquiry from an editor. Sometimes an editor initiated a request to submit after reading Roseliep's poems in respected journals.

Nineteen sixty-one was the watershed year in Raymond Roseliep's literary career. On April 29 he attracted major attention in *America*, a leading Catholic weekly. Thomas P. McDonnell, a freelance writer and a former newspaperman from Boston, presented "Three Unpublished Poets." His article opened:

> Poetry in the United States, during the last decade or two, has become very vigorous and qualitatively very accomplished, but many of our finest poets are known only through their underground reputations. By an underground reputation, of course, is meant the recognition gained through appearance in periodicals, and frequently, among those, in the ones least know to the public. An "unpublished" poet, therefore, may be defined as one who has not come out in print with a volume of his own.

McDonnell's article kicks off with Roseliep, identifying him as "a teaching priest in the English Department of Loras College in Dubuque, Iowa." He focuses on Roseliep's poems about his relationship with students but also includes darker work from one who, McDonnell says, is not "a poet of easy pieties." The poem chosen to represent Roseliep was "Wood Carving," syllabic in form with thirteen syllables in each line.[9] McDonnell mentions upcoming appearances in *Massachusetts Review* and *Critic*, and, in an inset, the upcoming publication of a book of Roseliep's poetry by Newman Press. He ends the section on Roseliep: "Here is a poetic talent, then, which quite exceeds a great deal of the book-published verse today."

---

9. Thomas P. McDonnell, "Three Unpublished Poets." *America* 105:5 (April 29, 1961), 212–13.

Book Publications

Roseliep hit his poetic stride—and broke out of the Catholic orbit—with the publication of his first three hardbound volumes, *The Linen Bands* (1961) and *The Small Rain* (1963), both by Newman Press, and *Love Makes the Air Light* (1965) by W. W. Norton. Wider audiences drew wider attention and inevitably a broader swath of criticism.[10] *The Linen Bands* received more than seventy reviews, many of them in the secular press. When Roseliep was asked by Dennis Hayes how he was treated in this bigger world, he responded, "On the whole, very well. I did get a few sour reviews, though; my students took pleasure in those."[11] Hayes subtitled his interview "The Method and the Art of Father Ray Roseliep, the Famous Priest-Poet." That hyphenation of Roseliep's person/persona was to dog him throughout his life, bifurcating him in ways he often did not appreciate. He admitted to Hayes that he did not truly know what a "Catholic poet" was, and as a priest he certainly could not escape being so relegated.

The Linen Bands

In the copy of *The Linen Bands* presented to his close friend David Locher on June 23, 1961,[12] Roseliep wrote in the margin of the title poem "If not the best in the book, certainly the most important."

The Linen Bands

I did not hear the nameless angels, or
the named, attend my ordination rite,
as grade school sisters often calculate
in 2nd nocturn flights. Instead, the floor
of our cathedral sanctuary picked
a leather and a mortal sound to press
within my ear, not waiting for surprise:
a priest came up to me on heels that clicked.
He carried, as a precious cargo, bands
of linen. Though I knew the moment spelled

---

10. Roseliep, a great saver in all ways, compiled the reviews in three binders, one for each book, preserved in LCARC 325, D:1.

11. Hayes, 10.

12. Handwritten note in David Locher's personal copy of Raymond Roseliep, "The Linen Bands," *The Linen Bands* (Westminster, Md.: The Newman Press, 1961), 3.

a symbol from our liturgy, and held
no shock, still I would notify my hands,
dozing in olive brighter than a tree.
The priest unbolted strands of white, and bound
my thumbs and fingers, like an open wound.
Thus I was tied to Christ, or Christ to me.

Today the other ceremonies dim:
the sober candle shadowing my face,
the calling of my name and how I rose,
the chanting to Augustine, Magdalen,
the Virgin, and the saints who terrify,
my body lying in a marble groove
of floor, the handing and the handling of
the instruments, a preface aimed too high,
an awful weight of hands upon my head,
the bee drone of the Latin in our Mass,
a chasuble as heavy as a cross,
my *hoc est enim corpus* firmly said.
But those are images for which I grope,
far in the mind; and if I now recall
their point and power, I seem to feel
the pull of thread as woven as a rope.

It would be poetry to open up
my store of feelings and to play a prank
with them, by saying I was wholly drunk
as an apostle on a flowing cup
of recent grape, as James perhaps, or Paul;
or that I gallivanted into night
with stars and music and a weaving gait,
as flushed as David after harping Saul.
No, rather I was like a man struck dumb,
and doomed to listen to the fountainhead
of silence. I remember how I slipped
from church to find my people who had come
to see the *miracle* (my brother's word,
exaggerated as his sudden kiss),

and how my mother wept with woman ease;
and how my hands, now free, were briefly stirred.

My hands are busy in a blessing way
since then, and they absolve and they unite,
and in our several sacraments, anoint;
they pour a water that is life. Today
I pause to wonder why they often shake
when lifting bread so light within the Mass,
or why, when sometimes touching other flesh
they want to yield: and yet they do not break.
Priest hands—ah there's the holy rub, as Will
might pun it—and I live to comprehend
the meaning underneath a stringy bond
that holds them to an unseen love, and hill.
Each time I watch a young man pray, then go,
my facile breath grows audible and tight,
and mind re-girds the will with strips of white
that have the burning quality of snow.[13]

Why would Roseliep deem this poem "so important"? "Tied to
Christ or Christ to me?" Hard and weighty words from that crucial
poem strike a mighty blow, causing readers to wonder, perhaps, what
arduous inner task this poet has in mind as he carries us on his journey.
Consider these words and their connotations, heaped one upon another,
from this one poem: *press, unbolted, bound, wound, tied, sober, shadowing, terrify, marble groove, instruments, awful weight, done, heavy, cross,
grope, power, pulls, woven, rope, drunk, harping, struck dumb, doomed,
silence, shake, flesh, yield, break, stringy bond, tight, strips of white burning.* Many of these nouns and verbs are combined into powerful phrases;
adjectives deeply affect the nouns they precede, such as "stringy bond"
or "burning quality." The harsh ending "k" of "struck" is swallowed
whole in "dumb." Poems from *The Linen Bands* surely need to be read
in whole and more than once, but the overpowering accretion of words
such as those few listed from just one poem give an ominous warning
and a perceptible tone of suffering and excruciating misery that might
suffuse our experience.

---

13. Roseliep, "The Linen Bands."

Roseliep is going to a crucifixion, not only Christ's but his own — "and I live to comprehend/the meaning underneath the stringy bond/that holds them to an unseen love, and hill."[14] "Hill," placed strategically at the end of the line and near the end of the poem, seems to signify Golgotha, the place of Christ's crucifixion. In his poetry, Roseliep often hangs himself on a cross of his own making.

Not all poems in *The Linen Bands* are crisscrossed with misery. Many relate his experiences with college students. Most early reviewers of *The Linen Bands* marveled at how well Roseliep understood these young men. No wonder: of a total of fifty poems a reader could count at least twenty-two connected with his students. The student-inspired poems are clustered in the early pages of the book, but references to young love dominate the entire text in one way or other, sometimes disguising the agonies of adolescent longing in an artwork such as in "Boy with Melon" or "Picasso's 'Boy with a Pipe.'" Other student-centered poems are couched in Roseliep's own adolescence or his struggle to shed it. One example is "Some Men a Forward Motion Love," which chronicles passage but not conclusion: "Childhood is over, and we shove/ourselves to manhood, linking arm with those/who feign a forward motion, or we move/from shadow into shadow, not from love."[15]

In his preface to *The Linen Bands*, John Logan comments extensively on Roseliep's "heat between the priest and the poet ... increased by the teacher in him." Logan comments about Roseliep's teacher-student relationships in the poem "Picasso's 'Boy with a Pipe,'" which Logan considers "one of the most beautiful of all ... behind which it is perhaps as hard to see the priest-teacher as it is to see the physician behind William Carlos Williams ... or the insurance salesman behind Wallace Stevens."

Logan seems to find that distancing is a hallmark quality of the way Roseliep touches his readers "with the remote idea." Distancing, however, does not seem to be the theme of most of Roseliep's student-centered poems. The dance of the words on the page would belie such a characterization. Consider "Picasso's 'Boy with a Pipe,'" in which Roseliep uses these words and phrases: "a youth in tights," "broods on shirt and trousers," "struggle with a ter-/acotta pink unruly as the flesh?" "the stamen of the flower damp/and sticky," "the right arm drops and pines/and

---

14. Roseliep, "The Linen Bands," lines 58–60.

15. Roseliep, "Some Men a Forward Motion Love," *The Linen Bands*, 38.

nearly points the hunger of the young." Roseliep has been engrossed in erotic description in most of this poem, but in the last lines he introduces himself quite pointedly: "Flowers play in circle on the wall, — / and brow, as I have said, / returning me to 'saltimbanque' [French for 'charlatan' or 'buffoon'] and boy and maybe god."[16] Very few of the student-centered poems, it seems, or even this art-inspired poem, are about "out there." Most of Roseliep's poems center on the poet's own inner struggles.

If *agape* (unconditional love) was the dominant love-struggle for Roseliep, his poetry would probably be far less interesting and provoking. If we took him at his word in explaining "The Linen Bands" and being "tied to Christ or Christ to me," we would, perhaps, not enter into that crucible of erotic love repressed which seems the true struggle of the poet—the priest-poet whose love life is often described as "sublimated." Roseliep cannot seem to reach that ideal. Like Sisyphus, he constantly pushes his rock of eroticism up Golgotha Hill. A critic of this first volume would be hard pressed to find more than seven poems of the fifty not dealing with Roseliep's love struggle in one form or other. [17]

Critics such as Dennis Schmitz, a former student of Roseliep's and an outstanding poet, recognized Roseliep's dominating conflicts in identifying particular poems as his favorites. Schmitz chose the trio of "Heels Wear Down," "Ragman" and "The Scissors Grinder."[18]

"Ragman" and "The Scissors Grinder" appear near the end of *The Linen Bands*[19] and, combined thematically with "Vendor," the first poem from *The Small Rain* (see comments in the next section),[20] give a window

16. Roseliep, "Picasso's 'Boy with a Pipe,'" *The Linen Bands*, 9.

17. Roseliep marked "SAVE" on only two documents that he deemed to be indicative of his true inner self: one a "Natal Horoscope Analysis" was completed by a request from Margaret Carpenter, a long-time correspondent deeply into personal horoscopes. "Father Raymond Roseliep 8/11/17 3 P.M. Farley, Iowa [the date, time and place of Roseliep's birth]." The horoscope was prepared by a professional astrologer, Robert Raymond Shanks from San Diego, Calif., or 11 rue Scribe, Paris, France. The second "SAVE" document, again requested from a professional by Margaret Carpenter, is a color analysis of a person—in this case, Raymond Roseliep—who, at her request, sent in various categorical preferences. In his own handwriting he marks the "most informative group" as that which shows "antipathy or rejection." The entire interpretation of this color analysis might require an expert and could only be definitely affirmed by Roseliep himself. However, red is the dominant color for the passionately driven Roseliep, and the resultant repression from his chosen lifestyle remained an essential conflict for him throughout his life. Raymond Roseliep—Biographia, LCARC 325, D:2:31.

18. Interview with Dennis Schmitz, April 2003.

19. Roseliep, "Ragman" and "The Scissors Grinder," *The Linen Bands*, 60 and 61.

20. Roseliep, "The Vendor," *The Small Rain* (Westminster, Md.: The Newman Press, 1963), 3–4.

on conflicting passions and deep insights into the poet. The three men chosen by Roseliep in these poems are anything but ordinary. Rather they are three pariahs, cast out from what seems the safe world of the poet's childhood.

"Seems" is the catchword. Nothing in Roseliep's world, childhood or otherwise, was really ever safe and secure. In almost every volume of his poetry, whether he is writing long-line syllabics or short haiku, he is the conflicted outsider, remote from love, from self, from peace. Even when he seems to be celebrating, he undercuts the opening tone of a poem with a sobering dark ending. Roseliep was indeed a contender in life. These three pariah poems, among some of the earliest he published, are a thematic triptych, pointing to a recurring question for readers: just who is this protagonist, so deeply rooted in agony? The pariahs could easily be seen as alter egos for the poet, giving us insights into his never-ending questioning of life, its demands and its meaning.

"Ragman," the first of the two outcast poems from *The Linen Bands*, opens on a dark note:

> The hoofbeat down the raveled tar
> came thudding softly on my ear,
> though I was young to understand
> my father's wonder at my fear.[21]

"Hoofbeat down the raveled tar" can easily conjure a black and foreboding devil figure. And the "beat" of the compound word is emphasized by the very regular iambic rhythm of the poem. Beat, beat. It reverberates to the very end: "loneliness with loneliness." Something in this ragman hypnotizes the young boy. He hears the ragman first: hoofbeat, then horn. The deep sadness of the vowel/consonant "or" is often used by Edgar Allen Poe who recognized this combination as one of the most mournful sounds. Roseliep's use of "or" in "horn," and again in "forlorn" are ominous warnings. A disjunctive "but" at the opening of stanza three takes poet and reader down a different sense path, one of *sight* in which the ragman's "shabbiness began to shine." The horn within the ragman's horn that the young boy heard awakened him to a world unknown to most ordinary butchers, bakers, or candlestick makers. Together, the ragman and young boy travel worlds apart where they share a "fellowship / of

---

21. Roseliep, "Ragman," lines 1–4.

splendid pain." The word "alive" stands alone at the end of line 13 and
may be the harbinger calling for the rest of the poet's life. Walt Whitman,
whom Roseliep celebrates in a variety of poems, asserted in "Out of the
Cradle Endlessly Rocking" that from at the time he saw the lonesome
thrush by the seashore—"my own songs awakened from that hour."[22]
When this poet Roseliep returns in his last stanza to the manhood of the
present, he asserts as well:

> Now I am older, still I clutch
> My rags of fatherless distress
> and climb a golden coach to share
> a loneliness with loneliness.

In *The Hero with a Thousand Faces*,[23] Joseph Campbell asserts that,
mythically, the traveler of life setting out on multiple journeys must "kill"
the imposed authority of the father before choosing another authority
figure as a guide. Is it a coincidence that "father" appears as progenitor
in stanza one of "The Ragman" and is left behind in "fatherless" of the
last stanza? Roseliep, in this persona, has chosen to abandon a safe past
and climb, instead, into the dangerous but "golden coach" and share the
ragman's lonely life journey.

Also in *The Linen Bands*, on the page opposite "Ragman," we find
the second conflicted pariah, "The Scissors Grinder."[24] Once more, the
poet-persona "hears" the approaching man who "belled the street/of
our moping town." This time his mother is the protector figure who
coaxes him to experience the extraordinary. Red, closely associated with
all things conflicting for Roseliep, is a dominant color in "The Scissors
Grinder": the boy is "singed" by his "bristly touch" and "razored glare."
Sparks from the grinder's wheel "seared" his bone and "at my feet in fiery
pools/splinters winced and bled." All seems too much at this time for the
young man. He doesn't climb aboard any golden chariot in this experience. Rather, the persona tells us, "I fled, I fled." Nevertheless, this fiery
man with his own kind of "hoofbeat" never leaves the boy:

---

22. Walt Whitman, "Out of the Cradle Endlessly Rocking," *Leaves of Grass*. The "Death-Bed"
Edition (New York: The Modern Library), 1892.

23. Joseph Campbell, *The Hero with a Thousand Faces* (Princeton, N.J.: Princeton University
Press, 1972).

24. Roseliep, *The Linen Bands*, 60 and 61.

I know I shall remember
until the day I die

the grindstone of a hairy hand
the blade of an eye.[25]

What remains is the man not the occupation. Once more a pariah takes him over, becomes a guide—even if not a particularly welcome one.

Although most critics reviewed *The Linen Bands* favorably, those who found fault could sometimes be vitriolic or, perhaps worse, dismissive. One of the most interesting and provocative set of reviews for this first hardbound volume of Roseliep's appeared in a 1961 issue of *Mutiny*.[26] Titled "Four Poets Take Note ...," Sam Bradley, Charles Philbrick, Gil Orlovitz, and James L. Weil gave lengthy assessments of Roseliep's strengths and weaknesses as a poet. A preface of sorts preceded the individual reviews: "Based on a reading of *The Linen Bands*, they could justly be termed 'creative criticism.' Certainly they are not the usual bland, brief surface-skimming that too often passes for a 'review.'" The editors went on to praise these four reviewers who, themselves, were poets, writing in isolation from one another and, according to Emile Capouya: "fulfill this ideal: 'In the very best case ... a review will endeavor to carry the book's argument one step further, amending or rebutting, making a conversation of what was hitherto a monologue.'"[27]

These reviews were definitely *not* monologues. One review in particular, from Gil Orlovitz, eventually—after letters from such well-known poets as Robert Bly— elicited an apology from both the editors of *Mutiny* as well as from Orlovitz himself for misreading in "The Linen Bands," not only the word "olive" as "love," but building an almost entirely false assessment upon his personal misreading. Orlovitz, moreover, wrote in acid tones in which he not only dismissed Roseliep but also T. S. Eliot, John Dryden, Robert Frost, and Ezra Pound.[28]

---

25. Roseliep, "The Scissors Grinder," *The Linen Bands,* 61, lines 17–20.

26. Sam Bradley, Charles Philbrick, Gil Orlovitz, and James Weil, "Four Poets Take Note," *Mutiny* 4:1 (1961), 19–26. *Mutiny* (Jane Esty, editor) began publication in the late 1950s and was known for its quality in choice of critics and writers. Roseliep published poetry in *Mutiny* and received critiques from well-known writers such as John Logan, who wrote the preface for *The Linen Bands*, 1961.

27. "Preface," Bradley et al., "Four Poets Take Note," 19.

28. Orlovitz, "Four Poets Take Note," 22–23.

Sam Bradley focused on the love conflict of Roseliep's, "how *eros* moves on to become *agape*." Among Bradley's favorites were "The Scissors Grinder" and "Some Men a Forward Motion Love." Bradley asserted:

> In the poem, "Some Men a Forward Motion Love," Roseliep takes the heart-guilt from a letter ('Still haven't finished childhood') and tries it out on his own fear, for he wants "no back-/ward steps." Childhood is not over for any mortal, not in this life, but the child comes to new experience and powers of response, and needs to say that it is over. "We shove/ourselves to manhood, linking arm with those/who feign a forward motion, or we move/from shadow into shadow, not from love."[29]

Charles Philbrick chose his favorite poems as well, giving brief attention to "No Laughing Matter," which "pleased me with its humor." Philbrick's tone was highlighted in this comment: "Many of the well-turned sonnets also touch me with their strength and trembling on the theme of love renounced."[30]

Perhaps the review that most fulfilled the expectations of the editors of *Mutiny* was the one by James Weil, a unique assessment with its own theme—that of finding what he titles "Poetry Through the Spectrometer." Among thought-provoking passages is:

> midway between the black and white there lies a grey, and on either side of it the blues and greens and reds and yellows, and between them subtler shadings of the intellectual and spiritual spectrum. His first collection of poems, *The Linen Bands*, may indeed be read as a beam of radiant energy dispersed and then brought to focus in a series of images arranged to reflect the "color" of an idea or mood.... This book has a prismatic quality—a quality which can be ascribed figuratively to the book's brilliant language and which is undeniably present in Dr. Roseliep's repeated reference to "light" and "dark" and specific colors. [31]

Weil claimed that more than half the poems in *The Linen Bands* had such references calling for "spectrum analysis." He asserted that the title poem "The Linen Bands" was the "only one almost entirely *white*.... Finally, 'mind re-girds the will with strips of white/that have the burning quality of snow' [last line of Roseliep's poem], and on that note we are prepared for the colorful struggle to follow." Weil dissected poems focusing on "green, gold, yellow and red" as the "most hectic" and followed with perceptive analysis of poems such as "From His Study Window" and

---

29. Bradley, "Four Poets Take Note," 19–20.
30. Philbrick, "Four Poets Take Note," 21–22.
31. James Weil, "Poetry Through the Spectrometer," "Four Poets Take Note," 24–26.

particularly "The Yellow Christ." Gray poems identified by Weil pointed out areas where Roseliep showed that his "wit is anchored to intellectual and passionate depth." Roseliep's "blue" poems, however, were most attractive and meaningful to Weil—poems of "such profound nostalgia and so beautifully direct they might have been written by a mystic." Weil began his catalogue of "ascending blue" poems with "Picasso's 'Boy with a Pipe'" and ended with "Satire of Circumstance," which he quoted in full. Weil predicted "[Roseliep's] second book will move along still *bluer* lines."[32] He also revealed a depth of understanding of the "quality of aloneness" noted by Thomas P. McDonnell in a review in *Four Quarters*.[33] Nonetheless, Weil asserted that, though sworn to celibacy, Roseliep, like Shakespeare's King Richard II, would fulfill the prophecy "My brain I'll prove the female to my soul." Fulfilling Weil's prophecy of more "blue" poems, one could easily categorize the very first poem of *The Small Rain,* "Vendor" (the last of the trio of pariahs, following "Ragman" and "The Scissors Grinder)" as deepest blue.

The Small Rain

Among those "bluer" poems to come, Weil would even say indigo for the "vendor," the most challenging eponymous pariah, in the first poem from *The Small Rain.* This time, the poetic persona is older, but still a very conflicted young man dealing fearfully with the last and most dangerous of this trio of crafty men. Hints of priesthood ("I strayed away from that confessional")[34] darken the present and his recalled childhood past.

VENDOR

On the New York Central from Chicago to South Bend
I saw him—at first from the back—and mistook him for
the conductor. His uniform was weary and dark,
his railroad cap might have come off the ark, and his shirt
collar was officially white under the stone grey.
On his tin tray he carried among the gimmicks some
cracker jack & tomato juice (and I had to wince
after cataloging them in files of Innocence

---

32. Weil, 26.

33. Thomas P. McDonnell, *Four Quartets* 10:4 (1961), 29–33.

34. Roseliep, "The Vendor," *The Small Rain,* 3, line 19.

& Experience). He rattled up and down the aisle
of our coach a mystical 7 times—I counted.
Of his visage children were aferd, very few
asking their mothers for a dime or two. Flesh sagging
from the bonework of his face and neck was the color
of frost bitten corn, his eyes had unhappy people
in them, and his drained lips crackled. The hands I had seen
before, on Halloween or in a home doctor-book
a boy will sneak through. He was hunched, rickety. And true.
(Little use to bury my head in Wolfe's epic of
the Angel—I strayed away from that confessional,
unable to put my ear by the stick crossed window
and help a man/boy say his fable.) The vendor held
me: I could feel him as a poem or candle-end.
So I was rather glad when we pulled into South Bend.

That night I took a cold shower and tried to send him
down the drain. I had enough ghosts of my own for bedfellows anyway, and would prefer sleeping with them.
But I didn't. I kept buying cans of tomato
juice which I poured into half filled waterpots of gin,
telling him a half truth about my fountain of youth.
When he wouldn't even wet his dryleaf mouth, I bought
a hundred boxes of his cracker jack, and I strung
the sticky kernels on christmas cord, though not too loose.
Round his neck I looped the noose and hung him on a hook
in the skyblue ceiling of the 7ᵗʰ coach where kids
whispered innocent transgressions into the latticed
ear of a priest (whose wooden face never seemed to care
what else was toppling in their parish). Then I cried out
to them with a loud voice, and they came wide eyed and stared.
Before I died, I dangled till my skin burned to husk.
The grinning bones were left uncoffined. In single file
those children passed, the vendor leading them up the aisle.[35]

    This poet is already on a literal journey, aboard "the New York Cen-
tral from Chicago to South Bend." This time, sight, the first sense, is

35. Raymond Roseliep, "The Vendor," *The Small Rain,* 3–4.

deceptive. The "vendor" is perceived as a conductor, ambiguously present-ed as a choice of an erroneous or true guide. This pariah sells "gimmicks," "cracker jack & tomato juice." The grown-up traveler perceiving the dubi-ous conductor adds symbolic meaning, calling to mind Blake's *Songs of Innocence and Experience* as well as a mystical seven-times journey up and down the aisle. This time he watches how other children view the vendor's "visage" and are "aferd." The descriptive words for the vendor's offerings are rife with sacramental sound: harsh consonants of k's—a bread of "cracker jack," to be washed down with an intoxicating wine of "tomato juice."

Among the words of an eerie personification for this dark man, the poet's 13-syllable line length and page width constrictions ironically plac-es the word "true" standing alone on one line.[36] What real-life revelation does this vendor sell for the grown man? "The vendor held / me: I could feel him as a poem or candle-end."[37]

The dilemma of a positive for poem and a negative for a candle about to extinguish is a strange either/or that the poet tries to exorcise by a cold shower. His dreams—nightmares, rather—keep the vendor before his sight, urging the poet to a confession he could not hear from someone else. The poet tells only half-truths, however, and eventually in his night-mare hangs the vendor from a rope of "cracker jack" strung on "christmas cord." He conjures the mystical seven once more in a coach where kids are confessing to a priest with a "wooden face," uncaring about "what else was toppling in their parish."[38]

Most nightmares wake us—but, echoing T.S. Eliot's ending words of "The Love Song of J. Alfred Prufrock," when voices "wake us and we drown"[39]—this poet-persona dies, watching his own skin burn to a husk. At the end, of poem and life, the poet is left "uncoffined" while the children pass by, led "up the aisle" by a Pied-Piper-like figure, the vendor himself.[40]

Roseliep commented about this poem—so often the choice for crit-ics' speculation—"I never suspected what that vending old man on the train meant till after I had written a poem about him—he uprooted a

---

36. Roseliep, "The Vendor," *The Small Rain*, 3, line 18 or 19.

37. Roseliep, "The Vendor," *The Small Rain*, 3, line 22.

38. Roseliep, "The Vendor," *The Small Rain*, 3, line 37.

39. T.S. Eliot, "The Love Song of J. Alfred Prufrock." *Prufrock and Other Observations* (Lon-don: The Egoist, 1917).

40. Roseliep, "The Vendor," *The Small Rain*, 3, line 41.

lot of suppressed material from my unconscious. And he still haunts me in that poem."[41]

Why is this Roseliep-conjured Pied Piper so threatening to the poet-persona? Does the answer lie in the telling of half-truths, which ultimately kills him for lack of giving in to passion, symbolized by the "red" things that his mother bought him? In that poem, even his mother seems to urge the young boy to forgo restraint.[42]

Certainly, as we follow Roseliep throughout his poetic career, these are increasingly important questions for readers to ask of the poet-persona. Roseliep titles a key poem, "Some Men a Forward Motion Love." He tells us first of a friend who claims he still hasn't "finished childhood"[43]; then, he asserts "My friend is I, / and I'm afraid of I, and want no back- / ward steps. Childhood is over, and we shove / ourselves to manhood, linking arm with those / who feign a forward motion, or we move / from shadow into shadow, not from love." [44] Even his assertions are undercut and leave readers wondering just where to find *truth* in the poet's revelations of self. The poet tells a deep truth in his words "I chose a lyre."[45]

What price does the poet-persona ultimately pay in taking either backward or forward direction? What is the inevitable result for him: "poem or candle-end"?[46]

"Vendor," the initial poem in *The Small Rain*, is described by Daniel Berrigan[47] as "a terror that walks by night." Berrigan goes on to say "The horror is gently fitted on the hand of the living like a dead man's glove; the wonderfully skillful internal rhyming, the deliberate shut and jostle of end syllables leave one with the eerie sense of having run all night down the coach aisles of a runaway train." Berrigan chose other poems as "best" in this second hardbound volume of Roseliep's: "Ways of My Exile," "Priest's Diary: Two Entries," "Hospital Visit," and "Elegy for Edward." Berrigan's choices are from each of the four numbered sections in *The Small Rain*. "Vendor," with its alter ego in the one who sells "cracker jack and tomato juice," offers a kind of protection from a direct facing of

41. Raymond Roseliep quoted in Martin A. Miller, "Of Rafts and Small Rain," *The Lamp* 62:2 (February 1964), 32.

42. Roseliep, "My Mother Bought Me Red Things," *The Small Rain*, 14.

43. Roseliep, "Some Men a Forward Motion Love, *The Linen Bands*, 38, line 11.

44. Roseliep, "Some Men a Forward Motion Love, *The Linen Bands*, 38, lines 11–16.

45. Raymond Roseliep, *Sun in His Belly* (West Lafayette, Ind.: High/Coo Press, 1977), 27.

46. Roseliep, "The Vendor," line 22.

47. Daniel Berrigan, "The Season of Youth," *Today*, May 1964, 29–30.

the self—at least until nightfall and nightmare; "Ways of My Exile" (also section 1) offers no such relief for the poet Roseliep. The word "my" in the title prepares us for direct address to the self. In later works (though seemingly not in this volume), Roseliep will almost always use a seasonal sectioning, and autumn is rarely a time of relief of any sort for the poet. "Ways of My Exile" is set in November—for the poet who "goes dryfooted and is bare this midyear / in my wandering."[48] Roseliep, like Wordsworth, was a walker. In this poetic journey he not only covered exterior ground, he went deep into his "unmanly grief," occasioned by the sight of a young boy "punting / his football over the telephone wires," all the time perhaps unaware of the young girl who is watching his prowess and who, according to the poet, "loves him" and is "a light forgotten."[49]

Roseliep focused on the outer world in sensuous detail: for the boy, "he is the seed springing out of due time and season." The girl has skin that "rivals / the last huddling marigold in its picket prison; / her body is tendril, floating, tenuous, brief in / the antique afternoon of my journeying." As the reader encounters this lonely traveler, however, all is most deeply focused on the treacherous inner world of the observer—ironically, the outsider. Roseliep carefully chooses his words for the ultimate impact of exile, an exile from what he often decries—love of *eros*. So often *agape* is not enough, not nearly enough. Roseliep hammers home his "ways of exile" in words and phrases that strike "hard,"[50] as Berrigan would say: *November, dryfooted, bare, strain, unmanly, falling, huddling, picket prison, antique afternoon, dry earth, deadleaf street, cracks, stinging, thighs of my older life, spatter, naked flesh of ground, night.* His final stanza is a crushing blow:

> November is no land for lovers. So I will pull
> my collar tight around my throat, spend a final glance
> on the girl whose name I know, wave
> only once, and show the boy tenderly to my grave.[51]

That final "boy" is not the dropkicking punter; it is the boy we meet over and over in Roseliep's poems, a boy he cannot truly exile, and a boy he can never become again, not even in memory. How often has he tried

---

48. Roseliep, "Ways of My Exile," *The Small Rain,* 10, lines 1 and 2.
49. Roseliep, "Ways of My Exile," *The Small Rain,* 10, line 17.
50. Berrigan, 29.
51. Roseliep, "Ways of My Exile," lines 25–28.

to bury this boy forever and "shove [himself] to manhood."[52] The priest's
white collar he pulled tight around his throat has the same kind of restric-
tion that "the strips of white [with] the burning quality of snow" had in
his signature poem, "The Linen Bands."

"Priest's Diary: Two Entries," chosen by Berrigan from Section Two,
takes impetus of place from very diverse deathbeds, one for a child of
seven, set in April 1944; and the second for an "Old Codger," set in
August 1947. In both, the priest-poet seems powerless to be the effective
oarsman for crossing over into another world. The ending of the second
entry gives us a tar-like image of the priest who will "spit the offal of the
Styx." Weird rhyme connotation could conjure the Pyx that holds the
white Host of the Body of Christ.[53]

Berrigan's choice, "Hospital Visit," from section 3, recalls another November, a time when Roseliep's mother was at Xavier Hospital. Autumn leaves
are the thematic center of this journey, from his initial picking of them on
Locust Street, to placing them temporarily in his pocket, to floating them on
the linen sheets covering his mother's hospital bed, to her placement of them
ringing a statue of St. Francis. The final crazy-quilt stanza uses those leaves as
a springboard of faith or at least hope of it—in healing:

> jump as a
> child or poet
> wild on the crutch of
> belief in the rained-
> down, colored leaf.

Nothing was ever an easy ending for Roseliep. His "crutch of belief" leaves us wondering. And he would definitely mean the pun for
leaf/ leaves.[54]

Berrigan's final choice, from section 4, "Elegy for Edward," blesses
a brother who has recently died. We are again in autumn, "the crumble
season / of oakleaves," and the speaker-persona seems to be the poet Roseliep, the "ramshackle brother" who grieves and remembers the brother
who was "moist from rummaging/ our father's cornfield where you
stripped the stolen ear...." One brother, Donald, could certainly be this
"rummager," to judge from family folklore: young Raymond suffered

52. Roseliep, "Some Men a Forward Motion Love," *The Linen Bands,* 38.

53. Roseliep, *The Small Rain,* 36.

54. Roseliep, *The Small Rain,* 49–50.

more than one kind of teasing from this older brother. The poet longs for a kind of sight he does not have, "hoping our younger brother drops by / long enough to pack His mud cakes on my stubborn eye." Capitalizing "His" seems to indicate that the poet-persona is hoping Christ will give him comfort through seeing.[55]

If the triptych of poems "Ragman," "The Scissors Grinder," and "Vendor" could highlight the theme of pariah in Roseliep's poems, there is another tantalizing tetralogy of poems in *The Small Rain* that center on the Roseliep persona of the hunter: "Hunter," "Leafing Through July," "No Horn in August," and "This Singular Moment."

If one ever met the poet Raymond Roseliep, or even if one only encountered him in a picture-portrait, this man would never be associated with "hunter." The poet Roseliep was much more the sensitive lover than the manly hunter. However, in four relatively contiguous poems in this second volume, *The Small Rain*, Roseliep focuses on this central image of the hunter. The first of these four poems actually bears the title "Hunter," but the word also appears in the texts of the other three poems. Why did this concept so intrigue Roseliep? In "Hunter" we have (at least we think we have) a real person with a weapon who has "killed a deer."[56] The "pride" of his killing and bringing home his trophy conjure for this persona the image of King Lear drunk on his madness. The poet prefaces the poem with a quotation from Shakespeare's play: "Lear. I will endure. In such a night as this!"

Of course, various factual elements of "Hunter" might make us wonder about the reality. Would you put a dead and bleeding deer into the trunk of your car? Most hunters tie the carcass to the roof of a car or in the bed of a truck, boldly proclaiming their prowess in killing. We might also question whether the pale antlers could that quickly (the same evening) be placed above his bookshelf. Why would the persona look "for a child to test my words"? When this hunter sleeps, he dreams and personifies fear as a frail boy who is "delicate as a new feather." Then this boy, unlike Lear in age but very much like him in emotion, takes us in dream to a world of terror. Storm, "unreasonable weather," makes the forest cry back "his alarm." Whose alarm is this? Is it that of the poet-persona who has killed his deer only in his imagination, or a recollection

---

55. Roseliep, *The Small Rain*, 68.

56. Roseliep, "The Hunter," *The Small Rain*, 65, line 1.

of some childhood experience, relived in a quaking manhood that barely endures "In such a night as this!"[57]

The hunter is distanced in "Leafing Through July."[58] This time the persona is associated with a butterfly which "riddles" him with "green thought." This hunter is a "goldheavy robber" of a "lavender wind-flower." The poet-persona had been reading Gerard Manley Hopkins's sonnet "The Windhover," which, in part, depicts a world that shines like "shook foil." The poet becomes one with the spiny plant, deflowered by the hunter's butterfly. He is left desolate, abandoned "in a flicker." The assertion of "O sacrament of earth and the hunter's butterfly"[59] does not ease the despoiling. Ultimately, a seemingly harmless insect is every bit as dangerous as a man with a weapon.

"No Horn in August"[60] is an ominous sonnet. August is the poet's natal month, and Roseliep barely disguises any persona in these 14 lines. The word "hunt" in various forms appears three times in this poem—in "the hunting dog of Autumn," in the "hunter" and "his cup" and finally in "laurel shimmering for the hunt."

The poet tells us that August has a growing problem. "Growing" has a double meaning in this poem: the growing associated with a season and the growing toward manhood. Once again, Roseliep, the poet, returned to the problem of becoming a man, leaving boyhood behind. His own birthdays in this particular poem "block the uncertain earth / with their half-away from a boy's gloom." Usually in a sonnet there is some sort of resolution given in the sestet. Not for this poet or poem. His manhood "refuses the hunter's cup / or laurel shimmering for the hunt." Instead, as the poem's title forewarns: "I have heard no horn in August drop" (line 12), and the ending refuses him or us "any jocular sound of the chase."[61]

The fourth "hunter" poem, "This Singular Moment,"[62] is one of Roseliep's loveliest *odd* sonnets—odd, because of the violation of a set form. There are just nine syllables to a line rather than the form's usual ten. The iambic rhythm is roughened and causes unpredictability. Slant rhyme also adds to the readers' unease.

57. William Shakespeare, *King Lear*, Act III, Scene 4.
58. Roseliep, "Leaving Through July," *The Small Rain*, 66.
59. Final line of the poem.
60. Roseliep, "No Horn in August," *The Small Rain*, 72.
61. Roseliep, "No Horn in August," line 14.
62. Raymond Roseliep, "This Singular Moment," *The Small Rain*, 73.

Direct address to a woman ("On my shoulder your hair is golden") at first draws readers close as we experience "woodscent" or "maybe the hunter's day folding." The poet gathers the woman into his arms and, then, almost immediately, begins to distance her and readers alike. Now there is a "space/opening and widening for us,/and a timepiece with more perfect chime." One might think this "hunter's day" remembered might be an ideal location for love until the distance is reinforced through moving the "I" to a "he." Another "boy or man/willing to give / what he draws from invincible love" becomes the ultimate lover. The poet-persona pays the price of the loss of "this singular moment." The season of "autumn" and the past tense in the final line erase the reality of love for the poet. In the sestet the slant rhymes of "face," "price" and "loss" underscore what is only a remembrance, and even that remembrance a "loss/of the autumn you gathered and wove."[63]

Boy or man? How often the poet Roseliep struggled with becoming. What deeper understanding of him can we gain from his life agony of searching and longing as we read various poems such as these, which focus on a central word such as "hunter"? Roseliep, himself, told us very little about who he was. We are always searching his poems for clues. When we find theme repetition, seasonal cycles turning and returning, we must pay attention if we want eventually to begin to know him. We, too, become the "hunter."

One of the earliest reviewers[64] of *The Small Rain* called the title of this volume "curious," then identified the words taken from an anonymous 16th century writer which begins (in a modern translation):

> Western wind, when will thou blow,
> The small rain down can rain.[65]

The reviewer omits the last lines of the ancient text, which portend the prevalent theme of absent love, once more, in this, the second hardbound book of Roseliep's poems:

> Christ, if my love were in my arms
> And I in my bed again!

---

63. Final lines of the sonnet.

64. Pete Geisler, "Fr. Raymond Roseliep Caught in '*Small* Rain.'" *The Lorian,* October 13, 1963, 3.

65. Anonymous, "O Western Wind" (1500). Accessed at http://pinkmonkey.com/dl /library1/west_w.pdf, March 15, 2014.

Although the text became part of songs that were used in Roman Catholic Masses, the intent of the original poem was definitely secular. Roseliep was confronted, more than once, about "human love," and to the student reviewer he replied, "How can a priest write of love between man and woman?" The reviewer summarized Roseliep's rather ingenuous explanation by writing: "This he easily explains away. The poet merely performs a transfiguration, if you will, into the form of the young man who is the real protagonist" and continues with Roseliep's direct words: "From there, the actual writing of the poem is no problem at all. The poet can now suffer the ups and downs of the young man's love affair."[66] If you believe Roseliep's explanations you would take it that "Roseliep's genuine love is for his students, as personalities and as 'the best raw material' for his creations. His works bring the student alive as only a true lover of this confused, struggling creature could."[67] Obviously, not everyone reviewing this book (or other books of the poet) would take Roseliep at his simple gloss.

Not all students were as polite as this Loras reviewer. In an interview with an editor from *The Witness*,[68] Roseliep himself admitted that he heard one of his students referring to the title of *The Small Rain* as "The Diminutive Drizzle." The fellow he was talking to agreed that was a good title for it, and he went on to describe the dust jacket as "the raincoat — so you won't get all wet like the poet." That dust jacket, designed by Roseliep's nephew, John R. Roseliep, features a tree that, according to Roseliep "sort of terrifies me ... looks almost as if it were suffering or in need of rain."[69] On the front cover of the hardback a man seems to be fleeing desperately from a tidal wave, certainly not a "diminutive drizzle."

The title poem itself received a variety of interpretations. One of the most provocative came from John Mullen in *Sketchbook*.

> The title poem is actually a series of twelve sequential statements on love experience, with correlating images from astronomy, cosmic forms, music and anatomy. This mysterious ladder of utterance leads to Dante's wheeling light, the most memorable gem of the *Paradiso*, and the reality which transfigures all the intervening harmonics. This piece, like every other dealing with the love theme, performs a kind of sacrificial act in which the ordinary becomes the extraordinary, and

---

66. Geisler, 3.
67. Geisler, 3.
68. *The Witness* (Dubuque archdiocesan newspaper), November 28, 1963, 10–11.
69. Geisler, 3.

matter is transformed by momentous contact with the human, which contact beckons and beats us until we die unto life. [70]

Mullen attributed quite a lofty interpretation to the poet who seems as parched as the earth that gets only a "small rain" to clean the sky and "untrouble" the man who still waits on his bed for a "simple / light to twine / my body / peaceful as a / star in rain / water." Then this poet-persona talks to himself a bit more, turning his thoughts from "too / many beloved, / moving / their earth gently." We do not know if the poet-persona ever moves from his bed actually to climb that hill, or if he remains to "do" all the rest in his mind—to grip at "resurrecting air" until a "snap" and a "creak- / ing sound" become a kind of new music so "light / will wheel to a / point / sharper than rain." It is ironic that the original Western wind poem ends with a wish to be "in my bed again." Roseliep, persona or not, seems to begin and end there.

Mullen and many other critics marveled once more at the poetic control that Roseliep had always exhibited: "*The Small Rain* is a collection of fifty-seven poems, ranging in form from the long-line syllabic, through experimental free forms, to the recently recaptured haiku."[71] Most critics who commented on the four numbered sections of the text were probably quoting, in some fashion or other, the statements from the inside cover blurb of *The Small Rain*. No editor was quoted nor mentioned in the stylistic comments, and we could wonder if Roseliep himself wrote the copy. This description of the structure of the text sounds very connected to the poet's voice:

> The fourfold arrangement of the poems in *The Small Rain* reveals the growth and versatility of a man who has passion for his craft. Section 1 has several fairly long works and the long-line syllabic poems which do not follow a pattern of stanzas. Section 2 contains syllabic poems of fixed stanza patterns varying from two to nine lines. A kind of penultimate movement or counterpointing to the other groups, section 3 represents recent experimentation in free forms. Syllabic sonnets, containing haiku terza rima with a syllable-count, a lone iambic sonnet and a single freer handling of the normal iambic measure ("Tour. In Rain") comprise section 4. Father Roseliep's long proved ability to use well the various forms, both open and set, is firm indication that he permits his verbal medium only the mildest tyranny.[72]

---

70. John Mullen, "Poetry, the Poet and Father Roseliep." *Sketchbook* (St. John's University, Collegeville, Minn.), spring 1964, 33–34.

71. Mullen, 34.

72. Roseliep, *The Small Rain*, front jacket flap.

A short paragraph of praise from Paul Engle, long-time director of the Iowa Writers' Workshop (1941–1965), was the only critical comments on the book cover or jacket. Engle, too, praised Roseliep's excellence of style: "[Roseliep] also brings to the forms of his poems the same sort of invention in rhythm and line which he brought to their subject matter."[73]

One critic[74] titled his review of *The Small Rain* "Human Love and Happy Anguish." He said, "In Roseliep's poetry we find that life is as beautiful as a flower, and so is his life, if we judge it from his poetry, which we are bound to do, for he invites us to do so as he shares with us the nostalgic recollections of his happy childhood." An oxymoron of "happy anguish" will never do for poems in *The Small Rain* that can be grouped into a wider variety of anguish than that of *The Linen Bands*. Although love can be a catchall thematic web, Roseliep's poems could easily be subdivided into such headings as: *Love Struggles* (perhaps 25 of the 57), *Alter Ego Struggles* (7 and counting), *Boy/Man Struggles* (at least 12), some poems about *Mother/Father/Brothers*, a few directly referring to *students*, some that just *name-drop*, and even a few that seem to center on *death*—obviously another wrenching struggle. The wresting/wrestling described in most poems does not seem to come from a happy childhood, as one might surmise from the powerful poem "My Mother Bought Me Red Things."[75] The young Raymond always seemed to have heard "the soft thud ... (shamefully astir) in [his] blood." Though his love for his mother was deep and abiding, he ended this marvelous tribute to her by saying: "Maybe tonight I can / clamber past boyhood and the growing years to meet these / abusive tears, violent as the red / velvet shroud she appointed to hang over my head."[76] Reading those closing lines, anyone who wishes to understand the true relationship of mother and son must recall that Roseliep claims in the very first line: "My mother bought me red things, *innocently enough*" [emphasis mine]. Red, always a controlling color in Roseliep's life, denotes passion and struggle, but—as painful as that struggle could be, it was a color in which he reveled.

---

73. Paul Engle, in Roseliep, *The Small Rain*, back jacket flap.

74. Editor, "Human Love and Happy Anguish." *The North American Mentor* 2:1 (Spring 1965), 9–10.

75. Roseliep, "My Mother Bought Me Red Things," *The Small Rain*, 14. (*See* Chapter Seven, page 264, for the text and a discussion of this poem.)

76. Roseliep, "My Mother Bought Me Red Things," final line.

Reading deeply into the poems of *The Small Rain,* one can always feel that tsunami coming after the man who flees.

Love Makes the Air Light[77]

*L*ove Makes the Air Light, published by W. W. Norton in 1965, just two years after *The Small Rain* and four years after *The Linen Bands*, continued to fulfill the poetic expectations for the priest-poet. This volume contained more of Father Ray's experiments in haiku and haiku-like poems.

The early sixties were prolific years for the poet, and snagging a major publisher added to his reputation, not only in the religious world but also in the secular. He had dedicated *The Linen Bands* to his mother, *The Small Rain* to his father, and—ironically—*Love Makes the Air Light*

> for my students
> > past
> > > present
> and to come[78]

In 1965 Roseliep was a professor of English at Loras College. At the time of publication of this volume, however, he most certainly would not have realized it was his last year teaching at the college and that no more students would come. The surrounding air for this priest-poet was not so light. The mid-1960s were a very difficult period for Roseliep. In August 1965, Roseliep entered St. Mary's Hospital in Madison, Wis., to recover from what he termed at that time a "nervous breakdown." Roseliep's mother died in June 1966, about a year after his return from St. Mary's. At the direction of archdiocesan authorities, for reasons not entirely clear, he did not return to Loras College to resume teaching, but rather was appointed chaplain of Holy Family Hall in Dubuque, a position he held until his death in December 1983.

Norton's edition of *Love Makes the Air Light* contained no effusive John Logan preface nor even a single paragraph of critical praise—just a short blurb that identified Roseliep as "poet and Catholic priest" as

---

77. "The title is a line taken from the first chapter of John Updike's novel *Rabbit Run,* and indicates truly the subject matter of every work included in the book." Dennis Hayes, "Love Makes the Air Light." *The Scholastic* (University of Notre Dame), January 21, 1966, 25.

78. Roseliep, *Love Makes the Air Light,* dedication 7.

well as a writer who had "exquisite care for language that marks the pure poetic gift."[79]

"Vendor" had often been lauded as the best poem in *The Small Rain*, possibly the best Roseliep ever wrote. "My Father's Trunk," the first poem in *Love Makes the Air Light*, caught many critics' attention as well. James Weil, editor of *Elizabeth* and one of Roseliep's most perceptive critics, wrote: "the longer-lined poems are all exciting and 'My Father's Trunk,' really superb, goes right through me."[80]

"My Father's Trunk," the opening salvo in this collection, addressed Roseliep's lifelong thematic center: "I wondered if it was mostly about love," a love that "makes the air light."[81] Pictures of Roseliep's father show him as a quite masculine man. Stout, even burly, John Roseliep does not look to be a man with whom to trifle. His softer side was surely brought out by Anna, and her sensitivity was passed on most to Raymond, the middle child.[82]

In the poem we climb up to the attic with Raymond, the grown man who sought to understand the enigma of his father. In the opening lines from the poem, Roseliep gives us an insight into the "closed" persona of his father. "His trunk was / a place where years were shut in him like the leaves / of a book whose title alone he displayed."[83] In his series of "hunting poems," the poet made it easy to wonder if those images were not physical realities for Raymond. The hunting of a timber wolf, however, was as real for the father as the brass knuckles and billyclub of his days as sheriff. Roseliep discovers these mementoes in this trunk sealed with locks he cannot open at first, literally or figuratively. He thinks the oval locket he finds and cannot open always held the image of his mother, but he is not sure. The gentler side that John Roseliep's second wife could evoke from him is captured by Roseliep in the images of John's bachelor sewing kit and how he twirled a bluebell "like a sparkler." The very existence of this trunk and its revealing contents is further proof of John's gentle side.

79. Roseliep, *Love Makes the Air Light,* front-cover blurb. In his hardbound copy Roseliep penned under the blurb, "written by Denise Levertov...." No acknowledgement was given for her by Norton.

80. Undated letter to Raymond Roseliep from James L. Weil, editor of *Elizabeth.* See binder containing reviews of *Love Makes the Air Light,* LCARC 325, D:1:1:11.

81. Roseliep, *Love Makes the Air Light,* lines 5 and 56.

82. Interview with Marcella Anderson Becker, summer 2003.

83. Roseliep, *Love Makes the Air Light,* lines 2–4.

Roseliep obviously made this attic trip often, but one might wonder if his father ever knew of these secret visits and whether he might have punished the youngster for snooping.

Perhaps the most powerful poetic moment for the Raymond's boy persona is revealed through the juxtaposition of the sounds of his friends playing outside while he puzzled out the "wilderness of myself" inside. Instead of going outside he played inside imaginatively. "With this strange fine figure of man" he took on various personae, oblivious of whether they would have truly fit his father. He brought that "giant of my childhood, built / so long of limb and entangled in those dark / lidded privacies" closer to him in his own private way, making the future poet Roseliep "equidistant / to 'love that makes the air light'" and allowing him to become at least "Chip of his strength."[84]

Kneeling mentally near Roseliep in the attic sitting cross-legged before his father's trunk, consider the echoing journey of another famous attic trip, that of Hart Crane, which Crane remembered in this deeply touching poem from 1926:

My Grandmother's Love Letters[85]

There are no stars to-night
But those of memory.
Yet how much room for memory there is
In the loose girdle of soft rain.

There is even room enough
For the letters of my mother's mother,
Elizabeth,
That have been pressed so long
Into a corner of the roof
That they are brown and soft,
And liable to melt as snow.

Over the greatness of such space
Steps must be gentle.
It is all hung by an invisible white hair.
It trembles as birch limbs webbing the air.

---

84. Roseliep, *Love Makes the Air Light,* line 56.

85. Hart Crane, "My Grandmother's Love Letters," *Hart Crane. Complete Poems and Selected Letters and Prose* (New York: Liveright Publishing Corporation, 1966), 5.

And I ask myself:

"Are your fingers long enough to play
Old keys that are but echoes:
Is the silence strong enough
To carry back the music to its source
And back to you again
As though to her?"

Yet I would lead my grandmother by the hand
Through much of what she would not understand;
And so I stumble. And the rain continues on the roof
With such a sound of gently pitying laughter.

Crane was most probably a homosexual, and his sexuality was deeply troubling for him. In his handling of his grandmother's love letters, he wonders finally about taking his grandmother "by the hand" through "what she would not understand." Crane's suffering is painfully palpable with only the rain for comfort, and even that is pity, a cold comfort indeed. Roseliep's memories of his father echo Crane's gentle warning: "Over the greatness of such space / Steps must be gentle."

The eleven-syllable lines of "My Father's Trunk" even mirror the last four lines of Crane's poem. The line length makes us linger in those attics of memories. Readers do not descend from the experiences. We are left there, first with Crane and then with Roseliep, to ponder Crane's grandmother and Roseliep's father:

My Father's Trunk

The soft grainy light of our attic opened
my father's past a little way. His trunk was
a place where years were shut in him like the leaves
of a book whose title alone he displayed
—I wondered if it was mostly about love,
though other strengths were there pressing a vision
on my landscape. I loved the hunters riding
in coontail caps through the ornamental path
inside the lid—I knew by heart the clipping
how he bagged a timber wolf in some woods near
Farley, Iowa, and I sported the brass

knuckles and dangled the billyclub of his
sheriff days, I aimed the elegant pistol
at spider targets—the topmost color in my
first spectrum was the greenpearl of the handle.
Under the sulphur whiteshirts with hard collars
and their beautiful musty smell and the old
leather smell of razorstrop were keys to locks
I could never open; an oval locket,
sealed tight as a dream, carried I always thought
my mother's image. I tried never to laugh
at the ohio matchbox with the sewing
kit of his bachelor days, and though it was
hard to picture the big fingers threading a
needle, I once saw that hand lift a bluebell
from its tower and twirl it like a sparkler.
The letter in the blue envelope he had
never opened bore a script daintier than
my mother's exquisite flourish, and when I
left the blue flap sealed, ordinary breathing
avowed the silence but did not disturb it.
Stale flower smell on another clipping brushed
me like rain: "a knot of English violets
enhanced the heliotrope gown" his bride wore
at their winter wedding, before "a long tour."
And every solitary honeymoon
to the attic filled my boyhood for a while.

One day I heard the plunk-plunk from our chestnut
tree, the gang all pocketing them for our pipes,
small fry on the block playing stickball, the flash
and thrust of limbs. I sat cross-legged before my
father's trunk and the wilderness of myself.
Signs I found in the tenacious silence of
things: I was the black-footed ferret, juggler,
harlequin: I was a touch on the padded
stairs, a balance of milkweed seed, Picasso
performance. With this strange fine figure of man
I had been playing follow the arrows and

capture the flag. Outside, someone was calling
ollie-ollie-oxen-free, and I was free
as a robin, a sun print on a swimmer,
the detached brownleaf and the unfallen snow.
Slyboots of that giant of my childhood, built
so long of limb and entangled in those dark
lidded privacies, I was equidistant
to 'love that makes the air light.' Chip of his strength.[86]

This poem, admired by many critics, is technically perfect in syllabic strength and gentleness combined, using soft sibilants throughout, and modulating harsher words such as "light" by adjectives such as "grainy" that not only give us a marvelous sight image but a softening of sound. Roseliep, who eventually would confine himself to much shorter lines and total poem length by choosing haiku for his dominant form, certainly knew already the power of *ba* (Japanese for "place"). The attic was a total world opening to the entire persona of the poet as well as a mini-biography of his often elusive father. He used every one of our senses to give a portrait of his father through himself to his readers: the sight and feel of the coonskin cap, the sound of the "plunk-plunk" of chestnuts being pocketed to make pipes, the smell of "sulphur white shirts" and the "leather smell of razorstrop." We could even feel the kinesthetic experience of the lifted bluebell taken from its tower to be twirled. Most of all, we are totally immersed with the son discovering the depth and even the delicacy of this father. Roseliep could certainly identify with his father's sensitivity but he also claimed he was a "chip of his strength."

Critics admired another set of poems, often called "The Barbara Poems" — "For Barbara, by Mistletoe," Note, with Glove," "The Singing Lesson," "First Communion," and "For Barbara, Eight."[87] The child celebrated in these poems was real; the Keohen family who befriended Roseliep often invited him to their home and visited Father Ray in his Holy Family apartment. Barbara was the youngest of the four Keohen daughters.[88] The winsome Barbara child was an attraction all her own through her inventiveness, youth, and trust in him, as well as a potent reminder of boundaries: "You are the fearless jailer / of my growing child

86. Roseliep, "My Father's Trunk," *Love Makes the Air Light*, 15–16.

87. The Barbara poems are printed together in *Love Makes the Air Light*, 34–39.

88. Interview with Marcella Anderson Becker.

day fear / that I should never revel / in the adventure of thorn."[89] All five Barbara poems are heightened in intensity by direct address to the child.

They also linger on the edge of trespass, situated in *Love Makes the Air Light* just after fourteen pages of highly erotic love poetry, all of them in direct address as well. If readers tried to believe the poet's attempts "never [to] revel / in the adventure of thorn," they would be sorely tested by such lines as: "Run me, love me / thru the spring hills / and shooting star / at our ankles"[90] or "Put your hand in my hand / and I love you / deeper than Triton's horn / or whirling grotto"[91] or "When your arms ring my waist / in their tendril / manner, casting a spell / of dark fruit / and rain damp flesh, keener than sickle / cut or grapefall / on a dry faith:"[92] or "Drop your red hair / over my quiet / hand, my arm. / On my breast show it / whatever you find / near a lover's blood, / a man's / terrible wait.... Fire / comes together"[93] or "My world without you, lady / is white and black and gray"[94] or "Though I never rest my hand / on the goldsun of your flesh, / I drain desire from my wish / only when I have wakened"[95] or "Sun is a lion / ... / love, come"[96] or "I love you / and kiss you with my mind. / Darling, / slip into sanctuary / where another angel / can not tread."[97]

In full text, the following poem immediately precedes the Barbara poems:

Poem in Midsummer

The bee is drinking at red
clover fountain
more sparkling than
my burgundy blood.

Host of narcissus
breaking over a green

---

89. Roseliep, "For Barbara, Eight," *Love Makes the Air Light,* 39.

90. Roseliep, "May Song," *Love Makes the Air Light,* 17, lines 1–4.

91. Roseliep, "English Sonnet," *Love Makes the Air Light,* 20, lines 1–4.

92. Roseliep, "Italian Sonnet," *Love Makes the Air Light,* 21, lines 1–8.

93. Roseliep, "Red Hair," *Love Makes the Air Light,* 22, lines 1–8 and 13–14.

94. Roseliep, "To His Dark Lady," *Love Makes the Air Light,* 24, lines 13–14.

95. Roseliep, "Platonic Lover," *Love Makes the Air Light,* 27, lines 1–4.

96. Roseliep, "Invitation to a Promontory Over the Mississippi," *Love Makes the Air Light,* 28, lines 1–2 and 17–18.

97. Roseliep, "When Lutes Be Old," *Love Makes the Air Light,* 32, lines 1–6.

vested body shatters
my day shine.

Darling, this slight
of hand can wreck our love.
What I speak of
is a single light."[98]

Many critics noted that all of the poems in *Love Makes the Air Light* are poems about love in one way or other. Most of those who comment, however, do not refer to the overt eroticism of Roseliep's tantalizing use of a variety of personae and the power of direct address to the lover at hand. The word "darling" for example, occurs infrequently in Roseliep's poetry, but in the two works preceding the Barbara poems, that word is used powerfully in addressing the beloved. The intimacy implied is overwhelming, making the innocuous titles highly ironic.

What are we to make of the young Barbara, innocent, naive—as some critics believe the poet Roseliep to be. Barbara, yes—Roseliep, never. This poet, "cross-legged before/ my father's trunk and the wilderness of myself" is all too aware of being "entangled in those dark/ lidded privacies"[99] and a struggle with how to love as agonizing as the emotions expressed in his haiku "Priest, to Inquirer" reveals:

This cassock whips my
legs through the four seasons so
I'll know who I am.[100]

If it were only that easy for the poet Roseliep.

The five Barbara poems remain an interlocking puzzle: just how should readers interpret this celibate priest's attraction to a young girl? From "The taste/ of your/ holly berry lips"[101] to "The glove you dropped/ (unwittingly) by my single bed/ on our Christmas eve visit,/ with your attending father.... Love/ later, not yet"[102] to "across your father's prize dahlia/ where honeybees wheel in their/ nervous dance, and

---

98. Roseliep, *Love Makes the Air Light*, 33, lines 1–12.

99. Roseliep, "My Father's Trunk," *Love Makes the Air Light*, 16, lines 54–55. The "dark-lidded" can be read as double entendre for the trunk and the poet-persona's eyes.

100. Roseliep, from a sequence, "A Scale of Haiku," *Love Makes the Air Light*, 41.

101. Roseliep, "For Barbara, by Mistletoe," *Love Makes the Air Light*, 34, line 103.

102. Roseliep, "Note, with Glove," *Love Makes the Air Light*, 35–6, lines 1–4 and 23–24.

I plunge into / the troubled waters of my being"[103] to this one of the
Barbara poems, quoted below in entirety:

FIRST COMMUNION

The other day
I took my pen-
knife, Barbara,
opened

a door of violet,
was careful
when I felt
the petal
lantern
my touch
(like your unburnt
flesh),

and made this song
for your Communion.[104]

Opening this poem to interpretation seems to be as dangerous as any
overtly sexual approach to a child. The phallic symbolism of the pen-
knife with the yonic symbolism of the "door of violet" leads only to a
highly charged verb "lantern" and the child's "unburnt / flesh." That this
poem seems a celebration of the child's First Communion only intensifies
the mystery of the intent of the poet. No veil of personae can mitigate the
expressed sexuality of this encounter.

The last poem in the Barbara sequence opens: "The horned toad
sleeps in your hand ... and your fingers caress him like a flower.... You
are the fearless jailer / of my growing child day fear / that I should never
revel / in the adventure of thorn."[105]

What should a reader think? Is the poet-persona pathetically dangerous or deeply poignant? Is any interpreter being overly intrusive
in finding strong phallic/yonic symbols throughout? Should a reader
ignore the overt Freudian undertone/undertow or look, instead, for a

103. Roseliep, "The Singing Lesson," *Love Makes the Air Light,* 37, lines 17–20.

104. Roseliep, *Love Makes the Air Light,* 38, lines 1–14.

105. Roseliep, "For Barbara, Eight," *Love Makes the Air Light,* 39, lines 1 and 9–12.

Jungian overlay of yin/yang with an innocent priest using a child as a lovely Muse?

Critics, if they addressed these poems at all, even superficially, were very cautious in assertions and quite forgiving about what might be the poet-persona's intent. When commenting briefly on the poems that are sexually charged, the Barbara poems among them, Bill Pauly said of Roseliep, "This priest who is poet ... even his fire does not burn, but warms and lights instead. He knows the road of passion and compassion, the vitality and commitment in love that keep it from descending to lukewarm charity on the one hand or lust on the other."[106] Dennis Hayes commented: "[Roseliep] handles the theme of love for a child both humorously and genuinely, with no hint of the usual triteness or sweetness associated with such poems, in what may be called 'the Barbara series.'" After quoting "For Barbara by Mistletoe," referring to "Note with Glove" and giving lines from "For Barbara, Eight," this critic consoled us with: "But fear not—Roseliep remains chaste, and Barbara and all his other friends intact. He really is not a sex maniac, just a word and form maniac."[107] Readers, perhaps, will remain wary.

Not all the poems in *Love Makes the Air Light* were of such intensity as the Barbara poems and those that precede the sequence. Roseliep often chose his students for a poem's jumping-off place, as well as his brother Louis and a few famous literary correspondents such as E. E. Cummings and Katherine Anne Porter.

Some critics believed Roseliep's third hardbound volume was his best; others thought differently. In an anonymous note in the *Virginia Kirkus Bulletin* an editor commented,

> Mr. Roseliep has published two other volumes of verse, and apparently is a college English teacher. Several poems are addressed to his students, or are about other poets, or spring from quotations. He is fond of the Haiku ... and other short forms, which are often academic, sentimental, about friends or children and full of somewhat contrived images. However, there is a handful of good poems. In boyhood recollections, or impersonal subjects, the short lines become simple, telling, and free of mannerisms; and in the few poems in which the poet gives himself enough room, he can create a moving,

---

106. William Pauly, "The Various Light," *Lower Stumpf Lake Review* (St. John's University Press), spring 1967: 8.

107. Dennis Hayes, "Love Makes the Air Light," *The Scholastic* (University of Notre Dame), January 21, 1966: 25.

rich atmosphere. It seems curious that he should have chosen to concentrate on what appears to be the least of his talents."[108]

One can wonder what this anonymous reviewer would have thought of the flood of haiku volumes that began flowing in 1976, beginning with *Flute Over Walden.*

In case any reader pondered how to leave this volume, Roseliep himself pointed the way in the final poem.

THE SMOKE SMELL OF SPRING

The smoke smell of spring and your smoky hair
Hum in the nostril,
that kid with the red cap fires a hardball
over the sun,
a housewife tinsels the branching clothes line
brighter than her sunburn,
a spider stubs a toe on rock
footlighting a ballet of violets.

In these middle years I hail my stance:
rise, move, turn,
a priest darkgolden,
oiled and wined for the dance.[109]

Roseliep presented himself brave-faced, addressing once more an ambiguous loved one, using the color red to signify his ever-abiding passion, noting the intricacies of a world he loved and affirming his priesthood as well as his ability to stand astride at least two worlds, "oiled and wined for the dance."

Poetry Contests and Awards

Not long after Roseliep began publishing his poetry, he began to win awards. The first came in 1962 when he was the third place winner in the 12th annual cash awards for poetry of the *Carolina Quarterly,* a literary magazine published by the University of North Carolina. He seemed to take off in 1968, reaping three awards: third prize for "Timothy" in the 1967 *Writer's Digest* poetry contest, announced in the

---

108. "Love Makes the Air Light," *Virginia Kirkus Bulletin*, September 15, 1965.
109. Roseliep, *Love Makes the Air Light,* 110, lines 1–12.

February 1968 issue and reprinted in *Shenandoah* in their August 1969 and winter 1970 issues.[110]

TIMOTHY

My student gives me his six pound son
as he once gave me his bachelor's
essay on 'Childe Roland to the Dark
Tower Came.' I hold him as a sack
of plums, then tenderly as a man
with a portion of first folios.
Soon this weight in my hands will become
a bee of a boy carrying his
own honey as his father and as
I had done—oh, he'll strip, run to swim
dark waters darker than his pubic
hair. I hand him back to his father, rummage my closet to see
     whether
I'd kept a horn that makes sad music.

Roseliep's dark themes of lost loves and a more sensual way of living are already evident in his earliest poems.

More significant for Roseliep was the Kenneth F. Montgomery Poetry Award in 1968, given by the Society of Midland Authors at their 53rd annual dinner and award presentations on April 6, 1968, in Chicago. Letters to and from the Society of Midland Authors, saved by Roseliep in his Awards folder, make it clear that Roseliep declined the invitation to attend the award presentation because by that time he was no longer teaching at Loras College and was continually strug-gling with his voice problems, making only rare—if any—public appearances.[111]

---

110. In the first printing of "Timothy" in *Shenandoah: The Washington and Lee University Review* 21 (August 1969), 30, the word "pubic," intended by Roseliep, was changed to "public" by the editors. Roseliep informed them of the error, and the reprinted poem in *Shenandoah* 21 (Winter 1970), 16, contained this footnote: "This poem is reprinted from the Autumn 1969 issue; line 11 contained a serious typographical error."

111. Letters from Arthur Weinberg, president of the Society of Midland Authors, April 1 and 19, 1968, to Raymond Roseliep. Mrs. William A. Schmid, who sent the check, wrote on March 22, 1968: "I re-read your poems in *Poetry*, and was taken as usual with the originality, lovability, and strength of them.... The check will be for $100.00."

In May 1968 for his poem "Swan," he received First Honorable Mention in the Leigh Hanes Memorial Poetry Contest sponsored by the Poetry Society of Virginia and announced at their annual meeting in Williamsburg. Exactly which poem was honored is not certain but may have been this haiku, from *Sailing Bones:*

> milkweed …
> Pavlova's
> swan

Many awards came to Roseliep later for his haiku and are discussed in Chapter Five, next.

Chapter Five: Haijin

unable
to get hibiscus red
the artist eats the flower

—Light Footsteps[1]

Haijin, very simply, is Japanese for "haiku person." The designation must be used sparingly, however, only for those writers who have achieved status in the world of haiku and have dedicated their lives to the genre.

Raymond Roseliep was a *haijin*. So was William J. Higginson, one of the earliest and most prominent members of the American haiku community, who said that "Iowans learned daring from Roseliep."[2] Higginson called the Iowan a "fine poet ... able to win 5-7-5 and freeform haiku contests in the same year, with interesting, sometimes startling poems."[3]

All readers, critics, and writers of haiku must come to some sort of definition of haiku, and more specifically of what Roseliep called "American haiku." He was not one unthinkingly to accept the definitions of others, even those generally taken as authoritative. He was quite familiar, for example, with R. H. Blyth's four-volume *Haiku* and two-volume *History of Haiku*. Roseliep marked a few passages in his personal copies of and drew an arrow to this passage:

> [Haiku] is the infinite grasped in the hand, before the eyes, in the hammering of a nail, the touch of cold water, the smell of chrysanthemums, the smell of *this* chrysanthemum. Haiku are thus an expression of the union of those two forms of living which Spengler

---

1. Raymond Roseliep, *Light Footsteps* (La Crosse, Wis.: Juniper Press, 1976).

2. William J. Higginson, *Haiku Compass: Directions in the Poetical Map of the United States of America* (Tokyo: Haiku International Association, 1994), 8.

3. Higginson, 8.

regarded as irreconcilable and mutually ununderstandable, the Classical feeling of the present moment, of restricted space, and the Modern European feeling of eternity, infinity.[4]

Roseliep, however, would eventually call into question the complete applicability of any definition of Japanese haiku to the kind of haiku being written in America, particularly his own. He was well acquainted with the landmark definition from the Haiku Society of America,[5] issued in 1973 and revised in 1976:

> An unrhymed Japanese poem recording the essence of a moment keenly perceived, in which Nature is linked to human nature. It usually consists of seventeen *onji* (Japanese sound-symbols).

After substantial research and discussion, in March 1993 the Haiku Society of America adopted a new definition of haiku that became the norm for the American haiku community:

> A haiku is a short poem that uses imagistic language to convey the essence of an experience of nature or the season intuitively linked to the human condition.[6]

Definitions, redefinitions, and clarifications of what an English-language haiku should be are a preoccupation of haiku specialists. One recent attempt comes from Charles Trumbull, who provided the definition he used when he was editor of *Modern Haiku*:

> Haiku is a brief verse that epitomizes a single moment. It uses the juxtaposition of two concrete images, often a universal condition of nature and a particular aspect of human experience, in a way that prompts the reader to make an insightful connection between the two. The best haiku allude to the appropriate season of the year. Good haiku avoid subjectivity; intrusions of the poet's ego, views, or values; and displays of intellect, wit, and facility with words.[7]

---

4. R. H. Blyth, *Haiku. Vol. I: Eastern Culture* (Tokyo: Hokuseido Press, 1949), xiii.

5. "The Haiku Society of America is a not-for-profit organization founded in 1968 by Harold G. Henderson and Leroy Kanterman to promote the writing and appreciation of haiku poetry in English. Membership is open to all readers, writers, translators, and students of haiku. The HSA has been meeting regularly since its inception and sponsors open lectures, workshops, readings, and contests." From the HSA website, http://www.hsa-haiku.org/about-hsa.htm.

6. Complete definitions may be found at "Official Definitions of Haiku and Related Terms," Haiku Society of America website, http://www.hsa-haiku.org/archives/HSA_Definitions_2004.html.

7. Charles Trumbull, e-mail, February 11, 2013. The *Modern Haiku* definitions of haiku and related forms may be found in "Submission Guidelines and Policies" on the Modern Haiku website, http://www.modernhaiku.org/submissions.html.

Haikuist and haiku blogger Dave Russo fleshed out his own definition with thoughts about haiku and potential guidelines for their composition. He wrote,

> There are many definitions of haiku, such as this one provided by the Haiku Society of America.... Definitions are a good place to start, and they can be used to strengthen or challenge our assumptions about haiku. Definitions are not good for settling arguments about what is truly a haiku. No single definition can do justice to the tides of tradition and innovation that have washed over haiku in the last 400 years.[8]

Quoting translator and former HSA president Hiroaki Sato, Russo put haiku definition in a historical perspective: "Today it may be possible to describe haiku but not define it.... [*The Encyclopedic Dictionary of Contemporary Haiku* (Tokyo: Meiji Shoin, 1980)] describes the history of the term, but makes no attempt to say what a haiku is. Both in form and content, all you can say is that a haiku, be it composed in Japanese, English or any other language, is what the person who has written it presents as a haiku."[9] Russo further ruled out any categorical definition:

> One of the early pioneers of haiku in English, Harold Henderson (1958) has written, "A definitive definition of haiku is probably impossible [as haiku] must be what poets make them, not verses that follow 'rules' set down by some 'authority' ... a strict definition is neither possible nor desirable."[10]

Russo delineated differences between Japanese and English haiku. He quoted from Columbia University Shincho Professor of Japanese Literature Haruo Shirane,[11]

> If pressed to give a definition of English-language haiku that would encompass the points that I have made here, I would say, echoing the spirit of Basho's own poetry, that haiku in English is a short poem, usually written in one to three lines, that seeks out new and revealing perspectives on the human and physical condition, focusing on the immediate physical world around us, particularly that of nature, and on the workings of the human imagination, memory, literature and history.

---

8. Dave Russo, "Haiku Definitions," North Carolina Haiku Society website, http://nc-haiku. org/haiku-definitions; accessed March 15, 2014.

9. Hiroaki Sato, "HSA definition reconsidered," *Frogpond* 22:3 (1999), 73.

10. Harold G. Henderson, *Introduction to Haiku* (New York: Doubleday, 1958).

11. Haruo Shirane, "Beyond the Haiku Moment: Bashō, Buson, and Modern Haiku Myths," *Modern Haiku* 31:1 (Winter–Spring 2000): 48–63. Also available online at http://www.haikupoet. com/definitions/beyond_the_haiku_moment.html.

Russo, though probably accepting that an end-all definition of haiku is impossible, still kept searching. In a comment to the online haiku anthology *Montage*[12] he wrote, "Just thought of another consideration in regard to the importance of haiku definitions—context. We all know this: I'm just adding a little to the conversation." That little turns out to be quite a lot when he offers differences for the various audiences to whom he might speak: a group of people familiar with haiku; people more familiar with haiku and its variations, who are reading collections of poems that purport to be haiku; and, finally: "If I am an editor of *Poetry* magazine, my working definition of a haiku might be: 'A kind of brief poem we do not publish unless the work seems to fit with the other poems we've selected for that issue.' It might help if the work was by someone we've heard of, like Tomas Tranströmer."[13]

Poems Morphing into Haiku

Most American poets begin their haiku careers by writing haiku for themselves, then for family and friends, before they start submitting their work to newspapers, magazines, and haiku journals. Collections in books are not the norm for most poets until much later. No so with Raymond Roseliep. He began writing typical lyrical poetry in school and producing full-length books of his poems in the early 1960s. In books of poetry Roseliep marked his journey from longer poetry to very short texts by including haiku and haiku-like shorter lines in interlocking stanzas.

Evidence of Roseliep's willingness, even as a beginning poet, to experiment with any poetic form was clear from an article in the "Poems for Our Time" column of the *Louisville Courier-Journal* dated August 9, 1959.[14] Poetry columnist Abbey Meguire Roach was not really a haiku critic, but it was clear to her that Roseliep was experimenting with content and style. She wrote about his "The Little Love You Give": "Here is another of those descendants of Robert Browning's penetrating human

---

12. Allan Burns, selector, "Comparative Haiku: Haiku of Dave Russo." *Montage* 34 (week of October 25, 2009). http://www.thehaikufoundation.org/2009/10/25/montage-34/; accessed March 15, 2014.

13. Swedish Nobel Prize–winning poet Tomas Tranströmer (1931–2015) for many years wrote haiku among his other poems. His 2004 work, *Den stora gåtan* (*The Great Enigma*, 2006), includes several dozen haiku. Dave Russo, "Haiku Definitions," North Carolina Haiku Society website; http://nc-haiku.org/haiku-definitions; accessed March 15, 2014.

14. "Articles About Raymond Roseliep," LCARC 325, D:1:35. The earliest of these saved articles in 1959 from "Poems for Our Time" in *The Louisville Courier-Journal* predates his publication of his first book, *The Linen Bands* in 1961.

presentations, done in one of the very latest modes, for styles in poetry as in all the arts and everything else are constantly changing, and difference and novelty add their own penetration and thrust as here. This is one to turn over in the mind."

At a quick glance it looks as though this poem might be another of Roseliep's ten-line syllabics.

THE LITTLE LOVE YOU GIVE

The little love you give is much. You see
it is not simple for a man of my
capacity — no, limitation is
the word — to have you in: for trust is strange
to my vocabulary or becomes
a game I seldom play, but hardly name.

What you are granting as a kind of loan
looks big, and I am poor enough to rank
it as a need. Since you are thrifty, I
would never take a gambler's chance and ask you in
where willingness is not a gambler's sin.

The room is narrow, yes. Arrange your coins
in double stock upon the table of
my soul: if you should win them back, please say
the loan is canceled (for security
is out of question).

Now my invitation stands;
friend stay as long as you can stay
if only for an ordinary day.

But, though often containing ten syllables, the lines began to vary visually, using a combination of short-syllable words plus a longer word. The internal rhyme was unexpected. Roseliep played upon the words "game" and "gambling," suggesting the erotic in lines addressed to someone, "I'll take a gambler's chance and ask you in / where willingness is not a gambler's sin."

Roach commented on Roseliep's "Cobweb Detail" on January 24, 1960: "This poem calls for careful reading. But when one has followed the testimony of all five senses to the beauty of law and order in one small phenomenon — one glimpses the loving care that must be back of all creation and how that Law and that Love are One." Though Roseliep used rhyme and rhythm in these seven stanzas, each stanza could be considered a four-line haiku. Two of the stanzas read

> Clock the ear
> by nervous strings
> till wind rubs
> where music clings

> Decode when you touch
> spun thought like this,
> almost aware
> of what Love is.

On June 19, 1960, Roach wrote about "The Day My Father Was Buried": "Dr. Roseliep has his own way of seeing and saying things, and is saying quite a lot of them in different ways in a variety of media." What a wonder if we could have followed Roach's particularly sensitive readings beyond 1963, when she ended her last critique with "The Scissors Grinder" writing this perceptive observation: "It is modern and something else yet again."

Joseph Joel Keith, a critic writing for the journal *Mutiny*, commented in 1961,

> Always the intelligent craftsman, Raymond Roseliep has grown for anyone who has studied his poems in quality journals, to become the inspired artist. And what is an inspired artist? It is a man, never content with the facility of his gift and a desire to rush into print, who would be a perfectionist.... It is a valuable device when a poet knows what he is doing.... Raymond Roseliep, finding the strictures of syllabics challenging, has chosen all patterns of this difficult form; and has succeeded admirably when he has created his own rhythms.[15]

It is not entirely clear where Roseliep first learned of haiku. He said he began working with haiku in 1963,[16] but already earlier in the 1960s he was writing shorter-line verses resembling haiku in both spirit and form. Two poems, "Spider" and "Flight 621," published in the *Delta*

---

15. *Mutiny* 4:1 (1961–62), 58–59.
16. Raymond Roseliep, "This Haiku of Ours," *Bonsai* 1:3 (1976), 11.

Epsilon Sigma Bulletin,[17] looked much like linked haiku, and most of the five three-lined stanzas can be read on their own merit; for example, the first stanza of "Spider"[18] (presented in full on page 202):

> Tender footed, tip
> toe in raveling harshlight,
> young-body ardent.

Even the four-line stanzas of Roseliep's "Flight" are akin to contemporary haiku. A sequence that he published in the December 1964 issue of the *Delta Epsilon Sigma Bulletin* was named "A Scale of Haiku." These poems bear titles and follow the 5–7–5 syllable count prevalent in many haiku of the early 1960s. "Spider" also appeared in Roseliep's *The Small Rain* (1963) with other three-line poems that began to be patterned like haiku. He repeated "A Scale of Haiku" in *Love Makes the Air Light* (1965) where many of his sequences are three-line and four-line shortened stanzas.

Roseliep most often wrote in a book the date he acquired it. In his personal library he had Harold G. Henderson's *Haiku in English*, the paperback version, with his date of March 1968, and Eric W. Amann's *The Wordless Poem*, dated December 1969. So in the 1960s Father Ray was aware of the best of haiku writing and commentary. It is likely that the priest-poet's correspondence with Elizabeth Searle Lamb—who was publishing in *American Haiku, Haiku West,* and *Modern Haiku* in the mid-1960s and became a charter member of the Haiku Society of America in 1968—was eventually a defining influence for all things haiku in his life from 1978 onward.[19]

Roseliep's poetry book *The Small Rain* (1963) already had several poems suggesting haiku. The title poem is one example. The first section reads,

> After the small
> rain
> has rained
> down

---

17. *Delta Epsilon Sigma Bulletin* 7:3 (October 1962), 84–85. *Delta Epsilon Sigma Bulletin* (later renamed *Delta Epsilon Sigma Journal*), the organ of the national Catholic scholastic honor society, was an important periodical for Roseliep throughout his publishing career. From 1951 to 1983 it printed forty-eight of his poems.

18. Roseliep, *The Small Rain* (1963), 70. "Spider" was one of Roseliep's many nicknames.

19. The first letters from Roseliep to Lamb that he saved date from 1978, although hers to him date from 1976. Some correspondence is undated.

and sky is
made
clean and I
am untroubled again

quiet
near the clock
spring of no-
time:

I will lie
waiting
for simple
light to twine

my body
peaceful as a
star in rain
water.

Trumbull suggests that at this point Roseliep was not yet writing haiku per se, but rather "tailoring his longer poems, quite possibly under the influence of haiku. In any event, Roseliep was shortening both his lines and stanzas. The stanzas ... in *The Small Rain* are not stand-alone poems—they're merely short stanzas."[20] Poems such as "Spider" and "Anointing," he suggests further, are "a clear step in the haiku direction."

> I'm aware of only about fifty haiku written in four lines published by anyone in English before 1970. In addition to Roseliep (*Love Makes the Air Light*, 1965) there are several each by two Japanese, Yone Noguchi (who calls them haiku) and Jun Fujita (who calls his tanka), as well as Costa Rica–born poet Álvaro Cardona-Hine and a few one-offs, including Gary Snyder, Cor van den Heuvel, and Mae Sarton.
>
> Anyone judging many of the shorter-lined poems as akin to haiku would find Roseliep already violating a number of haiku traditions. Perhaps he is among the first to write four-line haiku such as in "The Old King" or "Portrait of a King" (in *The Small Rain*). The interlocking multi-stanzas of "Spider" and "For My Last Anointing" wear a 5–7–5 outer coat, but those poems bear titles and are often overtly didactic.[21]

---

20. Charles Trumbull e-mail, October 28, 2013.
21. Trumbull e-mail, October 28, 2013.

Poems of Roseliep's that were clearly intended as haiku made their debut in his third book, *Love Makes the Air Light* (1965), nestled in with longer poems. The book includes ninety-six haiku and haiku-inspired poems, nearly all of them in titled sequences. One of the most intriguing is:

SONG FROM AN ENCLOSURE

They say you are
nearest when
far away.

I would like
to feel you if only
breath on my cheek

or quick
collision
of skin

to bother
belief, elusive-
my-love

O

room is wide and the world is
wide

Christ!
and it's that way
inside my fortress of flesh.[22]

This sequence has a typical Roseliep theme of the poet's ongoing conflict of the appropriate way to express his passion under the constraints of the life of a celibate priest. Consider also this sequence:

FOR DENISE, DISTRACTING

Girl sudden
as yellow rainfall
running a yellow

---

22. Raymond Roseliep, *Love Makes the Air Light* (New York: W. W. Norton & Co., 1965), 103.

vein thru the birdwing
in my poem,
you are tampering with

artifact and fact:
a bluejay
candled branch

breaks
when you kneel on the gray
marble of my mind.

I will leave confessional
foolscap
littered with birds

to take communion
in the late air
where light is at a premium.[23]

The lines, "you are tampering with / artifact and fact," relating to Denise, could indicate the difficulty Roseliep encounters dealing with his various attractions that he seeks to temper or sublimate in poetry.

Roseliep plays with structure in his haiku sequences, sometimes giving interior names or numbering sections or composing mini and humorous sketches of various people he knew such as the Keohen family,[24] opening with:

Mr.

The chocolate bat
over his bald head rings a
lopsided halo.[25]

Two haiku sequences, titled "A Scale of Haiku" and "Upon Cherry Stones," use a sequence title as well as individual titles for the haiku within the grouping. He employed the traditional 5–7–5–syllable format,

---

23. Roseliep, *Love Makes the Air Light*, 109.

24. Dr. Gerald Keohen was the Roseliep family physician and friend. His daughter was the subject of Raymond's Barbara poems — *see* page 78.

25. "Summer Night at the Keohens," Roseliep, *Love Makes the Air Light*, 73–74.

initial capitalization, and terminal punctuation. All of these haiku compositional details would soon be out of fashion, and indeed Roseliep himself soon dropped them in his own work. Because they lack seasonality and treat human nature, these poems would probably be called by purists senryu, haiku's humorous cousin. Here are two examples from "A Scale of Haiku":

PRIEST, TO INQUIRER

This cassock whips my
legs through the four seasons so
I'll know who I am.

AFTERNOON WALK

I look back to see
the figure I lightly brushed,
now veiled in black rain.[26]

Such haiku sequences abounded in *Love Makes the Air Light.* Most had a central theme, but they were often burdened with heavy titles, making poems into mini-sermons. Clearly, though, Roseliep was tending toward much shorter lines, abandoning his earlier syllabics and sonnets. His ongoing theme of love constrained, however, can make reading this text another entrance into an overriding level of pain in the poet's life.

Publication in Non-haiku Journals and Anthologies

Raymond Roseliep did not start publishing his haiku in specialized haiku journals until 1970. As he noted in a bibliography compiled in 1967: "My poems have appeared in more than a hundred periodicals since 1944." The most important and the most representative of this period in the priest-poet's publishing history were: *Commonweal, The Catholic World, America, Thoreau Journal Quarterly,* and *Yankee.*

The Catholic World

Gradually, haiku as well as longer poems began appearing in some of these publications. The most notable was the two-page illustrated spread in *The Catholic World* in 1969, titled "O Western Wind:

26. "A Scale of Haiku," Roseliep, *Love Makes the Air Light,* 40–41.

A Sheaf of Haiku by Raymond Roseliep."[27] These haiku were all titled and followed a strict format of three lines of 5–7–5 syllables. Roseliep's wit and proclivity to experiment were already evident in these eight haiku. A sample:

AFTER THE RORSCHACH

Do not forget to
put the tinker toy of me
together again.

O WESTERN WIND

Whose step on the rain
outside my bedroom window
Christ! I think I know.[28]

The letters between Roseliep and the editors of *The Catholic World* were brief and professional compared to the friendly, personal correspondence with later editors. Typical is one from January 20, 1967: "I am happy to accept your poem, 'Parents,' for publication as soon as the schedule permits. Payment will be forwarded to you shortly." Roseliep could be demanding and even acerbic in these exchanges with poetry editors, as in this exchange in 1969 with Rev. John B. Sheerin, CSP, of *The Catholic World.* When Roseliep's work did not appear in print in what he considered a timely manner, Roseliep wrote, "While I am writing, perhaps you won't mind my asking after my series of short poems entitled 'Some Small Creatures' which you accepted on July 21, 1967." He was assured that these haiku would appear in the April 1969 issue. Then when he saw the final version, Roseliep was surprised by the layout of the poems. He wrote to Sheerin, "I want to thank you for the remarkable way you presented my poems, 'Some Small Creatures,' in your April issue. Those line drawings were sensitive, charming, disarming, and

---

27. Interview with Elizabeth Searle Lamb, May 11, 2004. Most probably these pages caught the eye of Lamb who eventually became a life-long correspondent with Roseliep. In 1969 Lamb was writing a regular column for *Modern Haiku,* titled "Random Notes from an Anonymous Haiku-Watcher," but no record of her early correspondence with Roseliep exists in the Roseliep files at Loras or in the American Haiku Archive in Sacramento, which houses the Lamb papers.

28. Roseliep, "O Western Wind: A Sheaf of Haiku," *The Catholic World* (November 1969), 62, and reprinted with changed formatting in Roseliep, *Step on the Rain* (1977), 37.

marvelously imaginative. I only wish you had given the name of your artist on the page with the poems."

Roseliep asked for and received the name of the artist, Martin Charlot, and wrote a letter of thanks to him. This demonstrates the kind of personal involvement typical of Father Ray and, of course, was usually appreciated by his collaborators in publishing. Nudged by a note from Roseliep, Charlot also agreed to illustrate "O Western Wind: a Sheaf of Haiku": "I hope you might be able to give me a kind of repeat performance—with some of my haiku. These would adapt beautifully to the talent of your artist, and a page or a two-page spread would be unique indeed." In that same letter Roseliep had also admonished the editor: "I suspect you haven't the space (that's one reason, by the way, why I don't submit more often, wishing that you had the room for more poems—but I do understand; and I am glad you can print as many as you do; there are so few good Catholic markets, and you know that too)."

Perhaps it was Roseliep's urging that resulted in an entire issue of *The Catholic World* (January/February 1976), titled *Faith and Poetry*. Don Brophy, a member of the editorial board, wrote, "Many readers may feel it is unusual, and perhaps even mistaken, to devote an entire issue of *New Catholic World* to poetry. In the past this magazine has addressed itself to practical, pastoral matters like education, worship, human behavior, and moral attitudes. It has never pretended to be a literary journal. But now, suddenly, one whole issue is given to poetry. Why?" Brophy explains that many poets were asked to write short essays explaining what it meant to be an artist with religious beliefs in today's world." He ended his full-page introduction with these words: "Poetry is a kind of divine foolishness that attempts to capture the entire cosmos within the confines of a single vision. We are all poets in the end."

Roseliep's contribution to this issue was an essay he wanted to be titled "Against the Night." All essays in that issue, however, were to have the same title, "A Poet's Belief." Roseliep kept the theme of his preferred title, however, opening his essay: "While I rebel against the night surrounding us, my nature has its own way of attempting to achieve peace with itself and other natures and to bring order from The Chaos." He ended, "A Christian commitment, poetry helps me unearth the coherence of life. It completes and caps my being. It is my stand against the night." Roseliep directed that these words, "Against the Night," appear on his gravestone.

Two of Roseliep's poems appeared in this special issue, along with this essay "Winter Wedding" (including eight haiku linked by the poet's closeness to the winter season) and a full-page spread of a longer poem, "Drink the Wind," which ends:

> Kicking old steps
> behind you,
> artful dodger,
> make one hell of a dust
> on what ever guilty ghetto,
> run out of your shoes,
> drink the wind.[29]

Roseliep's last appearance in *The Catholic World* was an appreciative essay titled "Raymond Roseliep: Poet-Priest," by Harry James Cargas, in 1977.[30] By the time Cargas wrote this essay, Roseliep had asserted that he did not want to be labeled a priest. The essay begins, however, "The subject of the poet-priest continues to intrigue. So many people will ask of the man, are you a priest first, or an author?" Roseliep had written Cargas, "I write not because I'm a priest but because I'm a lover." Cargas was satisfied enough with that answer to label Roseliep's oeuvre "Acts of Love."

Thoreau Journal Quarterly

One of Roseliep's favorite periodicals was *Thoreau Journal Quarterly*,[31] edited for many years by the prominent and often acerbic critic, Lewis Leary. The relationship between the poet who had written *Flute Over Walden* and Wade Van Dore, poetry editor of the journal, might seem strange, and at first glance their correspondence was sparse if you were looking in editors' folders among Roseliep's personal papers.

---

29. Raymond Roseliep, "A Poet's Belief," *The Catholic World*, 219:1 (January/February 1976), 41–43.

30. Harry Cargas, "Raymond Roseliep: Poet-Priest," *The Catholic World*, 49:5 (December 1977), 228–29.

31. Henry David Thoreau and Ralph Waldo Emerson have influenced American haiku enormously. Many poets, including Roseliep, have followed their lead. Book-length examples include Robert Spiess, ed., *A Haiku Poet's Thoreau: Passages from the Writings of Henry David Thoreau* (Madison, Wis.: mimeographed, 1974); Mary Kullberg, *Morning Mist: Through the Seasons with Matsuo Basho and Henry David Thoreau* (New York: Weatherhill Press, 1993); Thomas Paul Lynch, *An Original Relation to the Universe: Emersonian Poetics of Immanence and Contemporary American Haiku* (Dissertation, University of Oregon, 1989); and Ian Marshall, *Walden by Haiku* (Athens, Ga.: University of Georgia Press, 2009).

The Van Dore file, however, contains evidence a strong professional friendship. In one early letter, dated April 30, 1976, Van Dore wrote "I expect to rent a car outside New York, then go up into southwestern N.E. to get a couple of names and see bluets, apple-blossoms, lilacs. Wish we could take this trip together to compare flute-notes on the natural goodies." At the time Van Dore was writing a review of *Flute Over Walden* for the journal.[32]

The voluminous correspondence between the two poets began around 1969. Roseliep's first copy of the *Thoreau Journal Quarterly* (April 1973) was a gift from Van Dore, and Roseliep began appearing in the periodical in July of that year, this haiku winning special commendation:

> Walden breathes evening:
> man by a buttermilk sky,
> stickman in the water.[33]

In October 1973 Van Dore had published an essay, "Thoreauhaiku," in which he introduced seventeen haiku of Roseliep's, concluding, "The *Thoreau Journal Quarterly* is honored in being permitted to bring out the first *Thoreauhaiku*, which are worthy of appearing in America's oldest or best magazines.... Surely, the quality of these poems justifies the term *Thoreauhaiku*, and I suggest it be adopted and used henceforth as a banner head on *TJQ*'s haiku page."[34]

Many of these haiku were chosen by Roseliep for *Flute Over Walden* (1976). Among them:

> Concord visitors
> 　drink the wine of morning air,
> 　　break the bread of words.

> We Swamp Gods bid you
> grace our toadstool Round Table,
> 　Lord Druid Thoreau.

---

32. *Thoreau Journal Quarterly,* 8:4 (October 1976), 31–32. Van Dore was a student of Robert Frost's at Amherst College in the early 1900s and became a lifelong friend, helping Van Dore publish a book of his poems and inviting him to live with the Frost family at The Gully, his farm near Shaftsbury, Vt.

33. Raymond Roseliep, haiku, *Thoreau Journal Quarterly,* 5:3 (July 1973), 24.

34. Wade Van Dore, "Thoreauhaiku," *Thoreau Journal Quarterly* 5:4 (October 1973), 11–13.

In April 1978 Van Dore, who wanted most of all to be acknowledged as an environmentalist poet,[35] published a "Declaration of Dependence," dated July 4th, A.D. 1976. Many prominent poets, including Denise Levertov, Richard Eberhart, Richard Wilbur, Louis Untermeyer, Stanley Kunitz, and Van Dore, as well as Raymond Roseliep, signed the statement "on nature so that, beginning in this historic year, it may become our salvation." On a facing page was Van Dore's manifesto on Thoreauvian concepts of the interdependence of all forms of life. This issue also featured eight of Roseliep's haiku under the title "The Haiku Moment," including[36]

> drinking
> a dipperful
> of moon

> first
> out of the jet
> a fly

Roseliep kept in touch with Van Dore until the early 1980s.

Yankee

A folksy, widely circulated monthly from the company that had published *The Old Farmer's Almanac* since 1792, *Yankee* also caught Roseliep's eye in the late 1960s. Over the years he published dozens of poems in *Yankee,* one last haiku of his appearing in the June 1984, a half-year after his death.[37]

> IN BROAD DAYLIGHT
>
> apricot stamen
> on the nun's veil
>   bee in pursuit

---

35. *See* http://www.beauxartsbook.com/Writers/Wade.html.

36. Raymond Roseliep, "The Haiku Moment," *Thoreau Journal Quarterly* 9:2 (April 1978), 29.

37. Editors such as Jean Burden often had a hefty stash of Roseliep's poetry in reserve for a future issue. Certainly, this last haiku printed by *Yankee* can be read as chosen by Jean Burden for a final Roseliep erotic pun. Stamen, a male flower part shaped very like a penis, rests chastely on a nun's veil. But, a "bee in pursuit" takes the reader, perhaps, to naughty thoughts.

With the helpful guidance of Jean Burden, *Yankee's* poetry editor, Father Ray now had the opportunity to share his work with a much more diverse audience. Their collaboration signaled a break from Roseliep's publishing primarily in the Catholic press. His first appearance in *Yankee* (August 1968) was titled "Zoo." The poem has four linked stanzas that suggest Roseliep's stylistic journey through shorter-lined poems to haiku:

Zoo

Too much color in the aviary
hurts my eyes and I kept going back
to the Bengal tigers in their strong

smelling room of damp cement.
I tried to forget Blake and his fierce
beauty concept, drawn by these tigers.

A year later I nudge ten billion
thought cells and their red eyed nerves:
Why did I keep returning? didn't fire

already run the length of my vein ways?
Tigers smooth with cream texture
flow and flow. I am still drawn.

This poem is rich with mythic meaning, drawing upon Roseliep's poetic linking of the color red with his personality. The question "Why did I keep returning?" is self-directed and uses the pun "vein ways" to underscore his obsession with Bengal tigers. Even the word "drawn" is not innocent, suggesting torture and the rack of his chosen life.

Burden's last letter to Roseliep was posted December 6, 1983, the day of his death. She often sent him personally created cards with her poems and various pictures of her and her cat, a fondness they shared. Her last poem was titled "Now in the Brief Hours." That poem ends

Warned of early snow,
we reap the scarlet poems,
falling from burning trees.

She wished him a "New Year full of Joy and Love."

Specialized Haiku Journals

Modern Haiku

In 1963, *American Haiku,* the first American periodical devoted entirely to haiku, began publication in Platteville, Wis., a scant 40 miles northeast of Dubuque, where Father Ray resided and taught. He certainly would have gotten word of this seminal publication, but apparently he never met James and Gayle Bull, *American Haiku*'s founders and editors; he certainly never published any haiku there.[38] To keep things in perspective, however, it should be noted that many other haiku publications of the 1960s and 1970s—for example, Jean Calkins's *Haiku Highlights* and Rhoda de Long Jewell's *Janus & SCTH*—did not contain Roseliep's work either. Clearly, he was being selective in where he sent his haiku.

Modern Haiku was founded in California in 1969 by Kay Titus Mormino; the first issue appeared in the winter of 1969–70. Mormino had been writing haiku for several years already, but she was dissatisfied with the quality of the work she saw in the existing publications. Under her editorship *Modern Haiku* quickly became the most authoritative voice in American haiku—and the place where most poets, Roseliep included, sought to place their work. In 1977 Mormino passed the reins of editorship to Robert Spiess in Madison, Wis. Spiess had been one of the editors of *American Haiku* in the mid-1960s and served with Mormino as associate editor of *Modern Haiku* from 1971 to 1977. He remained chief editor of *Modern Haiku* for an astonishing 25 years.

In 1977 Roseliep was first mentioned in the *Modern Haiku* column "Random Notes from an Anonymous Haiku-Watcher."[39] The columnist, Elizabeth Lamb, mentioned that "four 'Thoreauhaiku' [were published] in the *Thoreau Journal Quarterly,* January, 1975. These will be reprinted in his collection, *Flute Over Walden,* to be published later this year by Vagrom Chapbooks."[40]

The initial letter from Roseliep to Mormino was not preserved in Roseliep's *Modern Haiku* folder, but her first letter to him, dated January 5, 1970, was retained: "Dear Sir, I do not know how to address

---

38. Gayle Bull e-mail, October 22, 2013.

39. "Random Notes from an Anonymous Haiku-Watcher," *Modern Haiku* 8:1 (Winter–Spring 1977), 37.

40. Lamb interview. She first discovered Roseliep's haiku in magazines, notably "O Western Wind: A Sheaf of Haiku."

you. Nothing on your submissions or return envelope indicates this. I should appreciate your telling me in your next communication." When Mormino accepted one of Father Ray's haiku for her second issue,

> Hollyhock in hair,
> a nineteen-twenty snapshot
> alive near my bed.[41]

she urged him to subscribe to the journal. Then she gave the priest-poet a kind of haiku publication primer, directing his attention to—besides *Modern Haiku*—*Haiku West* and *Haiku Highlights* as well as *Janus & SCTH* and the Canadian *Haiku*. She also asked him to encourage others to subscribe to haiku magazines. There is no evidence that Roseliep ever tried to publish in the first two, though seventeen haiku of his were picked up by *Haiku* in 1969–1971.

Roseliep replied to Mormino on January 10: "I am a Catholic priest. I do not, however, use 'Father' or 'The Rev' in signing my poems. In biographical notes I am frequently identified as a priest." He went on to let Mormino know: "I do what I do deliberately—'breaking rules.'… I hope you'll make room for experimentation in *Modern Haiku*." By January 12, Mormino was thanking Roseliep for his subscription. She added, "I shall, of course, use your name without title, as you wish, in connection with your poems." She seemed receptive to Roseliep's "breaking rules," asking only for "poetic quality" in both haiku and senryu of all schools.

In her letter of May 3, Mormino was forthright in commenting on Roseliep's submissions: "Some of the enclosed are amazing; almost all are clever. Perhaps my perception is at fault, or my responsiveness, but I find none that I can call either haiku or senryu, or poems of any kind, because they lack (for me) emotional impact." She ends, "Won't you write some haiku that communicate a genuine emotion." Likely he did so: in August 1970 he received an Eminent Mention in *Modern Haiku* for this sequence:

EVE TRIEM

> lotus kimono,
> ivory elephant dance
> at her singing throat,

---

41. *Modern Haiku* 1:2 (Spring 1970), 28.

gold sandled, rose-toed,
silence of water broken
by leaf of poem[42]

The handwritten letter from *Modern Haiku* Associate Editor Helen S. Chenoweth, dated August 4, 1970, was deeply appreciated by Roseliep. He replied, "Thank you for such a charming, kind note."[43]

Roseliep's correspondence with Mormino ended before Christmas 1977, when she sent him a card that included her haiku, "The youngest child / lights the 4th Advent Candle / Joy! Emmanuel!"

The reclusive Roseliep never met any of these journal editors, though Roseliep and Spiess lived a scant 100 miles apart, in Dubuque and Madison respectively, and Spiess was active in haiku matters in Madison and Platteville, Wis. (even nearer to Dubuque) as early as the late 1950s.

Roseliep and Spiess never agreed on a definition of haiku, especially what American haiku should be. The two had a strained, on-again, off-again relationship, which the priest documented in his personal letters to Elizabeth Lamb. In March 1979 he wrote her, "I really think Spiess is doing well with MH, and think this his best issue yet, content wise and arrangement wise. Do you agree? What did you think of his review of me? My only reservation, if that's the word, is that Robert must remember that I too have my own concept of what haiku is and what it isn't." Roseliep often vented about Spiess when he rejected what the priest-poet considered his "top-drawer" haiku submissions. Once, when Spiess turned down all the haiku Lamb submitted to him in August 1980, Roseliep wrote to her, "What is happening there?" On the other hand, there was a sort of playful admiration between the two men as well as a growing willingness to share more than haiku in their relationship.

On the whole Roseliep fared very well in his dealings with *Modern Haiku*. Both Mormino and Spiess generally welcomed his haiku, reviews, and essays. Issue 2:2 (1971) carried three Roseliep haiku; then there was a three-year gap until 1975.[44] After that, however, Roseliep's work — usually one, two, or three haiku — appeared in all but three issues of *Modern Haiku*.

---

42. *Modern Haiku* 1:4 (Autumn 1970), 4.
43. Roseliep to Helen Stiles Chenoweth, August 17, 1970.
44. The years from 1966 to 1974 were personally very difficult ones for Roseliep.

The pace began picking up in 1981, with four haiku in the first and third issues, and a longer haiku sequence "The T'ang Dynasty," in the second. The first issue of *Modern Haiku* for 1982 contained a sequence titled "Eight Poems" plus a separate haiku, which won a Special Mention Award, while the second issue contained Roseliep's "Fourteen Poems" and another single, which again was distinguished with an Eminent Mention from the editors. This issue also included Roseliep's review of Hal Roth's book, *Behind the Fireflies.*

Six Roseliep haiku were included in the first issue of 1983. *Modern Haiku* 14:2 (Summer 1983) was dedicated to Mormino, who had succumbed to cancer. Fourteen of the priest-poet's haiku appeared in that issue, and as a group they were awarded a Kay Titus Mormino Award. In that same issue Spiess and Roseliep published "Author and Reader," an open exchange of letters with the two men's interpretations of a Roseliep haiku that had appeared in the previous issue:

> downpour:
> my "I-Thou"
> T-shirt

In the Autumn 1983 issue the two men again traded comments, this time on this Roseliep haiku:

> monarch drying
> for a flight I plan
> to join[45]

These wonderful exchanges showed men who were accomplished and professional enough to discuss deep emotions. Roseliep had come a long way since Mormino's admonition to write haiku with genuine emotion. Spiess and Roseliep expressed their soaring feelings and premonitions of death. From Spiess, for example, "my body is becoming more and more brittle with each passing day; and soon my spirit will journey along the invisible path that the butterfly's spirit has taken." Eerily, Roseliep was already in the winter of his life and soon, as he wrote, "When the butterfly takes off, I will thus be united with the act of journeying forth: my sentient being will automatically soar; my heart will go straight

---

45. Raymond Roseliep and Robert Spiess, "'Monarch Drying': Author and Reader," *Modern Haiku* 14:2 (Autumn 1983), 19.

up; and my soul that has been making gradual ascent toward the vast unknown will dreamily practice its final lift from earth — no less real than this oncoming kaleidoscopic black-and-orange expedition."

In April 1983, Spiess wrote to Roseliep requesting that they share again "accounts" of haiku interpretation of another Roseliep haiku. The Iowan's reply was filled with warmth and welcoming: "We had so much fun last time writing account of an RR haiku that I can't resist playing the game with you again."[46]

The 1983 letters bear witness to a growing friendship and professional regard. The two men shared quotidian details as well as their special love of the outdoors — Ray on a nature walk, Bob kayaking. Perhaps it was the shared musings on the "I-Thou" T-shirt that also gave rise to some of Bob's thoughts about the spirit and an afterlife. On May 9, 1983, he wrote, as always, in longhand, "One always regrets hearing about the death of another's loved one and knowing, if only to a certain extent, the grief that is so keenly felt by the person." Spiess's last letter to Roseliep was dated November 5, 1983, and ended: "Hope to get in a couple more days of kayaking. Thanks for the oak and maple leaves — they rest before my Buddha statue." The third 1983 issue of *Modern Haiku* — and the last in Father Ray's lifetime — showcased ten of his haiku, two of which received Eminent Mentions.

Issue 15:1 (Winter–Spring 1984) of *Modern Haiku* was dedicated to Roseliep's memory. Twelve of his haiku were published in this issue as was Spiess's review of *Rabbit in the Moon*. The Summer issue again featured a tribute to Roseliep with a two-page introduction by Spiess followed by twenty-three memorial haiku contributed by Roseliep's friends and admirers. Spiess closed the selection with his own farewell verse,

> His gift of a leaf
>   golden in the votive light
>   before the buddha

In 1985–1986, Spiess published more of the priest's work under the nom de plume "Raymond Ray," and in *Modern Haiku* 16:1, he remembered his friend once again in his review of *The Earth We Swing On*. Over the years *Modern Haiku* had included 261 Roseliep haiku (some of these in essays and reviews).

---

46. Roseliep to Robert Spiess, April 15, 1983.

Haiku and *Cicada*

The late 1960s and early 1970s was a period of great turmoil in English-language haiku. Poets and journal editors were rebelling against the rapidly ossifying "traditional" concept of haiku as a poem written in 5–7–5 syllabic form, on hearts-and-flowers topics, and full of perfumy, poetic language. In the vanguard of the haiku revolution were a number of Canadian poets who dared experiment with haiku form and content, focusing on human emotions, incorporating Zen, and using Oriental aesthetics instead of Western tropes. Poets from across the continent flocked to two journals begun in Toronto by Eric Amann, *Haiku* (1967–1976) and *Cicada* (1977–1981). It is not surprising that Roseliep the innovator was there too.

Two years after the founding of *Haiku*, in 1969, the first work from the priest was accepted by Amann. In all, he published seventeen haiku. Amann turned *Haiku* over to American poet and scholar William J. Higginson in 1971. Higginson's first issue as editor, 5:1, included three Roseliep haiku, among them,

> Yes: Spring:
> my cat's tongue
> hones a grassblade

Higginson, however, was less enamored of the priest-poet's work than had been Amann. He wrote lengthy critiques in a letter of March 1971:

> "Past Feather Myth" seems too loaded with puns, allusions etc.; and I intensely dislike suggestions that such work as this has anything at all to do with haiku ('haikuist'?) It does not. And the suggestion simply adds to the general public's confusion as to what haiku has been, and what it perhaps could be. The publication of such things in places like *Poetry* has so bollixed up even knowledgeable views on the subject that I would cheerfully shoot any clown who does publish such a thing.

Higginson did find three verses among Father Ray's submissions that he could accept, under the emphatic note "THOSE MORE LIKE HAIKU." Higginson ended with, "And ol' man, have you anything for spring?"

In a later letter Higginson accepted three haiku but opined, "Most of your things are too 'imaginative,' and do not *deal* directly or adequately with real objects or experiences. Try reading Williams, or Br. Antoninus."[47]

---

47. Higginson to Roseliep, May 2, 1971.

Because Higginson and Roseliep had corresponded before, this letter to Roseliep opened with an unusual remark:

> It seems strange that we have not corresponded before this, or at least that I do not have anything in my files indicating that we have done so. But perhaps my small review of your small book from Swamp Press [*Swish of Cow Tail*] in last *Modern Haiku* makes amends. In the meantime, I have been looking for an opportunity for some time to tell you how much I have enjoyed your haiku
>
> >   vasectomy;
> >   the doll's
> >   eye[48]   .
>
> which I first noticed during a discussion of the poem at a meeting of the "Haiku Society of America" last year. I believe it is one of your best. Despite the horrified countenances of most of the old-lady poets at the HSA meeting. I was quite shocked with the vehemence with which they attacked the poem! They would not even discuss the possible interpretations which I suggested—all in all it was one of the least enlightening discussions of a particular haiku I've ever sat through.[49]

Higginson asked Roseliep to write a preface for another writer's forthcoming book, but he declined, as he almost always did for such requests, because he knew how such writing took precious time away from actual writing and promoting of his own work.[50] The two men continued to correspond into 1983.

Meanwhile, Eric Amann had started a new haiku journal, *Cicada*, which flourished in Toronto from 1977 to 1981. Again Amann welcomed and promoted Roseliep's haiku. Their correspondence continued until Amann wrote in a short note to Roseliep in February 1982, "Dear Raymond: Due to increasing printing and mailing costs and lack of time on my part I've decided—regretfully—to suspend publication. Wishing you all the best success for your fine work in the future. Eric."

The premier issue, 1:1 (1977), included seven pieces of Roseliep's, including the often anthologized

>   after Beethoven   ′
>   he gets the furnace
>   roaring[51]

---

48. *Cicada* (Toronto), 5:3 (1981), 8.

49. Higginson to Roseliep, August 24, 1982.

50. Roseliep to Higginson, August 28, 1982.

51. *Cicada* (Toronto) 1:1 (1977). Four of the seven haiku were included in *Sailing Bones* (1978).

Over the years *Cicada* published seventy-five Roseliep haiku.

The tenor of their friendly and ongoing correspondence was exemplified by Amann in his letter of April 21, 1977: "I do hope that this first issue will please you; I've tried to give it a broad spectrum of appeal without sacrificing taste." A P.S. read: "Also: sheer nosiness, but what do you DO at Holy Family Hall?" Roseliep, of course, gave him a lengthy answer on April 26. "I had to give up college teaching, and here I have peace and time to write and keep in reasonably decent health." Amann knew that Roseliep was in touch with other writers of haiku so he sent "a few of our folders and subscription forms." Roseliep countered with: "I'll enclose a few circulars on [my] recent publications so you can see what I've been doing." And, as usual, Roseliep tried out the mettle of his new publisher by offering suggestions for future issues of *Cicada*, such as:

> I strongly recommend that when you carry reviews of haiku books you quote poems from them, with no comment.... You can do some squeezing—like placing the haiku side by side in two columns.... So glad, too, to see you work in some experimental things—those concrete poems are charming.... Glad to see that you didn't stick closely to just one season in #1.... You could reserve certain pages here and there [for seasonal haiku].

Amann took Roseliep's suggestions in stride, and they were off to a fine professional friendship. Amann commented on April 30: "*Flute Over Walden* is certainly different from the Roseliep I know and I still can't quite identify you with this type of folksy humor and I'm looking forward to *A Beautiful Woman* which I have ordered from ROOK PRESS. I've also ordered a copy of *Thistle* that you edited." When Roseliep sent him a copy of the special issue of *Bonsai* with his article "This Haiku of Ours," Amann responded in June 1977

> Your article is the most sensible thing I have read about haiku for a long time; it is also very encouraging to me, as I sometimes despair of the field; so I am glad to know that you have a firm and optimistic outlook for haiku in the Western world. I cannot of course quite agree with enhancing the haiku with similes, personifications, etc. without losing a very vital part of the essence. It seems to me that there comes a point where so much of the properties of a thing have been taken away and replaced that it ceases to exist.

Amann shared with Roseliep that he was a physician in general practice as well as engaged with literary and publishing ventures, so Roseliep promised to send him an article showing how he, too, was "blending (I hope) his two vocations [of priest and poet]."

Gathering materials for volume 5:3, Amann sent a postcard to Roseliep: "One of your *finest* submissions." He published fifteen haiku in the second-to-last issue of *Cicada*, October 1981.

On January 21, 1982, Roseliep submitted twenty-eight haiku for publication: "We've had 25 below zero weather twice, with a wind chill of 90 below. That's Canadian cold.... Here's another submission; hope you can dig out something you will like." On a small slip of paper, dated by Roseliep 2–2–82, were the words quoted above from Eric about ending *Cicada*. The last issue of *Cicada* in 1981 had none of Father Ray's work but did contain this haiku by Elizabeth Searle Lamb dedicated to her good friend:

> the frog's eyes
> looking in / out
> for Sobi-Shi[52]

Dragonfly

The haiku journal *Haiku Highlights* was begun in 1965 by Jean Calkins in Upstate New York, and the editorship passed to Lorraine Ellis Harr in Portland, Ore., in 1972. Harr, who usually published under her *haigō* (haiku nom de plume) tombo ("dragonfly" in Japanese) renamed the journal *Dragonfly* and restarted publication in January 1973.

Roseliep's *Dragonfly* correspondence folder is slim. He wrote Lamb, "[*Brussels Sprout* editor Alexis Rotella] hasn't grated on me so directly as had the Dragonlady ... whom I was glad and quick to abandon."[53] Only twenty Roseliep haiku appeared in *Dragonfly*, from issue 3:2 (April 1975) through issue 4:4 (October 1976), and of these, only one,

> the heat has let up
> since you came with your fans,
> green butterfly

was picked up by the poet (with slight modifications in format) for inclusion in a book-length collection.[54]

---

52. Elizabeth Searle Lamb, *Cicada* 5:4 (1982).

53. Roseliep to Lamb, February 4, 1982.

54. *Dragonfly* 4:4 (October 1976), 20; Roseliep, *Step on the Rain*, 17.

Harr was well-known for her prescriptive approach to haiku, propagating lists of rules such as "The Isn'ts of Haiku" and "Guidelines to Haiku Writing." Roseliep's *Dragonfly* folder contains twelve of Harr's rather harsh admonishments to Roseliep written at the bottom of a full-page copy of her "Isn'ts" on goldenrod paper. Probably she sent this page to everyone when responding to a submission letter. One early rejection letter from Harr read: "Dear Raymond R—I don't use poems in haiku form—only haiku. Keep with it." Their correspondence (rarely dated by Harr) began in 1975 and ended on Roseliep's part after this comment by Harr written in a July 1977 note: "You had a complaint, sir? Strangely—it has come to me via a grapevine that you are making 'unkind remarks' about me. Tusck! Tusck! (Certainly not the actions of a man-of-the-cloth)." She went on to defend her standards. Harr often suggested word and line changes for Roseliep's haiku, and once she scolded him, "You ignore season ... season word, interplay of images ... strong haiku emotion etc ... NAUGHTY, NAUGHTY, NAUGHTY!"[55]

After Roseliep's *Frogpond* article "Cry, Windmill" (*see* discussion below) was published, Harr tried one more time to correct Roseliep's peccadillos: "Hello, sorry you never saw fit to answer my last note to you." Roseliep obviously had had enough. His last letter to Harr is dated July 14, 1975. Though he signed it "With friendship," the priest dished out her kind of trenchant criticism for her book *Tombo.* At least half of the page out-Harrs Harr in cattiness. Roseliep, after what looks like a perfectly harmless and friendly opening, "Your *Tombo* is an enjoyable experience. How ever could anyone write so many haiku on one subject. But you did." He lists his six favorites. Then comes his first salvo: "How do you justify the use of the past tense in these?" He lists three haiku and goes on to criticize another group of seven: "In these I find unnecessary words: (I will underline them)." He comments with specifics: for the word "marvelous" he says: "This is especially weak—things should be marvelous without our saying so by using that very word." For another haiku of Harr's that opens with the words "How to explain/the way it looks" Roseliep says: "I'd explain it!" Again, about "The dragonfly eats/400 mosquitoes a day—/ yet, stays so slim!" Roseliep remarks, "And as interesting as this one is, I cannot see this is a true haiku; simply a factual note, with nothing before your immediate vision." The one page of onionskin copy shows one-fifth of the page is praise; the rest is caustic comment. Harr got in the last word, however, with a laconic, backhanded compliment about *Flute Over Walden* in the back-page "Books Received & Reviewed" section of the October 1976 *Dragonfly*: "Poems of intellectual vitality in the haiku form."[56]

Bonsai

Roseliep's contact with Jan and Mary Streif in Prescott, Ariz., began immediately after their announcement of their intention to begin a new haiku journal, *Bonsai*. In an answer to a Roseliep submission of haiku for possible publication in the first issue, the Striefs wrote on September 10, 1975, "We are sorry to have to return these, but they do not seem right for us." However, they gave him encouragement: "don't let us scare you off," and he submitted more haiku immediately, three of which were accepted.[57] These four haiku won *Bonsai* Quarterly Awards in the first four numbers (1976) respectively:

> arboretum
> center of silence
> / a leaf falls

> in the window
> move and you lose
> the cardinal

> stumble
> on a star in the brook
> all three crumble

> fish
> swallowing
> the moon

as did his concrete haiku "Boy in a red cap" (*see* text on page 129) won the award in issue 1:3. Roseliep continued to publish in *Bonsai* until October 1977, and the journal ended publication in 1978.

---

56. *Dragonfly* 4:3 (July 1976), 20 and 66.
57. Striefs to Roseliep, January 31, 1976.

Outch

Another of Roseliep's preferred haiku journals, *Outch,* was published from 1976 to 1985, first in the U.S. and later in Tokyo, by Nobuo Hirasawa. In his files Roseliep saved an unpublished promotional comment he wrote in April of 1978, which read in part:

> The gutsy courage is what I like about Outch. Its editors are unafraid to experiment with the venerable classical concept of haiku and to arrange these experiments side by side with the traditional.... We carvers of heads upon cherrystones are proud and delighted to have the display case of Outch for presenting our products. Deeply involved in life and living, we enjoy sharing our felt moments with people everywhere. As Zen Master Ikkyu declared, for all of us "Attention, attention, attention" is our highest wisdom.

On October 12, 1976, Roseliep told Hirasawa "In your first letter to me you wrote: 'Your Haiku remind me of good old days of Basho and Issa, which we are losing here in Japan'" and asks permission to use this quote in promotional flyers for his forthcoming *Step on the Rain.* He signed off with this haiku from *Light Footsteps:*

> spring breeze
> puffs through the skeleton
> of a bird

Another communication from Hirasawa, undated, was a promotional flyer with the salutation "My Dear Haijins," asking "for all of you who love haiku to publish your haiku here in Japan, the home of haiku, both in English and in Japanese. I have been dreaming of publishing a real international haiku anthology since I started my international haiku magazine *Outch,* in 1976.... The title would be *Haiku of the World, Volume I, North America.*" Roseliep sent him ten haiku, but the planned anthology was never published.

Roseliep kept Hirasawa's beautiful handwritten letters in a file with letters from others of his cherished friends. The first of these is addressed "Dear Haiku Friend and Rudolph's Big Father" and reveals the genesis of Roseliep's *haigō* "Sobi-Shi."

> I have been thinking and thinking of your Japanese name this week, Friend.... Now here's what I have in my mind for your name. Since your name means a rose lover, why not call yourself "So-bi," which means exactly rose. We usually call a rose "bara," but in the world of poetry we call it so-bi, and as a hai-go (haijin name) let's add "shi" as

most of great haijin do, like Kyoshi Takahama, one of the greatest haijin
of Meiji Period."

Hirasawa went on to add the kanji for "Sobi-Shi" and offered to have
a chop made of the new haiku name. Hirasawa, like Roseliep a cat lover,
shared news that his beloved Blackie had been stolen. At this time Roseliep was taking good care of a feral cat that he named Rudolph (hence,
Hirasawa's salutation).

Roseliep was a frequent contributor to *Outch* throughout its publication run. Most issues contained a page or two of the priest-poet's work.
In issue 2:1 (spring 1977), Hirasawa published a brief autobiographical
piece Roseliep had written and which included the statement: "I define
poetry as distilled significance, and the poet as an animal with the sun
in his belly." Issue 8:1 (spring 1984) was dedicated "to the memory of
Raymond Roseliep." The opening pages (pages are not numbered in this
issue) featured "a dirge" of six haiku by Hirasawa, including,

> adieu
> Sobi-Shi Ray
> no more words

and followed by six of Roseliep's haiku, the last of which read:

> nails where he left them
> a ladder's length
> of light

Hirasawa remembered his American friend:

> He was one of the most important members since Outch started in
> 1972. It is not too much to say that it is through his valuable advice
> that Outch has gained over two hundred subscribers all over the
> States, Canada and some other countries. Besides being an excellent
> adviser of poetry, he was a close personal friend of mine. He was
> such a good letter writer and never a week passed without hearing
> from him…. We promised that we would meet some day in the near
> future, but this is now a dream that will never come true.
>
> > Iowa leaves in my hand
> > Sobi-Shi, Ray
> > you're gone before we meet

High/Coo

Randy and Shirley Brooks published *High/Coo: A Journal of Short Poetry* in Battle Ground, Ind., from 1976 to 1982 in vest-pocket size. As in their later venture, *Mayfly,* founded in 1986, the Brookses were looking for "a few good haiku"—which was, of course, right up Father Ray's alley. Roseliep was communicating with the Brookses even before the publication of the inaugural issue of *High/Coo.* Randy Brooks had contacted Roseliep and told him "I really enjoyed your Thoreauhaiku."

Roseliep dominated issue 1:2 (September 1976) with seven haiku. He flaunted his experiments with haiku form,

Image

Amy Lowell's cigar
making a halo
over
her

his penchant for erotic haiku,

spider shuttling
between the breasts
of Venus de Milo

and even experimentation and eroticism together:

$$
\begin{array}{ll}
 & n \\
 & o \\
 & i \\
 & t \\
 & c \\
\text{the boy in swim trunks} & e \\
\text{with dragon design} & r \\
\text{and} & e
\end{array}
$$

Roseliep appeared in most subsequent issues of *High/Coo*—a total of almost 100 original haiku altogether. Most important for the priest-poet, perhaps, was a series of three short essays in which he advanced his contrarian ideas about the poetics of haiku. These essays are discussed in Chapter Six. Contact with Randy and Shirley Brooks continued until near the end of Roseliep's life.

Frogpond

In 1978 the Haiku Society of America launched its official journal, *HSA Frogpond* (soon retitled *Frogpond*). Earlier Leroy Kanterman's *Haiku West* had served as the unofficial organ of the HSA. None of Roseliep's work was included in *Haiku West,* but two of his haiku were accepted for the first issue of *HSA Frogpond*:[58]

> Maggie is dead
> her yellow hair blows
> the wild wood flax

> sickle:
> the child stoops
> to pick up the moon

HSA Frogpond 1:1 also published Roseliep's essay titled "A Time to Rime," discussed in Chapter Six.

During Roseliep's lifetime, *Frogpond* had four editors: Lilli Tanzer (1978–1980), Geoffrey O'Brien (1981), Bruce Kennedy (1982–1983), and Alexis Rotella (1983–1984). The priest-poet's correspondent friend Elizabeth Lamb took over the year after his death and served from 1984 to 1990. All these editors were receptive to Roseliep's work, and from 1978 to 1984 *Frogpond* published 170 of his haiku as well as reviews and short essays. Roseliep's essay, "Cry Windmill," a defense of the use of metaphor in haiku, from *High/Coo* 7 (February 1978) was reprinted in *Frogpond* 1:2 (1978).

Unfortunately, Roseliep did not preserve his correspondence with Tanzer, but letters to and from O'Brien were friendly and encouraging. O'Brien especially welcomed the haiku sequences that Roseliep began to send in June 1981. In those years, very few poets were writing sequences, and Roseliep's work must have been seen as avant-garde if not revolutionary. In fact, the next *Frogpond* editor, Bruce Kennedy, wrote a postcard on April 29, 1982, asking "While I'm thinking of it, some time in the future I'd appreciate hearing your thoughts on the sequence form. I find an increasing number of people writing and experimenting with it." He went on to ask Roseliep to clarify what he thought "this form is, or can be." Five days later, Kennedy had Roseliep's comments.

---

58. *HSA Frogpond* 1:1 (February 1978). Two Roseliep haiku publications are listed among available books.

Roseliep's opening was: "I agree with you that many writers put unrelated haiku together and call them a *sequence.* I would call such a grouping a *sampler.* There must be a unifying principle for a true sequence. There must be an organic unity." Roseliep goes on to specify "a single subject or theme, ... a logical progression.... I do believe that experimentation is most important. Such as having a variety of types of stanza forms within a given sequence—such as: a pattern of a three-liner, a two-liner, a one-liner; or any combinations of those shapes. There are many other kinds of experiment, too, of course. Here is one I used: "The Morning-Glory." (*See* text of the poem at page 149 below.) Roseliep ended: "And I like to believe (do, in fact) that each stanza holds up as a haiku if put in isolation from the others if the title is read as the starting phrase of each stanza."[59]

In that communication Roseliep also was indelicate enough to include a list of ten typos and editing errors in Kennedy's first sailing with *Frogpond* (including a misspelling of Roseliep's name in the contents) and suggests that "another pair of trustworthy eyes for proofreading" was needed. Roseliep expanded his suggestion in ways that might not have been conducive to a future working relationship. Kennedy's longhand reply on May 20, 1982, had a defense of himself: "Don't take this personally, I appreciate your comments and concern.... I'm just frustrated and very busy lately." A rather icy letter from Kennedy of June 23, 1982, rejecting all haiku Roseliep had submitted, added these comments: "I hope you'll take this in the right spirit, I'm sure you could send these out and get them published elsewhere but I am trying to tighten the standards of *Frogpond.* I know you can do better than this." One of the haiku that Kennedy rejected was Roseliep's soon-to-be-famous "downpour:/ my 'I-Thou' / T-shirt."[60]

Roseliep was not included in the next *Frogpond* issue, 5:2. He noted on the front page: "I have nothing in this one—my first miss." Perhaps he felt he had lost his touch when he again had to write on the title page of his copy of *Frogpond* 5:4, "I am not in this one.... Sigh!" He also had nothing accepted for Kennedy's farewell issue, 6:2.

Roseliep's cordial and professional relationship with Alexis Rotella was recorded in a few letters between them. She inherited what she

59. Roseliep to Bruce Kennedy, May 4, 1982.

60. Published in *Modern Haiku* 14:1 (Winter–Spring 1983), 53, and collected in Roseliep, *Rabbit in the Moon* (1983), 29.

called "the haystack" from Kennedy.[61] She liked Roseliep's sequences and included the six-stanza "Greentime to White" in *Frogpond* 6:3 (1983). The sequence, appearing in print only weeks before the priest-poet's death, gives a feeling of eerie premonition. The final haiku reads,

> our silence
> the where
> of snow[62]

Roseliep's correspondence with Rotella may have been correct, but he confided another dimension in a letter to Lamb dated January 26, 1982: "Alexis wrote the following to a haiku poet who wishes to remain unidentified: 'No one ever inherits haiku; it's there for the young and the old. Do you think that Roseliep and Lamb "own" haiku? I don't. They may act like they do; but that doesn't mean that they do.'" In their next exchange, Roseliep added, "I can't imagine what prompted that outburst from Alexis. I have been told that she cuts down people left and right—including those she corresponds with and gives the impression of liking. Probably a schoolgirl brand of jealousy is at the root of it."[63]

Brussels Sprout

Roseliep's correspondence folder for *Brussels Sprout* contains many colorful irregular pieces of paper with messages from Alexis Rotella, with whom Father Ray would interact during her tenure as *Frogpond* editor, 1983–1984. Rotella established *Brussels Sprout* in New Jersey in 1980, like *Cicada* intending to challenge established English-language haiku. The often lighthearted correspondence between Rotella and Roseliep began in 1981 and continued until her birthday message to Father Ray on August 15, 1983. Her card included a cutout picture of a cupcake and a few song notes on the envelope and a blue, handmade card inside: "A belated happy birthday to the Sugar Daddy of Haikuland!" She placed cutouts of a bubblegum wrapper, a six-pack of Orange Crush and a "scratch and smell the GRAPE SNOW CONE!" It gives off a strong odor of grape to this day!

In all, under its two editors, Rotella and Francine Porad, a Washingtonian who took the reins in 1987, *Brussels Sprout* published more than

61. Alexis Rotella to Roseliep, August 11, 1983.

62. Roseliep, "Greentime to White," *Frogpond* 6:3 (1983), 24.

63. Roseliep to Lamb, February 4, 1982. The priest-poet could get himself in trouble with this kind of remark, but Lamb was not the kind of person who would pass these comments on to others.

forty Roseliep haiku. Rotella was enthusiastic about Roseliep's work, giving him special attention in three issues. First was a sequence of eleven haiku titled "Whisper Song," including[64]

> whisper song
> not well known
> of the jay

in a special "Rose Anthology" in which Roseliep was represented by sixteen haiku. Roses, of course, were a subject of special significance for him:[65]

> in Sobi-Shi's glass
> the dark rose
> of a love ago

And then in Rotella's final issue[66] six moon haiku, all reprinted from elsewhere, including this one that evokes Santōka's "Into the begging bowl, too, hailstones":[67]

> beggar's bowl
> full
> of moon

Quirky, endearing messages continued to flow between Roseliep and Rotella. On a postcard dated May 6, 1983, she wrote: "Dear Raymond ... guess what? the haiku world wants my head because I'm prolific. How do you manage to keep yours?" She always signed herself with an outsized signature. Rotella attested to her spiritual journey by writing "the places I've been inside are of course indescribable. Still I carry wood, I boil water, I chop onions for a simple stew. When one comes out of the maze, how simple everything becomes. The struggle is over; the Sun does it all."[68]

---

64. *Brussels Sprout* 2:3 (1982), 2–3.

65. *Brussels Sprout* 2:4 (1982), 36–40. The haiku "in Sobi-Shi's glass" had previously appeared in "50 Haiku by Raymond Roseliep," *Uzzano* 9/10 (Spring–Summer 1978), and Roseliep, *A Day in the Life of Sobi-Shi* (1978).

66. *Brussels Sprout* 3:1 (1983), 42.

67. Santōka, trans. Hiroaki Sato, *Cicada* 2:2 (1978), 10.

68. Rotella to Roseliep, January 17, 1983.

Wind Chimes

A new haiku journal, *Wind Chimes,* begun by Hal Roth in Glen Burnie, Md., in 1981, continued for twenty-eight issues until 1989. Roseliep's work was featured or referenced in every issue until his death in 1983. and *Wind Chimes* 15 is dedicated to his memory.

The first saved letter in Roseliep's *Wind Chimes* folder is a thank you from the editor for Roseliep's praise of a Roth haiku: "river fog / a bell buoy warns away / the stars." Roseliep typed at the bottom of this first letter: "Received February 5, 1981, and replied the same day. (I have misplaced his letter and the carbon of mine!! good grief.)" Roth proved a sympathetic colleague and professional friend of Roseliep from the outset. What attracted him, at least in part, was probably Roth's use of poetics that other haikuists scorned, such as personification, puns, double meanings, and an opening out to a cosmos.[69]

Roth already owned copies of *Listen to Light* and *A Roseliep Retrospective,* purchased at Roseliep's earlier suggestion. "I have read them several times. My sincere wishes that they achieve the success they deserve." On April 22, 1981, he wrote again announcing "I am planning the publication of a new haiku quarterly to be called *Wind Chimes....* I invite you to be a regular contributor."[70]

Acknowledging Roth's "kind letter," Roseliep sent him a dozen haiku, adding: "One suggestion. In your first issue, ask haiku writers to submit brief, pointed criticisms of one or more haiku in each issue, explaining that you wish them for both teachers and students in high school. You are bound to draw some interesting comments, but you must assure the writers that the best of these, the most helpful, will be published." Roseliep continued in this letter to give more suggestions. In general he found in Roth an editor who was receptive to both encouragement and constructive criticism. Roth accepted ten haiku for the first issue. In his letter of May 11 he added: "I am also most grateful for your suggestions and look forward to receiving your continuing guidance and poems." Issue 2 had twelve of Roseliep's haiku, plus a review of *Listen to Light,* which quoted Denise Levertov's praise of the haiku of Roseliep's that had won first place in the Yuki Teikei Haiku Society's contest in 1980 and been included in *Listen to Light* later in the year. Her full remarks read:

---

69. Hal Roth to Roseliep, February 16, 1981.

70. Roth to Roseliep, April 22, 1981.

Pinned on a wall where one sees it at odd times, a poem like this of Ray Roseliep's:

> campfire extinguished,
> the woman washing dishes
> in a pan of stars

can remind one of the whole woven tissue of gladness which, in these dark days, one struggles to preserve.[71]

Alexis Rotella's *Butterfly Breezes* was also mentioned in the Books Received section and quoted Roseliep's contribution to that 1981 anthology,

> afternoon stillness
> a brawl
> of butterflies[72]

Wind Chimes issue 12 was designated "In Memoriam, Raymond Roseliep, Priest, Professor, Poet." The words "Against the Night," from a Roseliep haiku and that he had directed to be carved on this tombstone appeared at the beginning of the issue. Fittingly, the "In Memoriam" dedication fills the deep red cover of the journal. The issue contains various tributes to Father Ray, from the homily given by Rev. Robert Vogl, his Loras College colleague, to the homage from Robert Spiess, who shared not only his own praise but also a section from one of Roseliep's letters that ended "as we head for spring."

Roseliep never read Roth's last letter, dated December 7, 1983, which contained a proof of LeRoy Gorman's review of *Rabbit in the Moon* that was published in the memorial *Wind Chimes* 12. Roth began, one final postcard to Roseliep, dated December 10, "Today was a more beautiful day than one deserves in December...." And he wrote in an empty space near the top, "Space, like the day, gone too soon. Hal." Four days before his friend Hal sent this postcard, Roseliep too was "gone too soon."

Haiku Contests and Awards

Haiku contests provided a platform by which Raymond Roseliep could judge his own work against the best haiku being written

---

71. Denise Levertov, "Books Received," *Wind Chimes* 2 (1981), 63. Her comments were repeated in the blurb for *Listen to Light. See* a reviewer's comments on page 210.

72. Alexis Rotella, comp., *Butterfly Breezes: A One Time Anthology* (Mountain Lakes, N.J.: A. K. Rotella [Jade Mountain], 1981).

by others. The first award Roseliep listed in his meticulous records was from 1962, when he was a first-place winner in the 12th annual cash award for poetry of the *Carolina Quarterly,* published by the University of North Carolina in Chapel Hill. The first haiku award was an Eminent Mention for "Eve Triem" — significantly, one of his transitional, haiku-like poems, published in *Modern Haiku*[73] in autumn 1970 (*see* text on page 105).

Helen Stiles Chenoweth, editor for that issue of *Modern Haiku*, implored, "I must know — please? — is Eve Triem the pen name of a poetess or is your haiku a tribute to a poetess, dead or living. I'll be asked, no hounded! The haiku people will know I edited this Autumn number when Kay [Titus Mormino]'s[74] tribute comes.... She was elated that I'd selected your "Eve Triem" for "eminent award."[75] Roseliep responded immediately: "Eve Triem (her real name) is very much alive, in Seattle, Washington."[76] Triem, a friend and long-time correspondent with Roseliep, had lived in Dubuque for a time.

"Christmas," a sequence of three-line linked stanzas was published in the January 1971 issue of *Yankee,* which gave it a third-prize award for "Yankee's Poetry Awards of 1970."

Thereafter Roseliep received many prizes for his haiku. Of special note because the "Walden" haiku in the April 1973 *Thoreau Journal Quarterly* was published before the appearance of his first all-haiku volume, *Flute Over Walden,* in 1976 is this haiku:

> Walden Pond idles,
> Its lord reads by kerosene,
> A hawk of train screams

Perhaps the priest-poet got his greatest pleasure to have tied for first place in the Harold G. Henderson Haiku Contest of the Haiku Society of America in 1977, the second year of the competition. Roseliep and Elizabeth Lamb were often amicably competitive in this contest. Roseliep took a first again (unshared) in 1982 and won an honorable men-

73. *Modern Haiku* 1:4 (Autumn 1970), 4.

74. Mormino was on leave of absence from *Modern Haiku* recovering from two critical surgeries that, according to Chenoweth, "almost took her from us." Chenoweth to Roseliep, August 14, 1970.

75. Chenoweth to Roseliep, August 14, 1970.

76. Roseliep to Chenoweth, August 17, 1970.

tion in 1979; Lamb won first place in 1978, a second place in 1981 and third place in 1982, 1991, and 1993. Roseliep's three Henderson Award–winning haiku were:

reaching into sky
the girl breaks the wish-
bone of geese   1977

never expecting
the lilies in November
nor the small coffin   1979

horizon
wild swan drifting through
the woman's body   1982[77]

Roseliep also won first place in 1980 in the contest sponsored by the California-based Yuki Teikei Haiku Society of the U.S.A. and Canada with his "campfire extinguished" haiku (cited on page 123. The poem was reprinted in *Listen to Light,* (*see* pages 167 and 210). The YTHS focuses on traditionally structured haiku (*yuki teikei* in Japanese means "season and fixed form"), and "campfire extinguished" is a perfect 5–7–5-syllable haiku with a season word ("campfire" — summer), yet it uses Western-style hyperbole in "a pan of stars." Father Ray was being both traditional and nontraditional at once.

A year later, Roseliep took a first place in the Season Word category of the Hawai'i Education Association Annual Contest, with

No wave today
from my friend in the caboose;
autumn wind[78]

---

77. The Henderson Award winners, and those of the HSA Gerald Brady Award for Senryu, were recorded in the Society's journal, *Frogpond,* and were collected in Haiku Society of America Twentieth Anniversary Book Committee, eds., *A Haiku Path: The Haiku Society of America 1968–1988* (New York: Haiku Society of America, 1994). These three winners appeared, respectively, in Roseliep's books *Sailing Bones, Listen to Light,* and *Rabbit in the Moon.*

78. This haiku was included in the biennial HEA contest chapbook, Darold D. Braida, comp., *Na Pua'oli Puke'ekolu* ("Joyous Blossoms") 4 (1983).

Not infrequently Roseliep's haiku were honored with best-of-issue awards from haiku journals, such as the four that were selected for the *Bonsai* Quarterly Award over the years (*see* page 114). In 1983 Roseliep's fourteen haiku in a series that included these two short sequences were awarded *Modern Haiku*'s Kay Titus Mormino Award: [79]

WILD GEESE

sky
of
themselves

hearing
only
themselves

beyond
our
selves

WINTER SET

i.
pressed in concrete
her hand and mine
iced

ii.
over her bed
this old lover . .
a nerve kicks in

One unusual prize, the Poetry in Public Places Award, 1980, underwritten by the National Endowment for the Arts and the New York State Council on the Arts, came in the form of 28″ x 11″ placards that showcased Roseliep's triptych "The Morning-Glory," which had been featured on New York buses (*see* text on page 149).

---

79. *Modern Haiku* 14:2 (Summer 1983), 6–8. This issue commemorated Mormino's death.

Other honors garnered by Roseliep over the years[80] included second prize in a contest from *Outch* (1977); an honorable mention from *Poetry Nippon* (1977); a biennial Merit Book Award from the Haiku Society of America for *Sailing Bones* (1978); a mini-chapbook award in the *High/Coo* contest for 1979; a best-of-issue award from *Cicada* 4:3 (September 1980); the Shugyō Takaha Award (grand prize) in the Yuki Teikei Haiku Society contest (1980); a second prize once again from *Yankee* (1982); and an eminent mention award in *Modern Haiku* 13:2 (Summer 1982) for this haiku:

> my mother's picture—
> bluejay with its autumn
> "tull lull"

Roseliep's Books and His Critics

Over the years, Roseliep dealt openly with the praise and criticism of both the content and style of his haiku. In a letter to Elizabeth Lamb on June 16, 1981, he wrote: "I believe it will be years before I get a full, balanced, 'consensus of critics' type of evaluation, perhaps after I'm dead; but at least it's fun thinking about it. What price glory." He grappled with criticism during all his professional life. On October 24, 1983, in another letter to Lamb, he reflected,

> I'm most aware of what I'm doing in haiku, and am getting to feel a little more independent, a little more removed from some of these self-appointed purists and critics. I'm not willing to write cute little nature ditties, nor flat clichés that so many think are "standard." I'm having too much fun doing my own thing, and even getting lyrical when I am moved to sing. If we don't keep going west we're going to land up in a backwoods that won't even appear like dear old classical Japan. End of my homily for today, dear Elizabeth.

Roseliep often shared evaluations of his critics through letters to Lamb. *Modern Haiku* Editor Robert Spiess probably ranked first among the objects of Roseliep's complaints. As pointed out above, Spiess was both an admirer and a critic of Roseliep but was especially critical of the priest-poet when he strayed too far from what Spiess felt were established rules. Other editors and critics about whom Roseliep complained included Spiess's associate editor Chuck Brickley, Lorraine Ellis Harr of *Dragonfly*, Canadian critics Anna Vakar and Rod Willmot of Burnt Lake Press, and Australian Janice Bostok of *Tweed*.

---

80. Roseliep Biographical Notes. LCARC 325, D:2:27: 10–11a.

Roseliep was always meticulous about documenting his poetic pro-
cesses and personal growth. His first small brown notebook, "Poetrie #1,
2.27.67 to 8.27.68," contained observations and various lists, as well as
contemporary words and some quotations from other writers. In 1971
he added larger notebooks, specifically labeled "c/o Lit. Exec. R. R. Notebook for poems." He kept these notebooks until his death; the last one
was found by his bedside. Many variations of a single haiku might appear
on a page. Sometimes he listed an exact date for a final choice, circling or
boxing it in red pen or putting a check mark or OK by a favored version.
He usually crossed out rejected variations with a blue marker but did not
delete them. The last haiku in the final notebook, labeled 12-3, had eight
variations. He finally chose

> over
> the dice throwers
> a wheel of stars

That final version did not differ from one on a previous page except to
center the word "over." Roseliep sometimes put much emphasis on word
placement within a haiku, and he was quite distressed if any publisher
changed even one space of a layout. He often wanted to control a reader's
eye movement, as in his visual poem "Boy in a red cap" on the next page.

Roseliep also kept lists of his publications of individual or groups of
poems and haiku. Not infrequently an influential person such as Elizabeth Kray, executive director of the Academy of American Poets, would
ask him to send a bibliography of his work. By 1981 he had compiled a
list of 90 haiku and non-haiku periodicals. Twenty-seven were devoted
entirely to haiku. A penciled note on one bibliography update read: "90
counted, 10-21-83."[81]

In his "Articles" folder, Roseliep placed the list published by Randy
Brooks in *Haiku Review '82*.[82] Elizabeth Lamb had compiled a special
section titled "Raymond Roseliep's Contribution to Haiku In English,"
with a thorough introduction, a list of "Critical Works on Raymond Roseliep's Poetry," a list of his books, a selection of his award-winning haiku,
and a checklist of "many of today's best literary periodicals"[83] in which

---

81. Biographia. LCARC 325, D:2:25.

82. *Haiku Review* was published every two years from 1980–1987 by Randy and Shirley
Brooks's High/Coo Press in Battle Ground, Ind.

83. Lamb listed 85 separate publications in which Roseliep was published.

Boy in a red cap

          s
        q
         u
           i
            r
             t
              i
               n
                g

                  a

                   y
                    e
                     l
                      l
                       o
                       w

                    a
                     r
                     c

                  o
                  n

the very first snow[84]

---

the priest-poet had published. In the 1984 edition of *Haiku Review* Lamb wrote, "This review-essay[85] ends with the two latest books by priest-poet Raymond Roseliep whose sudden death in early December of 1983 has shocked and saddened so many members of the haiku community.... In any event, Raymond Roseliep has, as priest, as poet, as teacher and friend, enriched the world in which he lived."[86]

---

84. *Haiku Magazine* 3:4 (1970); reprinted in *Bonsai* 1:3 (1976), 21; Bonsai Quarterly Award.

85. Elizabeth Searle Lamb, "A Rich Harvest: Haiku Books of 1982–1983." *Haiku Review '84* (Battle Ground, Ind: High/Coo Press, 1984), 2–15.

86. Lamb, "A Rich Harvest," 15.

Flute Over Walden[87]

Haiku form (though retaining the strict 5–7–5 syllable count) and content changed substantially in Roseliep's first standalone book of haiku, *Flute Over Walden,* published in 1976 by Sparrow Press. This book established a seasonal structure for his haiku-only texts, using the procession from spring to winter in haiku while quoting excerpts from *Walden* to mark the sections.[88]

Reading *Flute Over Walden* can be demanding, requiring much more, perhaps, than short praise or criticism with a haiku or two as examples. Haiku can be deceptively spare in form, yet as concentrated as a handful of granola. Newcomers to the genre might wonder at the prodigality of a poet who devotes an entire page to a mere three lines, until they accept this challenge of intensity and the rest of the world is shouldered aside.

True to the content as well as to the three-line, 5–7–5-syllable structure, Roseliep gave us miniatures of the season and the self: a shutter snapped on the essence of a moment. Nothing there was didactic. Trained as this priest-poet was to the pulpit and the sermon, Father Ray did not preach, but presented—and entered in.

Roseliep's choice of the title *Flute Over Walden* might suggest that his haiku were no match for Thoreau's philosophical musings during the more than two years he spent at Walden Pond. But the poet played on his word-flute, showing a depth of emotion not felt in his tentative earlier haiku. In the brief introduction Roseliep told us, "The voice in the poems is sometimes the Waldener's, sometimes mine, and I hope also my reader's. Sometimes maybe all three. Once it is the swamp gods." Yet for all this oneness and identification, Roseliep was not pantheistic; his haiku were not Nature's voice—rather, they were the conscious observer's recognition of simple things. More than recognition, they were celebration.

Roseliep did not disturb his reader with excessive capitalization, and punctuation was minimal. Here, finally, he captured the Orient's ideal way of Truth—a journey chronicled most appropriately by simplicity. Wallace Stevens could easily find here his own "Man on the Dump," waving a prized possession—"The the."

---

87. Raymond Roseliep, *Flute Over Walden: Thoreauhaiku* (West Lafayette, Ind.: Sparrow Press, 1976).

88. Jan Bostok, editor of *Tweed* magazine, in an article from 5:2 mistakenly attributed those prose divisions to Roseliep instead of Thoreau: "The poems are divided into four sections prefaced by short prose pieces. I find these pieces sometimes more interesting than the poems."

Poems in *Flute Over Walden* were not a symphony of sound; they were, as the title tells us, the voice of the flute, one note following one note. Nothing too much. Roseliep's first haiku burst from its seventeen-syllable seams:

> moon, find my bedroom,
>> the sweet Walden ghost tramping
>>> its pine-needle floor

Wait, the poet seemed to be saying, as we begin to turn the page. Do not move too quickly to the next poem. Take time, slow down, enter in: it's evening, the moon is just rising. Be a watcher with me for the kind of light that Hawthorne knew was magical, a precursor of the land of romance; no boundaries there; and yes, ghosts, mergings, all sorts of wondrous happenings. Roseliep seemed to say, "The Walden ghost is here; my bedroom is cabined now along Walden's shore, a pine-needle floor beneath Thoreau's feet, your feet, my feet. And we have yet to meet the swamp gods."

Hushed, emptied of that all-too-realness, we can go, with Thoreau, to a magic woods to find seasons, nature, self. Thoreau, himself, gave us the deep motive: "I went to the woods because I wished to live deliberately, to front only the essential facts of life, and see if I could not learn what it had to teach, and not, when I came to die, discover that I had not lived."

Flute Over Walden is also Roseliep's testimony of being truly alive to each moment. He gave us seasons—external, internal. Excerpts from *Walden* are the seasonal markers: Thoreau's first spring sparrow, his hoe, his pumpkin "chair," and his wintered cabin were the landmarks of Roseliep's own seasonal journey.

Nature's miniatures abound. Roseliep delighted in the "velour bumblebee," the "carpenter titmouse," an "arc of perch," an "asterisk of daisy," the "hearth-born cricket," and the "wassailer bullfrog." Experiencing his poetry, we often lose exact identification: where we are and who. Sometimes Roseliep put us on the surface of Walden Pond, sometimes in the middle of the night just awakened by a bean sprout who "hacks away darkness." Once we find ourselves at a toadstool table, surrounded by—no, not surrounded, but one with—

> we Swamp Gods bid you
>> grace our toadstool Round Table,
>>> Lord Druid Thoreau.

Incongruities of Nature were frequently the springboard for Roseliep's fancy:

> pale blue butterfly
> lifting diaphanous skirts
> above skunk cabbage

Juxtapositions of this type can make us laugh—sometimes at our own
seriousness. Lest we take ourselves too intently, we need only listen:

> Walden Pond quiets,
> a man reckons his account,
> a bullfrog *tr-roonks*

Roseliep often made us search our own lives for meaning. Consider

> lichen's for a nest,
> brown thrasher, not a trapeze—
> ask any white spruce[89]

You may never have seen a thrasher's nest, but it seems that Roseliep
had. It takes some looking. If perchance you live by the edge of a woods
or watch your backyard birds often, you may wonder if Roseliep meant
the thrasher's movements when he wrote "not a trapeze," or the way the
nest moves, or both. Ask a white spruce, perhaps? You can no longer ask
the poet, but, if you could, he might just tell you where to find that white
spruce. Who cares about thrashers anyway? Or beansprouts? If you ask
those questions, the *Flute Over Walden* (or *Walden*) may seem but an excla-
mation point following nothing. If you'd look for a white spruce, however,
there's a long and arduous journey—no beginning, no end. Roseliep's last
Thoreauhaiku was a first, a preparation for reading or rereading:

> hush, Walden spirit,
> helicopter hummingbird,
> my grasshopper blood

Quieted, we begin again. Thoreau's loon, making a plaything of the sky
and water, dove down to rise, beaded. A flute song rose too and touched
Walden on those wings.[90]

---

89. The word appears as "lichen's" in *Flute Over Walden*.

90. Donna Bauerly, "Flute Over Walden: A Review," *Delta Epsilon Sigma Journal* 21:3 (1976),
98–101.

In many ways, loon-like, Raymond Roseliep took off on a multi-leveled journey after *Flute Over Walden,* encompassing land, sea, and sky in what was truly a flock of haiku chapbooks.

Raymond Roseliep's poetry books received a gratifying amount of attention from the critics, but his haiku texts were reviewed by far fewer editors and critics, reflecting, perhaps, a ghettoization of haiku in the poetry world and a lack of sympathy for and understanding of haiku among poets and critics generally. Most of the dozen or so reviews of *Flute Over Walden* were positive, though often scanty and general in comment, only pointing to a few examples of favorite haiku. One of the first editorial comments came from a newsletter, *Conservation Call:* "*Flute Over Walden,* also very typographically attractive, is a 49 page booklet of 'Thoreau Haiku,' lambent jewels of poetry written by Father Raymond Roseliep, resident chaplain at Holy Family Hall, Dubuque, Iowa.... Father Roseliep's work shows him a worthy peer of most great Catholic priest-poets such as Gerard Manley Hopkins, Daniel Berrigan, and Brother Antoninus."[91]

Though Roseliep resisted being known only as a Catholic priest-poet, he surely welcomed the long upbeat review from *America,* an important Catholic periodical. After recognizing "honorable" chapbooks as being important for making "poetry that might never otherwise be published available in an inexpensive form," the reviewer exclaimed, "Other poets may claim larger acreage, but few have cultivated such verdant gardens at more refined heights. Here, for once, the medium and the message are at one."[92]

Flute over Walden, mentioned first among the "Books Received," elicited another short comment, in *John Berryman Studies:* "A fine collection from the master of western haiku and senryu."[93] Though this encomium is brief, it was the catalyst for a long relationship between the priest-poet and Ernest and Cis Stefanik,[94] editors of Rook Press, which later published several chapbooks for him. Roseliep often worked this way: he sent free copies of his works to editors to bring himself and his poetry to their attention, "just in case." He was bold enough to make outright requests for future publication of his works — and he was often successful.

The most effusive review of *Flute over Walden* came from Wade Van Dore in the book review section of the *Thoreau Journal Quarterly:* "How

91. *Conservation Call* (San Diego, Calif.) 37 (November–December 1976).

92. James Finn Cotter, "*Flute Over Walden: Thoreauhaiku.*" *America* 135:6 (1976): 129–30.

93. *John Berryman Studies* 2:3 (1976).

94. Roseliep to Ernest Stefanik, May 24, 1976.

delighted a word must be when poet Raymond Roseliep uses it! What a surprise when it is caught in his net of awareness—then deposited in a Thoreau-haiku. Adroitness is a religion here. This poet is so nimble-souled, he is able to divine the exact nook of meaning that a word wants to be tumbled into.... Roseliep's style is like a flickering of granite embedded in the inch-lines. When he writes, jewelry takes a holiday."[95]

The Juniper Press chapbooks

From 1976 to 1979 Roseliep busied himself with producing chapbooks. Through his own diligence he had attracted the attention of Juniper Press, Rook Press, and High/Coo, and their efforts resulted in several publications a year during this period.

Walk in Love

Searching in various haiku magazines for outlets for his work, Roseliep had contacted a variety of small-press publishers in 1974 before he wrote to John Judson of Juniper Press on November 1, 1975. After a typical introduction, showing particular knowledge of the editor and his publishing—in this case Judson's successes after their work together on *Voyages to the Inland Sea*—Roseliep asked, "Could I interest you in a MS for your Juniper series? I have just prepared one, which I call *Walk in Love*.... A book of love poems. By a priest (Maybe in this modern day of church-change, that isn't so startling)."[96] Roseliep always requested acknowledgments of publications in which he had already placed individual haiku intended for the present manuscript as well as the announcement of his forthcoming book, *Flute Over Walden*. He often worked on more than one manuscript at a time. Keeping track of replies and rejections alone was almost a full-time job.

Judson replied with a handwritten letter, "I'd love to see your ms., but I must warn you in advance that I'm booked up for several years...."[97] The poems that Roseliep sent to Judson caused the publisher to jump the line for Roseliep, however. Judson eventually chose twenty-three poems for *Walk in Love*, most with short lines and many of them not haiku but something close to it. For example the final poem reads,

95. Wade Van Dore, "Book Review" [*Flute Over Walden*], *Thoreau Journal Quarterly* 8:4 (1976), 4.

96. Roseliep to Judson, November 1, 1975.

97. Judson to Roseliep, November 23, 1975.

RE-ENTRY

This is the room
where I lived and died:
lightly! dust puff
at my side,

across the threshold
crossed so much,
air skin soft
to a touch:

lightly! footstep
barely stir,
a lover's breath
be whisperer.[98]

Roseliep's poem uses rhyme, four-line stanzas, and a title—but the stanzas are easily read as haiku. Each could stand alone in self-contained meaning.

Haiku was even more present in "Lorenzo's Bride." The first stanza reads

Whiteflower-still
you fill the valley
of my arms tonight,

The entire poem, consisting of six three-line stanzas, is one sentence that ends

mute
as my favor
on your marble throat.[99]

Walk In Love received only three reviews. Joseph Zderad wrote in *Encore,*

Roseliep is a master haikuist and no book of his is without at least a few of them.... Precision, the exact single word, must fascinate and challenge the poet.... The language is rich. One longs for the full-bodied longer poems, for lyrics fully orchestrated (such as his earlier

98. Roseliep, "Re-entry," *Walk in Love* (La Crosse, Wis.: Juniper Press, 1976).
99. Roseliep, "Lorenzo's Bride," *Walk in Love.*

poem, the marvelous "My Father's Trunk"), but that is clearly not now the poet's way.... With remarkable economy he paints entire landscapes with a mere brushful of words, writes years into a sentence, a lifetime in a poem.[100]

Vincent Heinrichs commented in *Chicory,*

> Readers familiar with the poetry of Raymond Roseliep know that he demands attention by his careful control of form and intensive use of language. *Walk in Love* meets our expectations, for the seeming simplicity of these twenty-three poems is beguiling. There pulses through this slim but masterful collection an undercurrent of quiet intensity about the relationship of art to the poet and to life.... In "River Song"... the speaker invites "love" to accompany him, to enter with him the "river," the dark place.... Love is necessary to fashion a defense against confusion of darkness. That defense is form.... Love becomes the means for the individual to create a stay against the night.[101]

Heinrichs ended his insights into love and its centrality in Roseliep's life by quoting a three-line poem titled "Chicago Picasso":

> Wings for passage, ground
>   for anchor. Art is. Only
>   love frees the sprung ribs.[102]

John Judson's notification in *The Plains Booklist* (summer 1977) merely cited the other two reviews. Other Roseliep chapbooks typically also received very little critical attention.

Light Footsteps

The smallest of Roseliep's chapbooks was *Light Footsteps,* a Juniper Special, published in 1976 as a surprise birthday present from John Judson. Two hundred fifty copies were hand set and hand printed. Judson ended this 2½″ x 3″ publication of seven Roseliep haiku (plus a poem of his own) "For Raymond, by Early Sun." Roseliep noted to himself,

> I thought he had it in mind to print a selection for his magazine *Northeast.* Instead, he surprised me, made a selection from this manuscript and put together the mini-chapbook which he called

---

100. *Encore* 11 (spring 1977).

101. Roseliep used the words "against the night" in more than one of his publications, most probably for the first time in the poem celebrating his mother "For a Seventy Fifth Birthday," (*The Linen Bands,* 1961), and again in his essay, "A Poet's Belief, *The Catholic World,* 219:1 (January/February 1976), 41–43.

102. Vincent Heinrichs, "Quiet Intensity." *Chicory* 1:1 (1978), 4–6.

Light Footsteps. I did not know of its existence until his package of
complimentary copies arrived as a birthday gift. He sent them a little
after the birthday, 15 September 1976.[103]

This tiny tome, which bore a price of 75¢, elicited one substantial
review—far longer, actually, than the text of the book—from Louis
Mannere in *Chicory*:

> The seven haiku that compose the text of *Light Footsteps* create the
> impression that Raymond Roseliep has filled hundreds of notebooks
> with haiku, and now he has distilled those thousands of poem that
> delineate his lifetime in art into this rare brew.... In these poems the
> poet has committed a part of his life (whether real or illusory) to
> language, and in his hands the language assumes a life of its own....
> The subtle effect of heightened awareness in these poems derives
> in part from the poet's departure from the traditional seventeen-
> syllable form in order to achieve great compression and concision.
> It is as though Roseliep is saying that sometimes seventeen syllables
> are too many to offer a scene, to express (or arouse) an emotion,
> and to invite a spiritual insight. Further, his concern for diction in-
> fuses these poems with life, allowing images to enlarge into meta-
> phor, and metaphor into symbol. For example, in the metaphysical
> "the first snow / took me indoors / of my real self" the unexpected
> verb causes the image to unfold like leaf from bud, from the par-
> ticular to the general, from the personal to the universal. Roseliep's
> departure from the 5–7–5 syllabic pattern may also have its source
> in his desire to make the poems more accessible through the use of
> natural speech patterns, that is, to create music of stress, duration,
> and the distribution of vowels and consonants rather than relying
> solely upon the number of syllables in each line. In "the silence. /
> a bee is singing / right into rock" there is a harmony of manner and
> matter that produces the sensuous pleasure of music which would
> have been undermined had the poet's first concern been with count-
> ing syllables.... The booklet is now out of print, but perhaps when
> Roseliep publishes his collected works he will include a section en-
> titled *Light Footsteps* as a significant part of his impressive canon.[104]

Roseliep always welcomed reviews of his haiku chapbooks and mention
of his other activities, especially in *Modern Haiku,* even if he had to swallow a few bitter pills along the way. He could always repeat a well-worn
adage: "No publicity is bad publicity."[105] Usually, however, reviewers

---

103. "Note to myself" on the carbon copy of a set of new haiku Roseliep sent to Judson, *Light
Footsteps* folder, LCARC 325, B:4.

104. Louis Mannere, "A Rare Brew," *Chicory* 1:1 (1978), 10–12.

105. Writers such as Oscar Wilde embellished this thought, but perhaps Brendan Behan said
it best: "There's no such thing as bad publicity except your obituary."

were quite balanced in their approach. Indifference from the critics was especially hard to take, however. In a book note on *Light Footsteps* for *Modern Haiku,* Willene H. Nusbaum had written, "None outstanding, but all are well done and for the modest price of 75 cents would make a nice remembrance for a poetry reader. One reviewer of this tiny book, George Ellison, at Unaka Range, said that 'John Judson surely designed it for midget meadow mice.'"[106] Roseliep always carefully noted his appearances in any haiku journal in his neat handwriting on the title page. One could wonder what he thought as he penned in the pages for his own haiku, noting his own completely positive review of Gary Hotham's new book, *Without the Mountain,* ... and the brief dismissal, "nice," from Nusbaum!

Sky in My Legs

The single review in Roseliep's files for *Sky in My Legs* (Juniper Press, 1979), which was written by Robert Spiess, opens

> Having 48 pages, this mini-chapbook in the Juniper Press series is a "thicker" issue than the previous ones of haiku that have come to my attention....
>
> As the acknowledgement page lists twenty publications, these haiku have had wide acceptance. And as the case with his other haiku books, in this one, also, Raymond Roseliep's haiku and senryu nearly always employ fresh images.
>
> > the spider locks
> > the folded hands
> > in the coffin

In connection with the last haiku,

> > water (Lord!)
> > at the heart
> > of all things

Spiess adds, "We are reminded of the view of the philosopher Thales (7th Century, B.C.) that the original Principle of all things is water, from which everything proceeds ... a divine force that fills all things."[107]

---

106. Willene Nusbaum, review of Raymond Roseliep, *Light Footsteps, Modern Haiku* 8:1 (Winter–Spring 1977), 45.

107. Robert Spiess, review of *Sky in My Legs* (1979), *Modern Haiku* 10:3 (Autumn 1979), 52–53.

The Rook Press chapbooks

Father Ray began a long and endearing relationship with Ernest and Cis Stefanik in 1976 when Roseliep asked: "Is there a chance that I could interest you in a chapbook for your Rook series? I have several in the planning which I could tell you about, but would like to know first if you'd be interested."[108] In less than a week, Roseliep had a welcoming yes from Stefanik for *A Beautiful Woman Moves with Grace.* Roseliep and the Stefaniks collaborated four more times: *Step on the Rain* (1977), *Wake to the Bell* (1977), *A Day in the Life of Sobi-Shi* (1978), and *Sailing Bones* (1978).

If you looked in the Roseliep files at the four folders marked for Rook Press, you might surmise that there was little correspondence with the Stefaniks. However, certain hints would tell you to look more deeply into other categories in those voluminous files. An evolution from the beginning salutation on March 1976, to Ernest and Cis Stefanik to "Ern" and "Erno" by July 1977, along with the creative change of his own signatures from Raymond Roseliep to Rookily in February of 1977, mirrored their growth from editors to friends. Even the folders for each of the five chapbooks published by Rook Press are slim,[109] containing usually a review or two. When you look, however, in the folders for personal communications, you hit pay dirt. Two thick folders labeled Stefanik, Ernie and Cis, yield a long and progressively deep commitment to one another during the years of Roseliep's publications with Rook Press.

Ernie was especially creative and playful in varying salutations for Roseliep. Among them, he opened many letters with such salutations as: Rainy, Rey-Knee, Rainy Ray, Bardic One, Ramon, Raimondo, Père Ray, and Brother Francis. One envelope, addressed to Felix Rudolphus (the names of two feral cats attended by Roseliep at his Holy Family Residence) is filled with 8½" x 11" cat paw prints!

In addition to the several chapbooks Rook Press published for Roseliep was a series in 1976 of eight poem cards, titled Bard Cards, featuring Roseliep haiku. He enjoyed sharing these cards with friends and correspondents.

In June 1982, Sister Iva Halbur, OSF, published, through Mount St. Francis, four Roseliep haiku poem cards titled "Only the Attentive,"

---

108. Roseliep to Stefanik, May 24, 1976.

109. *See* Chapter Seven: Raymundo. Selected Correspondence about the five chapbooks from Rook Press.

"People Who Care," "Sharing Stillness," and "Tonight." Sister Iva was a noted local artist, featured in *Julien's Journal*[110] as well as the Fort Dodge newspaper, *The Messenger.*[111] By 1982, Sister Iva had created 172 cards. Her studio, "the open eye" gallery, was located in Holy Family Hall, a separate wing near the residence of Raymond Roseliep. The article in *The Messenger* opened: "A Catholic nun competing with Hallmark and American Greeting? That's exactly what Sister Iva Halbur, OSF, does out of her art studio ... this Franciscan's ministry."[112]

A Beautiful Woman Moves with Grace

Chapbooks rarely receive much recognition from reviewers, even in the haiku journals. *A Beautiful Woman Moves with Grace*, however, was noticed by reviewers. Writing for *Chicory,* Josef Zderad, commented:

> It's hard to say if there are twenty-eight poems or twenty-nine. Isn't the title itself a poem? Economical, but every word is rich. And right. Moves with grace. Beautiful women never stride, amble, step, or even walk. They move.... This kind of caring for the exact word is a hallmark of Roseliep's poetry. One profits by studying the words, by re-reading the poems and trying to substitute some word in the poem with another (though rarely, if ever, succeeding). Many of the poems here urge a person, beckon, invite, perhaps dare one to write poetry. We experience what Juan Ramon Jimenez meant when he said, 'The true sign of poetry is contagion.'[113]

One of the most beautiful poems from *A Beautiful Woman Moves with Grace* was:

BLOODROOT

Woods dance the dance of
light-gowned ladies white
as your hand,
          jeweled
with a little gold
they hide from evening
when your eyes close too.[114]

---

110. February 1982, 7–8. A local magazine most often featuring the arts.
111. August 18, 1982.
112. Halbur, Sister Iva, OSF. LCARC 325, B1:H.
113. Josef Zderad, "Poems That Urge, Beckon, Invite and Dare." *Chicory* 1:1 (1978), 7–9.
114. Roseliep, "Bloodroot." *A Beautiful Woman Moves with Grace,* 28.

Roseliep kept clips of two other reviews of *A Beautiful Woman Moves with Grace,* one by poet Mary Lammons in *New Letters,*[115] which opened, "Like the title, these poems move with grace, gliding thorough sounds and rhythms, evoking music in their movements. Roseliep handles language like a mother holds her child—tenderly, guardedly, and sometimes with an excitement which grows into a swirling embrace." Daniel Rogers's review in the *Delta Epsilon Sigma Bulletin*[116] proclaimed, "Roseliep immediately assumes the reader's ability to accept and respond to his own humanness, to what he has unconsciously suspected ever to be the case, namely, that 'A Beautiful Woman Moves with Grace.'"

Dusk and Ocean

Editors Ernest and Cis Stefanik wrote on the back cover of this tiny publication: "This edition of Raymond Roseliep's 'Dusk and Ocean' is limited to seventy-five numbered and signed copies as a keepsake for the contributors to *Into the Round Air* (*Thistle* 5)." This keepsake consisted of heavy cardstock, folded once, with the title on the front accompanied by the photo of a mollusk by Bill Pauly. Inside is a sheet bearing the title poem, handwritten and signed, with the copy number and a personal dedication to each contributor. The poem once again involves the poet's struggles with passion and its expression:

> Dusk
> and ocean
> cat-lap on
> the beach
>
> Love,
> you air-
> skate
> my rock
>
> pad
> waiting
> the strike
> of your

115. Mary Lammons, review of *A Beautiful Woman Moves with Grace, New Letters* (Winter 1982–83), 107–8.

116. Daniel Rogers, "The Promise of Ambiguity in Recent Works of Roseliep," *Delta Epsilon Sigma Bulletin* 22 (May 1977), 62–65.

arrival
though
I
hear

the thorny
oyster
close a door
only[117]

Wake to the Bell: A Garland of Christmas Poems

*W*ake to the Bell (Rook Chapbook No. 11, 1977), had a lovely, brightly colored kneeling angel on the cover with red (Roseliep's favorite color) stitching on its robe. The selection of this cover illustration, taken from a 13th-century stained glass window in Lincoln Cathedral, England, bore witness to the dedication of the editors, who hand-tinted the angel. Roseliep acknowledged five separate publications for some of the Christmas-themed poems. "Cradlesong" was first printed in this chapbook:

sleepy butterfly,
wake
to the bell
sweet sky,

wing
the tallest hill
weighing
a limb

or two
of the dark
rose
tree

where older
children
place a dice
chime

---

117. Raymond Roseliep, *Dusk and Ocean.* (No place [Derry, Pa.]: Rook Society, 1977). Single folded page.

and you dance free,
weightless,
transparent
in no time

Echoes of many of Roseliep's themes and even some recollection of words used in the past tell the reader that this poem does not merely reflect its title. Phrases such as: "dark rose," "older children," "dice chime [game]," and "in no time," as well as a butterfly definitely out of season in a Christmas poem indicate dark underpinnings. Such poems as "Vendor" and all of the Sobi-Shi poems as well as the still slumbering Zen poems of *mu* from *The Still Point* seem held in this seemingly simple cradle song.

Roseliep received just one review, "Heralds of Christmas," by the editor of *Julien's Journal,* Marie Udulutch: "Reverend Raymond Roseliep is a man who lives Christmas all year long, a person whose constant challenge seems to be to control and direct his mental and spiritual energies and make them effectively serve himself and other people.... He is a perfectionist who is full of love."[118] In the interview for this critique, Roseliep wrote about his limited, autographed editions: "It's enough to have a small sharing ... even if one other person hears and understands, that's enough."[119]

Step on the Rain

The release of *Step on the Rain* (Rook Chapbooks No. 12) received a fair amount of recognition. *Outch* editor Nobuo Hirasawa, who had supplied the bamboo-brush kanji for this edition enthused, "Raymond's haiku reminds me of good old days of Basho and Issa, which we are losing here in Japan."[120]

Elizabeth Lamb reviewed the chapbook in the summer 1978 *Modern Haiku.* Though they were fast friends, she remained always the objective critic. After praising the beautifully presented chapbook and Hirasawa's brushwork, she wrote,

> And the poems themselves take one into many areas of Roseliep's inner landscape as well as the outer reality, as they move from the beautiful opener:

118. Marie Udulutch, "Heralds of Christmas," *Julien's Journal* 2:11 (1977), 24 and 26.
119. Roseliep to Marie Udulich, February 1977.
120. *Outch* 2 (Autumn 1977), 14.

turn to the field
a woman is singing
or a perfect bird

to the stunning close from which comes the title:

whose step on the rain
outside my bedroom window
Christ! I think I know

She continued,

The range of this collection is such that a course on haiku-senryu
writing could well use it as text.... Roseliep, whose haiku and other
poetry has been widely published, is a risk-taker. Not every experiment succeeds ... he is, it seems to me, trying out many of the poetic
devices common to non-haiku poetry to see what can be made to
work with haiku-senryu.

The least successful poems are those which depend on personification, or direct a comment to a person. A few skirt perilously
close to a quality of cuteness.... Not all are readily accessible at first
reading, but yield up a growing resonance as one lives with them.

the first snow
took me indoors
of my real self[121]

Selma Sefanile, closely and carefully reading *Step on the Rain*, commented, "Many poems are companion pieces, showing a unity of vision,
a wholeness, 'spring breeze' is related to 'winter wind' and to three others
on death.... There is a skilled, kireji-like use of the cutting word tech-
nique, a looking forward as well as back in 'O Western Wind.' Notice
how the word 'Christ' resounds: 'whose step on the rain/ outside my
bedroom window/ Christ! I think I know.'"[122]

Bill Pauly reviewed his mentor's chapbook for *Uzzano*:[123] "Raymond
Roseliep's newest collection of haiku is an excellent touchstone in this
rejuvenation of the traditional three-line poem. The work here offers
a refreshing diversity and texture; it unfolds lively, moving dioramas
which take us through the four seasons as well as untold seasons of the
self, where we 'live inwardly/ to hear/ the pop of a bud,' for example,
and where 'trees/ are walking/ with us.'... He is unflinching, too, in his
use of startling images usually not associated with haiku: 'the blind cat
hears/ the peacock unlocking/ bluegreen eyes,' and 'stumble/ on a star in
the brook/ all three crumble.'"

121. *Modern Haiku* 9:2 (Summer 1978), 14..
122. *High/Coo* 2 (November 1977), 22–23.
123. *Uzzano* 9/10 (Spring–Summer 1978), 14.

Pauly helps give credence to the many poetic devices that Rose-liep dares to use: "Careful use of alliteration, assonance, consonance, enjambment and even occasional rime underscores Roseliep's versatile word handling and his emphasis on sound values in haiku."

Into the Round Air

Nineteen seventy-seven was surely a bountiful year for Raymond Roseliep and Rook Press. This time around, however, Father Ray was invited to compile and edit *Thistle 5*, an anthology of poems by famous authors, colleagues, former students and correspondents who included Jean Burden (long-time editor and friend from *Yankee* magazine), Richard Eberhart, Gary Hotham, Colette Inez, Ted Kooser, Elizabeth Searle Lamb, Frank Lehner (his Loras colleague and editor for years of *Delta Epsilon Sigma Bulletin),* John Logan, James Minor, Bill Pauly, Daniel J. Rogers, Dennis Schmitz, William Stafford, Eve Triem, and Virginia Brady Young.

The Stefaniks wrote an opening note of thanks: "Raymond Roseliep, who agreed to be Guest Editor of *Thistle 5*, exceeded our expectations in soliciting poems for his issue; and so, with his willingness and assistance, we decided to change the format of the magazine to that of an anthology. The Guest Editor suggested *Into the Round Air* for the title, a phrase selected from Josephine Miles's "Pearl," which appears in this collection."

A Day in the Life of Sobi-Shi

Seven of Roseliep's Sobi-Shi haiku were gathered together by the Stefaniks and published in a handsome 5 ½ x 8 ½ format on a single laid paper sheet folded in four with oversize mustard-yellow wrappers featuring calligraphy by Roseliep's friend Nobuo Hirasawa. The haiku had all appeared in the *Uzzano* collection[124] although they were reordered for this edition:

> in Sobi-Shi's glass
> the dark rose
> of a love ago

>   seeing some fireflies
> Sobi-Shi turns from the street
> of red lights

---

124. Raymond Roseliep, "50 Haiku," *Uzzano* 9/10 (Spring–Summer 1978).

Year of the horse:
Sobi-Shi's heart goes thudding
softly through the wood

   waiting for her
his eye on the wind
   Sobi-Shi blows the conch

another hill
to climb
inside Sobi-Shi

stuck in the mud
   Sobi-Shi's horse
and the moon

Sobi-Shi
has no more to say
     the frog said it

The Stefaniks arranged the haiku to emphasize the centrality of the woman
and apparent lover. The last three can be read as Sobi-Shi's difficult leave-
taking from a woman who became, perhaps, more distanced in this arrangement, casting all in memory through the "love ago." Of the six
Sobi-Shi haiku, two—"waiting for her," and "in Sobi-Shi's glass"—specifically refer to a "her," although the "dark rose / of a love ago" hardly
prepares the reader for the eroticism of the "fireflies" haiku that follows.

The spacing of the haiku makes the reader look back, even if Sobi-
Shi had seemed to turn away. The other three haiku did not specifically
name a love, but, in the presence of the haiku that did, they took on the
weight of that lover.

Bill Pauly opened his comments on *A Day in the Life of Sobi-Shi*—
the only review of this chapbook in Roseliep's folders—by giving a bit
of its backstory:

> This sequence of seven haiku, first seen in the April 1978 *Uzzano*,
> is the work of Raymond Roseliep, dressed in his haiku singing robe

and wearing a haiku-name (haigo) that christens him "a man of art who loves the rose." In this persona, this other self, Roseliep moves us through a brief story of love remembered:

> in Sobi-Shi's glass
> the dark rose
> of a love ago

Packed with nuance, this pivotal haiku sets the tone and direction of the sequence with marvelous word play on the author's name. It also creates initial tension between light and dark that prevails in later poems, and inseparably fuses the dark rose, Sobi-Shi, and the 'love ago' in a central, controlling metaphor.

Pauly admitted, as Elizabeth Lamb had written,[125] "I am not always sure of this 'other man of the rose' by echoing her words: "I am left with questions and wonderment after this day with Sobi-Shi, and this I take as a good sign of how his fleeting scene has moved me."[126] As "a man of art who loves the rose," Sobi-Shi was simultaneously at one with the poet, a doppelgänger or alter ego. Sobi-Shi's conflicted journey from 1978 until his death was typical of Roseliep's life, on or off the page.

Sailing Bones

Compared to the small number of critiques for many of Roseliep's chapbooks, *Sailing Bones* (1978), another Rook Press chapbook, attracted the attention of four magazines: *High/Coo, Tweed, Poet,* and *The Plains Booklist.* In *High/Coo,* Hortense Roberta Roberts opened with one of the haiku:

> Lucy is dead
> the light
> in her clock

and continued, "At first glance a Roseliep poem may reach one as a simple, albeit startling, observation, then change before one's eyes from living picture to metaphor to metaphysical." Roberts called attention to Roseliep's sense of humor: "When Roseliep laughs at life's tricks and incongruities, his humor is neither cutting nor cruel.... [O]ne laughs with, not at, the poet: 'wrong bed — / best run / I said.'" She concluded, "A non-poet has asked me its meaning. At the risk of turning poetry into inadequate prose, I'll try to translate it. The dictionary meaning of bones

---

125. Lamb to Roseliep, November 7, 1978.
126. *A Day in the Life of Sobi-Shi*: Reviews. LCARC 325 D1:3.

is 'the skeleton within the body.... The body, living or dead.' Surely not dead, for these are sailing bones, moving to wind and water, alive with faith that the pilot light can rekindle the snuffed candle."[127] Lamb wrote,

> Raymond Roseliep ... goes sailing through a repertoire of modern haiku techniques, allowing each poem to find its own structure.... Following a number of haiku chapbooks that have appeared in rapid succession, these haiku seem to show a surer touch and more even quality than some of his others.
>
> Haiku, senryu, poems which are so much a blend of the two— every poem from:

> > the white crocus!
> > and I haven't changed
> > my clothes

> to the blithely irreverent verse of his alter ego:

> > alone in the rain
> > Sobi-Shi opens
> > his little rainspout

> > ...

> Roseliep tries no experiments here, no one-line haiku, no concrete verse. He simply hones his perception to a fine point and makes unforgettable use of his way with words. The book itself, handsewn into a two-color cover, is a credit to The Rook Press. And many of the poems inside those covers, once read, simply refuse to let go:

> > rain
> > erasing
> > the clown's face[128]

The reviewer for *Poet* 20 (8, 1979), 99, writes: "Sobi-Shi, the haigo, or haiku-name of the author ... is implanted in a number of the lines, adding an additional mood to these miniature brush strokes ... poems that invite participation, another aspect of these abbreviated, subtle weavings."

The Plains Booklist 17 (Summer 1980), simply quoted from the *Modern Haiku* review by Chuck Brickley of *Firefly in My Eyecup* (in which he called Roseliep "the John Donne of Western Haiku") Hortense Roberta Roberts's observations in *High/Coo,* and Elizabeth Lamb's in *Tweed.*[129]

---

127. Hortense Roberta Roberts, "Sailing Bones: Haiku by Raymond Roseliep," *High/Coo* 4:13 (August 1979).

128. Elizabeth Searle Lamb "Contrasts: Four New Books in Review." *Tweed* 7:1&2 (September/December 1978).

129. A copy of a typed note typically from Roseliep, marks the place of this review by asking the publisher to put both Roberts and Lamb (whom they quote) on their mailing list, "both are good book buyers."

Correspondence between Raimondo and the Stefaniks dwindled after Rook Press closed its doors. The priest's note on May 16, 1979, read, "Dear Doc ... I am of course saddened to hear of the demise of old Rookery, and I too, chant with you, Requiescat in pace." He continued, "The important thing is that you regain your health and vigor." He ended with: "I send love to you, Cis, and the chillun."

Sailing Bones included "The Morning Glory," a three-stanza sequence:

THE MORNING GLORY

> takes in
> the world
> from the heart out

> funnels
> our day
> into itself

> closes
> on its own
> inner light

Yankee Magazine had published the poem in their June 1978 issue and as a single broadsheet.[130] Then, in 1980, it was selected for display on buses in New York as part of the Poetry in Public Places project (*see* page 126).

The High/Coo Press chapbooks

Sun in His Belly

High/Coo Press was interested in publishing poem cards and chapbooks in addition to the journal of the same name. Randy Brooks's letter of July 19, 1976, replied positively to Roseliep's query about the possibility of doing a chapbook. Brooks asked for 36–50 poems or more for a selection. He welcomed both new and previously published haiku "Your enthusiasm," Brooks added, "is an uplift."

Roseliep, as always, wasted no time. Nine days later he sent the requested haiku: "I have put the poems into a pattern that makes sense (to me), and hope you will like the pattern." Brooks was no slouch either; his

---

130. Raymond Roseliep, *The Morning Glory* (New York: Poetry in Public Places, ©1978 Yankee Magazine). One-page broadsheet. A copy of the full-sized bus placard may be found in LCARC, Room 325.

letter of August 3 enthused, "Shirley and I are just thrilled with *Sun in His Belly.* This is an excellent collection of poems, and we would be honored and pleased to print it as our first chapbook." The Brookses' modus operandi was very much in synch with Roseliep's and soon became another publisher after the poet's own heart. Their letter is filled with the kind of specifics that Roseliep often demanded from himself and other publishers; for his part Randy Brooks thanked Roseliep for helping promote *High/Coo* among his haiku friends and for recommending Bill Pauly as another candidate for a chapbook.[131]

Sun in His Belly was a showpiece. Bound in canary yellow, the cover sported a photograph by Pauly and calligraphy by Sr. Mary Thomas Eulberg, two poets whom Roseliep, at various times, mentored. Most of the poems were haiku, and those that were not were short enough to fill a page but not overrun it. In the forty-eight pages Roseliep unleashed his just-short-of-scandalous poetic devices: haiku that were concrete or acrostic, puns, rhyme, and name-dropping. Any of them might be written in two, four, or five lines rather than the expected three. In the poems he also celebrated friends and was unabashedly self-referential:

VARIATION ON A THEME

house aflame
house aflame
rembrandt on the wall
tomcat in the hall

what to save
what to save
oil   fur   fire
I chose a lyre

Then, as a closing, a typical Roseliep signature:

ESCHATOLOGY

While all your bowers
crisp in heat, gardener Christ
have one more rose leap

---

131. A recommendation that was realized with Pauly's *Wind the Clock by Bittersweet in* 1977.

For *Chicory,* Hortense Roberta Roberts wrote the one review of *Sun in His Belly* that Father Ray filed away.[132] She noted that this was the fourth published collection of Roseliep's poems to appear in the past year, and she found it as exciting as his others. All the poems are brief, she wrote, but that is "not to imply that they are either slight or negligible. I know of no other poet, with the possible exception of Emily Dickinson, who can say so much in so few words." Roberts opined that the book's first poem was both explanation and introduction:

> wind keeps carving
> a head
> from mountain rock
>
> the man watching
> guides his knife
> to cherrystone.

"He has retained the fresh wonder and observation of a child with a man's wisdom and experience." She ended the review, "If you try to catch and hold [his poems] in hard prose they are no longer themselves.... You need to be quiet, to watch and listen ... they will come to you and belong. Even with those you can't quite comprehend, you can love the sight and sound."

The Books Received section of *Bonsai*[133] only presented bibliographic information about *Sun in His Belly* and these two poems:

> missing my woe
> the elevator girl said
> "Watch your step"

> BOWL
>
> My crystal
> magnified your nectarine
> long after it had
> shriveled like a head.

---

132. Hortense Roberta Roberts, "He Carves Heads on Cherrystones," *Chicory* 1 (1978), 13–15.

133. *Bonsai* 2:1 (April 19, 1977), 32.

Firefly in My Eyecup

In 1979 Chuck Brickley lauded Roseliep's metaphysical and philosophical approach in his new chapbook from High/Coo Press, *Firefly in My Eyecup.*[134]

> Raymond Roseliep is the John Donne of Western haiku ... the wit, the conceptual nature of his haiku, and the tension between the sacred and the profane which underlies much of his work, have more in common with Donne's conceits than with, let's say, Basho's internal comparisons.
>
> Nowhere are these aspects of Roseliep's work so well focused as they are in his most recent, and perhaps most brilliant sequence to date *Firefly in My Eyecup*. As an example of his wit, there is:
>
> > skylight
> > june bugs
> > moon-walk
>
> of his complex metaphor:
>
> > winter bees grow still
> > in my dream of honeycomb
> > empty on your hill
>
> and of his conceptual insight:
>
> > glass
> > is the way
> > your soul looks
>
> In each of these poems Roseliep, contrary to the traditional stance of haiku poets, looks progressively inward.... The last poem, in fact, reads like a line from Donne. It functions as a haiku only insofar as its brevity requires the reader to extend the metaphor into his or her own conceit.

Brickley adds in-depth commentary on four other haiku in the sequence of sixteen. For the ever-puzzling persona of Sobi-Shi in

> the call girl watches
> Sobi-Shi threading
> a needle

he notes, "In the best tradition of senryu, there is no moral condemnation in this poem, but rather, a worldly and humorous acceptance of the way things are. It may be that the call girl is innocently watching

---

134. The review, one of three in *Modern Haiku* 10:3 (Autumn 1979), 38–39, was written by Chuck Brickley.

Sobi-Shi thread a needle, but in his mind there is something else going on here. Tongue in cheek, he tries to concentrate on the task at hand."[135]

The haiku that follow the Sobi-Shi haiku become a bit singed by their near presence:

> by her bed
> night enters
> his boots

and

> rainy morning
> Renoir's
> sleeping lady

The Still Point[136]

Although *The Still Point: Haiku of "Mu"* — softbound, 5½″ x 8½″, and comprising 50 pages — might be considered a chapbook, critics referred to this publication from editor Robert Schuler and Uzzano Press as a full-fledged book. It was dedicated to Nobuo Hirasawa, one of whose calligraphic works graced the cover. In a prefatory note titled "Mu," Roseliep made it clear that the idea for the book came from his Japanese friend.[137] Roseliep, recuperating from surgery in the summer of 1978, detailed a strange inner journey after receiving a note from Hirasawa, who had sent an *omimai,* a gift to comfort a bedridden person, whether in the hospital or at home. The *omimai* was his brush drawing of "*mu,* done as he said in his 'most Zen style.'" Hirasawa went on to explain that *mu* means "nothing, none, empty." Roseliep continued, "Over a period of half a year, I began exploring the honeycomb and catacomb of *mu* as themes for the haiku moment." Perhaps anticipating more than usual criticism, Roseliep concluded,

> *The Still Point* is experience and experiment. American haiku will
> cease to be adventuresome if we should suddenly stop for breath.
> Like old Basho's frog, we must keep plunging. Eastern and Western
> frogs do, of course, and not all of them make the same sound.[138]

---

135. Ibid. A shortened version was published in the High/Coo catalog No. 1, Spring 1980.
136. Raymond Roseliep, *The Still Point: Haiku of "Mu"* (Menomonie, Wis.: Uzzano, 1979).
137. Hirasawa's kanji were also featured in *Listen to Light.*
138. Roseliep, "Mu," *The Still Point.* Introductory words, no page number.

Any reading of *The Still Point* must proceed at a snail's pace with pauses for reflection and gradual movement from cover to cover to a conclusion that is not an ending. The central image of each haiku can hold the reader for a long time, but probably not at first reading. The mind keeps flashing one unusual "image" in black and white. And suddenly, breathless (because you've been holding your breath), you might recognize that you are in the middle of a Zen experience of nothing, without the usual image at the center. Subsequent readings of Roseliep's *The Still Point* might keep you breathless. At one point in the reading of his *mu* you might wonder if you could remember how to breathe anymore:

> glass
> goes into the light
> it gives

Roseliep, however, quickly drew us earthward through these words, just across the page, of the poet, rapt in prayer:

> past my priedieu
> the vermillioned whisk
> of Wallace Stevens[139]

A priedieu is a small wooden desk with an attached shelf for one person to kneel and pray, common in many priests' private quarters. The "vermillioned whisk" is, most probably, fantasy.[140] The "whisk" of the deep red he perceives is particularly resonant to the child Roseliep, whose mother bought him "red things" such as "a fire engine to pedal with my bare summer feet."[141] The conjunction of prayer and the intrusion of red, connoting passion, are deeply embedded in the poet's life. In many ways, Roseliep could never escape being a priest-poet. Celibacy and passion are not easy bedfellows, and—for Roseliep—they are often the center of his writing and life.

---

139. Roseliep refers to the use of "vermilion" in Wallace Stevens' poem "Le Monocle de Mon Oncle." The "glass" haiku and "the vermillioned whisk" are at the exact center of *The Still Point*. Roseliep, ever fussy about the placement of his haiku, must have deliberately chosen the exact center of the book for these haiku.

140. If, instead, the poet is kneeling in a sanctuary or sacristy, the "vermillioned whisk" might come from the red piping and buttons on a cassock that a monsignor wears.

141. Raymond Roseliep, "My Mother Bought Me Red Things," *The Small Rain* (Westminster, Md.: Newman Press, 1963) 14.

Reading and rereading his haiku of *mu*, one might wonder at the power of Roseliep's seemingly simple expression, which carries the reader so swiftly to his "Therewhere." The gathered experience can be likened to the reaction of a dog on the mirror who panics because there seems to be nothing below him.

Roseliep said the fifty haiku of his text (including a triptych dedicated to Hirasawa) "arranged themselves." Even knowing the process of Zen only a very little, one will understand that this meant there was an intricate patterning, but one recognized through the inner silence that was completely open to the innate order of things. Essences. The only way to arrive at a true understanding of this arrangement is to go by the way Roseliep went. Your "eyes" need to see the poet and yourself gradually moving from the periphery of the concentric circles (made by Bashō's frog in the old pond, perhaps?) to the center where that same frog plopped in.

First, Roseliep quieted us down:

> not winding the heart
> nor minding
> the mind

Then he arranged our bodies:

> my lotus legs
>> from somehow
>> to no-how

He invited us to look (really):

> eyes
> unwatching
> burn surprise

He gave us the gift of himself. Roseliep, the "man of art who loves the rose" —

> the rose in hay
> wintering
>> cellar of my self

What had happened thus far, four haiku of *mu* into *The Still Point?* Much "un" doing: "not-nor-no-un." A paradoxical active participle "wintering" naming the kind of passivity that is dynamic. Word play that is serious: "winding" (long i) or "winding" (short i)? Doing neither, of course. "No-how" or "know-how"? Both, of course. "Cellar" or "seller" of self?

Roseliep, taking us along, moves, unmoves to the center of his experience (his volume of haiku as well as his priestly life). Centers are important places. Confucius once said that if you want to be safe, go to the heart of danger. *The Still Point* is dangerous territory. All around, the reader is threatened by "hanging"—suspension. "Therewhere." In that safe-dangerous center we find these haiku:

> the Mass priest
> holds up bread
> the still point

> holding bread
> hands
> are empty

These haiku of *mu* are mutually complimentary. Most Catholics are still aware of the doctrine of Transubstantiation. What was once bread is no longer bread. It may look like bread, feel, smell, and taste like bread, but after the words of consecration the priest is no longer holding bread. In that respect his hands are empty, but his hands (his being) are filled with Jesus Christ. Yet, the true priest is empty—more so than hands filled with nothing material. At that still point is All. The rush, the weight, of everything: world, afterworld, is crushing. No possibility of an escape in symbol, though that alone would be powerful enough; the reality is Eternity, now.

If we make it past this center, we must still work our way back to the far edge of the pond, cresting circle after circle. A warning: we could get caught in something this simple:

> hummingbird
> breathstop
> world a-turn

If we do make it back to land, it is night in the outer world—

> shapes of night
> shape
> shapeless night

(It was "cockcrow" at the entering moment.) Our souls are given back to us:

> the luna moth leaves
> bequeathing my soul
> to me

And our spent bodies (souls) have only enough energy to hear:

> the cricket cries
> our point
> of rest

Readers might curse Roseliep for *The Still Point*, because it clings like a burr one keeps brushing from finger to finger, drawing a little blood each time. The inner demand of this *mu* can be overwhelming. The corresponding responsibility, awesome. Yet, Roseliep gave his readers (and here one could bless, not curse him) for the rest of one's life:

> a frog to sit with
> and not say
> a word

After such a trip to a silent nowhere, keep hanging on. There are more dangerous places to negotiate.

The Still Point received fewer reviews than *Flute Over Walden,* yet Roseliep was probably gratified to find this book critiqued in the haiku journals, notably *Modern Haiku* and *Cicada.* Praise for *The Still Point* was more muted than usual, however, perhaps because the poet was now stretching out, taking more chances in expanding his idea of haiku both in form and content. Bob Boldman, no stranger to haiku, reviewed it in *Portals*:

> *The Still Point* is Raymond Roseliep's latest collection; on its pages
> are both the bones and the spirit of the poet. A step beyond pictures
> and even beyond the limitation of haiku, sometimes it's rough, others
> polished and distant, but the images always stand as poetry, not just

haiku.... It is fashionable to praise him, for he has done immense good in haiku literature, but the reason I admire Roseliep is because of his sense of self and his sense of order in the universe. There is always a boy and a marvel to be discovered in his work which somehow transcends my thoughts on whether it is good or bad. Like all else I marvel, it simply is. "holding bread / hands / are empty."[142]

Chuck Brickley, another critic well versed in haiku and Zen, reviewed the book for *Modern Haiku*: "R.H. Blyth once wrote that if he had to choose between haiku and Zen, the Zen would go overboard. In *The Still Point*, Raymond Roseliep chucks the haiku. All but abandoning his usual practice of relating man and nature, he assembles here over fifty koan-like poems under the sub-title: Haiku of Mu." Brickley quoted three "*mu*-sings [that] move toward pure conception" and a withdrawing from "Eliot's 'turning world' in order to isolate and focus on its 'still point.'" Yet Brickley says "It is in the many excellent senryu in this book that Roseliep comes closest to flowing with the event of his environment and, more usually, his imagination.... Blyth's throwing the Zen overboard would have been in the spirit of Zen. In the best of *The Still Point*, Roseliep remains true to the spirit of haiku. 'the corpse / the sea untangles / itself.'"[143]

Daniel Rogers opened his review of his friend's new book with a memory: "W.H. Auden, wearing his bedroom slippers and sipping a whisky, chatted with a group of us in Dubuque, his poetry reading just completed. He told us that a man seated there among us was for him one of the best haiku poets in America. Today, poet Lucien Stryk can well put the case even more strongly. 'Roseliep would be appreciated as a fine haiku poet anywhere, especially in Japan. He's the American Issa....' The poems invite us to respond from 'where we are' and to open those invisible eyelids that keep us from seeing more than we're accustomed to." Rogers ends his review, "In the open space of each page: a few words, shaped as simply as some white-on-white art form, as some early painting of a grass or bloom of Georgia O'Keeffe's."[144]

Rod Willmot in *Cicada* observed,

> Finally, the meatiest in this group is also the most troublesome: Raymond Roseliep's *The Still Point*. Haiku usually implies a focus upon particulars; any sense of the general or the abstract that we might receive — intimations of high meaning, or symbolism, or an indefinable

---

142. Bob Boldman, "Book Reviews," *Portals* 3.2 (1980): 9.

143. Chuck Brickley, "The Still Point: Haiku of 'Mu,'" *Modern Haiku* 11:2, 32.

144. Daniel Rogers, review of *The Still Point*, *East West Journal* (January 1981) 89–90.

expansion into the cosmic—is usually an effect of our reading. But Roseliep tends to focus immediately on the general and work down to the particular, if he gets there at all.... I think the key to Roseliep's work is to be found in the many poems, his best ones, dealing not entirely with either the particular or the general, the concrete or the abstract, but with the intersection between them ... he takes both together and seeks the 'still point' of their sudden juncture."

and singled out this haiku:

> the Tao
> catches
> a silverfish[145]

Willmot referred to *The Still Point* again in his essay "The Structural Dynamics of Haiku—Part III" in *Frogpond*. There, his Sixth Proposition reads, "In haiku, the prime direction of synechdochic implication (or inference) is upwards, from being towards meaning, and not the reverse." Wilmot continued, "In Raymond Roseliep's 'time / is what / is still' the meaning-level is stated directly, as a generality, and if that is all we get from the poem (according to the Fifth Proposition ["Haiku is stretched taut between 'it means and 'it simply is.'"]) then we are not experiencing a haiku." Wilmot goes on to look for a particular *instance* and, obviously, he does not find one, allowing that the reader could do so and therefore "it might be a haiku after all."[146]

Donna Bauerly began her review by recalling a visit to the site of the Dachau Concentration Camp. After hurrying past a number of huge black-and-white photographs of the victims, progressively more abject, she felt "shut down with overload.... The first reading of *The Still Point* took me to that same place.... I was frightened upon recognizing the sameness of experience. Breathless again. At one point in the reading of his 'mu' I wondered if I could remember *how* to breathe anymore:

> glass
> goes into the light
> it gives[147]

---

145. Rod Willmot, review of six haiku books including *The Still Point*, *Cicada* 4:2 (Spring 1980), 27–30.

146. *Frogpond* 4:1 [1981], 32. The haiku is from *The Still Point*, 7.

147. Donna Bauerly, review of *The Still Point*, *Delta Epsilon Sigma Bulletin* 25:2 (1980), 59–62.

Listen to Light

After publishing *A Roseliep Retrospective: Poems and Other Words By & About Raymond Roseliep* in 1980 — *see* below —, Alembic Press followed with one of the most beautiful hardback presentations of Roseliep's all-haiku texts, *Listen to Light*.[148] Critics quickly took notice of this book, which featured on the cover and frontispiece a bamboo brush rendering by Nobuo Hirasawa of the kanji for "light."

Even before readers delved into the journey through 200 haiku, "Firefly," a triptych of light on the back panel of the jacket beckoned with the pronoun "we":

> the scheme
> is
> light
>
> we
> are all
> in it
>
> some
> where
> out there

Five kanji signaled the way the journey was to be structured. Hirasawa's depiction of "light" was pictured opposite the title page, and other kanji prefaced the four seasons: "firefly" for spring, "skylark" for summer, "owl" for autumn, and "crow" for winter. Roseliep haiku celebrating those seasons opened each section:

> opening spring
> that bird
> with the corkscrew voice

---

148. Raymond Roseliep, *Listen to Light* (Ithaca, N.Y.: Alembic Press, 1980). More than fifteen journals took note of *Listen to Light,* including *Modern Haiku, Frogpond, Brussels Sprout, East West Journal, Parnassus, Wind Chimes, Library Journal, Choice, Coda: Poets & Writers Newsletter, Muse-Pie, High/Coo, The Christian Century, August Derleth Society Newsletter, The Christian Science Monitor, Delta Epsilon Sigma Bulletin,* Alembic Press releases; and locally in Dubuque the *Telegraph Herald* and *The Witness.*

heat wave:
tearing lettuce
for rain sound

autumn stillness:
the cracks
of your hand

One of the winter haiku leads to another search—

lost flake
　　　　soul
is it you?

Was the poet telling of his own seasonal cycles? The "soul" of the lost flake takes readers back to spring and the "firefly" in which the poet describes his own boyhood and adolescence. The newborn seasonal world of spring is frequently seen through the boy-poet's eyes, watching

the black hen
eating outside
her shadow

The young boy in springtime is already aware of death, another season, but that note is gently sounded:

in the widow's veil
stars
blown from dandelion

Brother-loss is the first intimate death the poet records for spring and the light fades momentarily at the close of "Firefly" when in

AFTER DUSK

asleep
the firefly
is fueling

> sparks
> however small
>   light lovers
>
>   our bodies
> listen
>   to light

Light! Readers follow the maturing poet in the summer of "Skylark,"
which opens with "morning song" and closes with dawn after the death
of his father.

> with his going
> the birds go
> nameless

The loss in those lines — three "gones": the father, the birds, the names.
This is the threat that Roseliep gave us before in *The Still Point.* The
haiku of *mu* — the "nothing; none; empty." The fearsome, awesome state
of Zen preparing for enlightenment. So the light comes:

> dawn
> at my fingers
>   I join my body

And a skylark fittingly ends its own season, rising into the light as does
the poet at dawn.

   Another bird alights to take the summer bird's place. The haunting
notes of the owl's voice pervade the autumn reverie in *Listen to Light,* and
loss is over all.

> autumn stillness
> the cracks
> of your hand
>
> the space
> between the deer
> and the shot

Perhaps the most poignant loss is captured in this haiku:

> never expecting
> the lilies in November
> nor the small coffin

Consider this haiku of *mu* at its sharpest. The "never" lives next to "expecting," canceling out life. The "no" in November with lilies, an Easter rebirth flower, out of season. The "nor," again a negative, preceding the small coffin—a child, a stillborn infant.

Roseliep does not erase this pain of loss. The next few haiku, instead, reinforce emptiness: in a "moonless wood" or "not seeing," in "distant weeping," and a "white orchid/on her coffin." Roseliep revisits his father's grave and makes readers catch their breath at the sight of the poet (momentarily a boy again):

> my mother stock-still
> before the balloon I put
> on my father's grave

When

> dawn
> scraps
> us

at the end of the "Owl" section in *Listen to Light,* Roseliep's fellow travelers could wonder if light is still a friend, a stay against a final dark?

"Crow," that blackest of birds, with overtones of another black bird that croaked "nevermore," stands almost as a barrier to the final season. The first winter haiku is not encouraging. A call goes out to "screw our courage to the sticking point" for the rest of this haiku journey. The stillness in the first pages of the winter section is frightening; the "she" in various haiku, a warning. One parent stands still between the poet and his own death. Could the mother who gave her son red things be ironically this same person:

> she chops firewood
> after his homily
> on hell

His mother's death comes preceded by life,

birthcry!
            the stars
            are all in place

The haiku that follow build in intensity of remembrance and anguish; then

        the cry
        is here
        where I buried it

and finally

            ghost of my mother
        on the clothesline waving:
            flour sack dishtowel

The journey proceeds inexorably, now toward the poet's own death. The black crow is the kanji for this fourth and final section. Extremes of black on white abound:

        winter garden
            the white
            eggshells

and

        night walk:
        eyes
        of the hills

Visiting Mount Calvary Cemetery in Dubuque, one could read Roseliep's epitaph—his height, his depth, and his final plunge into the vast waters of eternity—rebirth.

SOBI-SHI WRITES HIS EPITAPH

Six
foot
two:

six
foot
dark

Big
Dip-
per!

We get as close to eternity as we can on this earth when the priest-poet consecrates the bread to "whiteless / light." That "lost flake" appears again, cycling us to a final eternal burning:

light
lights
light

A trinity of flame!

Readers, be careful where you put this volume of light. It may ignite from spontaneous combustion. Sometime in the dark of winter, while you are asleep, it may flame forth and consume itself. In its crackling, listen to light, but don't be surprised if, from the shadowy ashes, a firefly goes off into its own light of spring—and be comforted, for "we / are all / in it / / some / where / out there."

A few excerpts from the reviews show how widely recognized Roseliep had become by 1980. Chuck Brickley in *Modern Haiku* wrote: "Is it really necessary to respond in kind to the extremes of Roseliep's problematic style? His latest collection, *Listen to Light,* demonstrates that the real significance of Roseliep's development lies not in the extent to which he has experimented with the form, but rather, in the extent to which he has succeeded in employing his experiment in the service of genuine haiku and senryu insights."[149] Brickley was generous with his selection of Roseliep haiku, even though many were in service to Brickley's ongoing argument with Roseliep's "stylistic excesses." Ten haiku, however, were cited for their excellence, ending with

ordering my tombstone:
the cutter has me feel
his Gothic "R"[150]

---

149. *Modern Haiku* 12:2 (Summer 1982), 32–34.

150. Roseliep wrote a full-page defense, probably never published, of this haiku, titled "Some

In 1981 in *Frogpond* Hiroaki Sato reviewed four books by various authors, one of them *Listen to Light*.[151] He wrote of Roseliep's "sophistication" that combined two traits common in Japanese haiku: "One is the obscure point of reference that makes the piece incomprehensible."

> in the lettuce core
> the distant weeping
> of a man

Sato believed that Roseliep could say much more but ultimately "the reader must be left in the dark...." The other trait is the apparently arbitrary selection of images that make up a piece. Sato gives this example:

> under
> El Greco
> the brown bag lunch

Sato wondered, however, "why not da Vinci, Hokusai, or Courbet instead of El Greco? The likely explanation is that a brown bag lunch under an El Greco painting is what the poet saw, but the piece lacks [a] kind of inevitability...." One might wonder if that reviewer had ever seen bodies emaciated from deprivation as portrayed in El Greco paintings. He concluded, "Most haiku in *Listen to Light* evince neither difficulty, however, and the book makes good reading in large part because of Mr. Roseliep's no-nonsense yet perceptive approach to the haiku form."[152]

A short essay by Jerry Kilbride in the next issue of *Frogpond*[153] addressed Sato's comments. "At first emotionally, and then intellectually, I relate the elongated and uneven shape of the paper bag with the torsos and limbs of El Greco figures and to the shapes of the clouds over Toledo." Kilbride went on to make many more connections between the brown bag and qualities of a painting that might have been "Saint Martin and the

---

observations of the review of *Listen to Light* in *Modern Haiku*, by Chuck Brickley." He concludes, "The final paragraph that notes that my book 'also contains a generous selection of Roseliep's finest haiku and senryu' seems almost like an afterthought, or a bit of have-to-back-bending. I hope not."

151. *Frogpond* 4:3 (1981), 34–35).

152. *Frogpond* 4:3 (1981), 34.

153. Jerry Kilbride, "A Few Words in Defense, and Appreciation, of Two Haiku by Raymond Roseliep, "*Frogpond* 4:4 (1981) 34.

Beggar." He also defended Roseliep's "lettuce core" haiku by referring to St. John of the Cross, Georgia O'Keeffe, and stars over Gethsemane, or "the cold and lacerated heart of the buried Christ while Peter weeps."

David Andrews, review editor for *Brussels Sprout*, recognized that "Raymond Roseliep is one of the foremost Western haikuists in the world today. As a poet of superb creativity his work is widely enjoyed and admired. Because he is a major haijin, and *Listen to Light* is a major recent work (in his list of 18 books), a 'major' review—in addition to those elsewhere—seems in order." Andrews went on to list the "Key Qualities of Roseliep Haiku—Originality, Brilliance, Perception, Sensitivity, and Humor." He presented one haiku illustrating each quality: for humor,

> after *Tosca*
> a mosquito
> aria

At a time when many editors were debating definitions of haiku, Andrews suggested that Roseliep's book contained "at least three (or four or five) main types of poems, which can be briefly illustrated as follows: "Classical Haiku, Experimental Haiku, Senryu, Haiku-Stanza Poems and Brief Contemporary Poems." Examples from Roseliep's haiku were given for each, and Andrews returned to a starting point with

> the blind man's
> yellow pencil
> in the rain

Andrews dug deep into Roseliep's controversial "campfire extinguished" haiku, which had won the Shugyō Takaha Award in 1980 (*see* page 125). He began,

> This is a brilliant haiku, whose beauty breaks forth with suddenness in the third line. It also is pure Roseliep. And so it might be interesting to take a closer look at this poem, to see how it meets one of the basic (but flexible) criteria of haiku: is the poem believable? Although much of art is, as Coleridge said, based on "a willing suspension of disbelief: (and thus accepting the art work on its own terms), classical haiku usually has a basic authenticity, especially those that are not based on whimsy or fancy. And so, of each haiku we can ask, Does it work?—or, in this case, does it hold water (or stars)?

Andrews then explored four ways the fire could have been extinguished. Each seems plausible. The reality of the rest of the haiku depends upon this dead fire, and the fact of the dead fire has been denied by at least one critic of haiku.

The second line, Andrews said, raises important questions, but problems of believability can be dismissed by having the woman "just now ready to wash the dishes—or is now washing dishes in what was, a moment ago, a pan of stars." For line three Andrews asserted, "This is the basic question: on a dark, moonless and starry night—in an open setting—can the stars be seen reflected in a body of water?—such as a still pond, a horse trough, or a camper's pan?" After admitting his own lack of personal experience and quoting Lord Byron: "And the sheen of their spears was like stars on the sea," he judged: "I would assume that, in some cases, they could be. If so, this prize-winning haiku would seem to pass all the tests of believability."

Andrews concluded, "One might well prefer that such a brilliant haiku as this one not be subjected to such scrutiny. It may seem too much like pulling off the rose petals to count them. But fortunately, in the world of art—whether it be a Beethoven symphony or a Roseliep haiku—the art work can be analyzed and still retain its power."[154]

Although Roseliep sometimes came under fire for his endorsement of Western poetic devices in haiku, he also received considerable praise from well-known writers and respectable critics of haiku. Alexis Rotella came out entirely on his side in her review of *Listen to Light* in *East-West Journal* (1983). Quoting this haiku,

> the wren
> moves apart
> from its song

she wrote,

> When the song is sung the wren is no longer connected with its music, just as what we contribute to the world is really no longer connected to us. Our names seem to be convenient tools for naming the parts of the whole, a way of cataloging the gifts of the One Light which become a part of the Whole. Roseliep himself is an aspect of the Light. It is clear by reading this collection that he knew exactly what the Universe was doing through him as the poetry moved apart from his pen."[155]

---

154. David Andrews, "Listen to Light." *Brussels Sprout* (1981) no issue number or pages listed.
155. Alexis Rotella, review of *Listen to Light*, *East-West Journal* 13:7 (1983), 77–78.

Reviewing for *Parnassus,* Colette Inez added, "The devilishly good poetry of Raymond Roseliep—or should I say angelically good poetry?—is a natural resource of Iowa. The resident chaplain of Holy Family Hall has by now gathered a clique of admirers for whom *Listen to Light* is yet another credential for an American Haiku master."[156]

Library Journal's reviewer, Rosaly DeMaios Roffman, expressed her view that "Haiku in English can easily slide into being artificial, but at its best—as in this collection—the form becomes a vessel for that quintessential showing-not-telling at which the Japanese excel." Roffman recommended the book as "Essential for collections wanting to represent the haiku form."[157] *Choice,* also important to book-buying institutions, was not quite as generous. Their unidentified reviewer spent most of the space allowed criticizing former Roseliep publications and dismissing many haiku in *Listen to Light:* "Once the nonhaiku have been deducted, what remain—roughly a third of the total—are vivid evocations of specific experience.... 'i.v. dripping, / the chirping sparrow's [sic; Roseliep wrote "chipping sparrow"] / one pitch.' On balance, *Listen to Light* is a handsomely printed volume that deserves to be studied carefully by those interested in English-language haiku."[158]

R. G. Rader, editor of the new journal *Muse Pie,* opined, "Coming so soon after the publication of Roseliep's Retrospective ... it is no longer difficult to believe that lightning does strike twice in the same place. In *Listen to Light,* we indeed listen to light."[159] Hortense Roberta Roberts in *Delta Epsilon Sigma Bulletin* 26:2 (1981) pointed out that

> Roseliep's poems have become even more sparse of words than much of his earlier work and have somehow gained in strength and vision.... A non-poet friend looked over my shoulder as I was rereading the book and remarked, "So few words on the page!" "Yes," I told her. "But they say more than most full pages of fine print...." He can write a whole story in three brief lines: "in the widow's veil / stars / blown from dandelion.'"[160]

In *High/Coo* Sanford Goldstein sounded a minor negative note: "But since I feel a haiku is basically an epiphany moment and since 'real'

156. Colette Inez, review of *Listen to Light, Parnassus* (fall/winter 1981), 244–46.

157. Rosaly DeMaios Roffman, review of *Listen to Light, Library Journal,* May 15, 1981, 1082.

158. *Choice* (July–August 1981), 180.

159. R. G. Rader, review of *Listen to Light, Muse-Pie* 1:1 (1981), n.p.l.

160. Hortense Roberta Roberts, review of *Listen to Light, Delta Epsilon Sigma Bulletin* 26:2 (1981), 58–60.

epiphany moments are rare, it is difficult for any haiku collection to sustain itself.... On the other hand, it has always seemed to me that Roseliep is at his best in the area of senryu." Goldstein found other aspects of poems that didn't fit into his notion of haiku, among them intellectualization, which "sometimes mars for me many of his haiku, though if he called them three-liners, this objection might not be raised."[161]

What almost all the reviews of *Listen to Light*— even those that were entirely positive— missed, was Roseliep's careful seasonal structuring and why he had taken the time to do it. The priest-poet wanted his readers to embark with him on a yearlong external and internal journey through listening. The title "Listen to Light" is an immediate call to readers' sense of hearing, paying close attention to what can be experienced through that sense. This is a kind of synesthesia, the concept of "perceiving simultaneously with more than one sense." What a curiosity: the "sound of red" or the "weight of silence." And here now is the poet Roseliep inviting us to "listen to light."

Swish of Cow Tail[162]

Roseliep's books came in all shapes and sizes; they came in raucous red (*The Linen Bands* and *A Roseliep Retrospective*) and in cool, flame-lit blue (*Listen to Light*); and they come softly (*Love Makes the Air Light*). They even come accordion-pleated like this one, *Swish of Cow Tail,* which, if you're not careful at first opening, will spill out into your lap announcing itself by name: Swish! Ed Rayher and Swamp Press gave us a noisy little book with many reverberations. It began to talk to you even before you opened the cover. Roughly textured paper spoke to your fingertips, readying you for the movement of the rooster-tail-rooster on the title pages. Or was it a cow tail? Search your flower books to find such a creature, for here is the first of many question/surprises that lure you outward from this wee volume. Just what sort of cow swishes the peach petals?

The Roseliep–Rayher correspondence is as interesting as any you will find between poet and publisher. Rayher wrote his undated letters on 5"×6" Swamp Press notepaper, all undated. Roseliep penciled in the dates upon receipt. On June 4, 1981, Rayher wrote, "I was sitting down to plan your book when I discovered that I had misplaced your poems"

---

161. Sanford Goldstein, review of *Listen to Light, High/Coo* 5:20 (1981), n.p.l.

162. Raymond Roseliep, *Swish of Cow Tail* (Amherst, Mass.: Swamp Press, 1982).

and asked for a replacement copy. He said he was planning on producing the book in three to six weeks. Roseliep assured Rayher, "You didn't lose my manuscript; you sent it to me in April, asking that I type up the poems you had picked and send them to you in June. So here they be." A few days later Rayher answered, "Yes, we send out review copies.... I must admit that I don't read the haiku mags much — so if you want to make me a list of good places — that would be great." By June 20, Roseliep had sent three single-spaced pages of addresses. The drawings by Jon Vlakos[163] occupied much of the subsequent correspondence. Rayher wrote, "I like them all — but feel I should have your reaction. I think the 2nd to last illustration is a bit off — perhaps too much humanized and so out of tune with the book." Roseliep was quite negative about the illustration for the title page. Vlakos was asked to redo it, and Roseliep was satisfied with the result and the rest of the illustrations.

On February 2, 1982, when *Swish of Cow Tail* had been printed, Rayher wrote: "Glad you liked it, I do, and people are raving about it. It will sell out quickly." Roseliep was exuberant too, and the next day he replied, "What a way to begin Monday; the arrival of your box of cow tails. I am absolutely DELIGHTED with your work. Each one is a work: of art. I do want you to know how much I appreciate the love's labour that you have put into my wee book. The accordion was a merry surprise. I am pleased with everything — the colors, the papers, the typefaces, the arrangement, the bindings." Correspondence between Roseliep and Rayher tapered off after the publication of *Swish of Cow Tail.*

The seven haiku that comprise *Swish of Cow Tail* might seem to be simple nature moments caught in essence, in centrality: tulip tree and peach petals. Some are senryu, nature-centered in the "I" of the poet such as in the "pear blossom thief" below. But all are Roseliep-stamped with a dynamism that moves the reader from one kind of nature (out there) to another kind (in here).

The illustrations by Vlakos are mirror images of the haiku. You can open *Swish of Cow Tail* in many ways. You can take the pages one at a time; Dedication (with haiku), rooster haiku, rooster illustration. Or you can spread out four pages: a rooster to your far left (on the last of the title pages) and a rooster to your far right, two haiku in between. You can catch another

---

163. Ed Rayher to Roseliep, September 14, 1981. Vlakos illustrated many books for Swamp Press and Rayher called him "our illustrator."

four-page spread with a pear blossom thief haiku to your left, prostrate and mirrored thieves doubled and centered, and a tulip-tree oboe's sound to your right. The vivid colors and the rich textures of these illustrations keep bouncing you around from word to picture to word and back again.

A steamy male sensuality pervades *Swish of Cow Tail.* With the pages spread fully out to their four-foot length, the haiku are bounded by a strutting rooster at the opening and a reclining bearded naked ecstasy-exhausted male at the closing. Such thrown-to-the-wind caution is contrasted in what is perhaps the central haiku,

> I catch
> the pear blossom thief ...
> wish I hadn't

Echoes of Augustine, his lusty adolescence, and his son, the Adeodatus he never rejected—these are the reverberations of the haiku man and his wistful recollection.

Seasons move in *Swish of Cow Tail,* but the microcosm is all spring. Beginnings and endings catapult into the reader's presence with the agility of Issa's flea, from the rising of the early tulip to the falling of the peach petal, a nature-death required for fruition. Every time you shove these pages back in place, you will want them to spill out again. This is Roseliep's paradigm of life. He gives us once more the whole of experience, his and the world's—in the twinkling of an eye—in *Swish of Cow Tail.*

Father Ray filed only four reviews of this mini-chapbook. One, in *Modern Haiku* was by William J. Higginson:

> For lovers of haiku the antics of Raymond Roseliep present something of a puzzle. How is one to respond to such a poem as
>
> > flea ..
> > that you,
> > Issa?
>
> This flea is the dedicatory poem.... Are they "haiku?" I'm not sure Roseliep cares. He writes very short poems—prolifically. In this particular group of seven there are one or two that don't make it, for me. And there is one that ends in trite superficiality:
>
> > in white tulips
> > the rooster's red head
> > flowering ...

But there are also three of these, in addition to the Issa-flea, that I think are perfect haiku in their exactness, their total 'no comment' approach to the always miraculous, always appalling events of everyday life. I'll leave the others for you to find; here's my personal favorite:

> the banker
> cancels
> a moth

Ounce for ounce, this is the best collection of Roseliep's haiku I have seen.[164]

Editor Hal Roth in *Wind Chimes* 4 (1982), 62–68, called *Swish of Cow Tail* "the latest jewel in the collection from Swamp Press...." "the delicate illustrations of Jon Vlakos combine with the poetic talents of Father Roseliep to make this treasure a festival of sight and touch and a joy to the soul."[165]

In her review essay for *Haiku Review '84*, Elizabeth Searle Lamb wrote, "Both the hard bound and paper editions of this mini (roughly 2 ¾ inches wide by 3 inches high) chapbook are gems!" She quoted part of Higginson's review and ended with the title haiku

> swish of cow tail
> peach petals
> fall[166]

The unnamed reviewer in the inaugural issue of *Inkstone* (autumn 1982) opened with, "Visually this is a marvelous little paperback," but continued with reference to

> the banker
> cancels
> a moth

"the [banker] poem, like the rest in the book, is far below the quality that we have come to expect from Roseliep and I feel that anyone buying the book with the expectation of finding his best work; rather than for the beauty of the book itself, or to complete their collection of his works, will be disappointed."[167]

---

164. William J. Higginson, review of *Swish of Cow Tail*, *Modern Haiku* 13:2 (Summer 1982), 31–32.
165. *Wind Chimes* 4 (1982), 62–68.
166. Randy Brooks, ed., *Haiku Review '84* (Battle Ground, Ind.: High/Coo Press), 1984.
167. Review of *Swish of Cow Tail*, *Inkstone* 1:1 (summer 1982).

Rabbit in the Moon[168]

Throughout 1983, Raymond Roseliep eagerly awaited the publication of his new book, *Rabbit in the Moon,* to be published by his friend David Dayton at Alembic Press in Ithaca, N.Y. The priest-poet had just begun inscribing notes in hardback copies to friends and reviewers when, on December 6, death came for him.

As always, much of the original concept, the selection of haiku, the structuring of the manuscript and all the other planning, the excitement and, finally, the reality were shared through Roseliep's exchange of letters with Elizabeth Searle Lamb. For example, Roseliep had requested that Jon Vlakos, whose work on *Swish of Cow Tail* he had admired, do the illustrations for this new book as well. Dayton absolutely refused to use Vlakos's work, however, which caused much anguish for both poet and illustrator. In a letter to Lamb on January 16, 1983, the priest foresaw the problem, "I am dying to see what Vlakos does for the drawings; am a bit terrorized, in fact, though he promised me not to get too sexy. (There's enough of that in the haiku. In a good way, I always intend.) One of life's most sacred workings."

Alembic Press gave its usual care and attention to the promotion of Father Ray's text. Dayton sent out full-page ads on quality stock accompanied by textual comments and a reproduction of the cover, letters with a detailed description of the content, and an order form to subscribers of the journal *Alembic* and customers of the press. Numerous book lists, including the Academy of American Poets *Semi-Annual Checklist of Poetry* for spring 1983 and *Small Press*[169] ran notices for *Rabbit in the Moon.*

Readers of *Rabbit in the Moon* may just as well get used to such dizzying movements as a leap of a rabbit or buddhas in the broccoli for they abound in the collection:

> rabbit in the moon
> in our broccoli
> small buddha voices

This puzzling haiku, explicable only partially by Roseliep's reference to a Buddha tale, marks the end of the spring section. In ten words the poet takes part of Earth out of itself and propels it to the heavens. He brings

---

168. Raymond Roseliep, *Rabbit in the Moon* (Plainfield, Ind.: Alembic Press, 1983).

169. *Small Press* 1 (May/June 1984).

the voices of an Eastern god into a Western kitchen-garden temple and casts a magical light over all these leapings.

Roseliep wrote many volumes of poetry, but never did he ask readers for so much energetic movement as he has here. Reading *Rabbit in the Moon* requires a mental and spiritual agility akin to the animal in his title haiku.

The largest motion in the book is the cosmic seasonal one. Once more the poet cycles a year, giving these haiku markers:

> hole in my sock
> letting spring
> in

> rose
> body language
> of the bee

> autumn frog
> what it is
> the smile hides

> snow:
> all's
> new

However, the poet gives us more than the seasons. He walks around his own life, gathering markers of physical and spiritual growth. Some of the boy haiku in the spring section are easy to understand:

> my father's back
> loaded with me
> and other frogs

Others are more elusive. In "Out of the Cradle Endlessly Rocking," after his boy-encounter with a mourning bird, Walt Whitman declared "My own songs awaked from that hour." The reader might wonder if Roseliep was telling that he, too, heard his poetic call in the boy-spring of his life:

looking for the bird
who called
my name

It would be easy to say that all the youth haiku are in the spring section of *Rabbit in the Moon,* and that Roseliep has simply matched personal growth seasons to the moving on of the year. A careful reading, however, reveals that the motions are much more complex, especially in light of Roseliep's previous poetry. A critical analysis of the poem "Some Men a Forward Motion Love" in 1980[170] gave some insight into his youthful questioning:

"Still haven't finished childhood" was the clause
that closed his letter; then he added, "In
more ways than one." By childhood he had meant
those Joycean trips through alleys of the mind
I beg to leave unlanterned. He explains,
it takes a child to catch a child: and swears
by it. I do not tell him I am more
the usual coward who transfers a fear.
This lighting back perturbs me like the search
through darkness for a blacker cat not there.
Let midnight wicks inform a virgin's fool-
ish wait, or scholar's watch. My friend is I,
and I'm afraid of I, and want no backward steps. Childhood is over, and we shove
ourselves to manhood, linking arm with those
who feign a forward motion, or we move
from shadow into shadow, not from love.[171]

This early poem still seems central to the entire motion of Roseliep's life as he shoved himself "to manhood." In many ways this poet remained the boy-man, ever capturing the wonder of first discoveries, ever growing up through remembrances as though life all happens now, not then.

---

170. Donna Bauerly, "Raymond Roseliep: 'Where Are You Going? Where Have You Been?'" in Dayton, ed., *A Roseliep Retrospective,* 29–44.

171. Roseliep, "Some Men a Forward Motion Love," *The Linen Bands,* 38. *See* page 55 for additional comment on this poem.

For example, when we read about his "first burr haircut" in the spring section of *Rabbit in the Moon,* it is easy to see Roseliep the child. But when we enter the winter section and read

> so small a child
> pushing clouds
> from the moon

we might be inclined to think other child than Roseliep. Roseliep often mingled the personal child of self with a generic child in many of his texts. With a stab of poignancy and self-recognition we realize the child in the man holds back the specter of death, and that death itself might well be the

> stranger in town
> the otherness
> of the moon

Roseliep called the complexity of motion in *Rabbit in the Moon* his "loopings." (Akin to leaping of the rabbit, we take it, for it is easy to identify this creature as an alter ego much like Sobi-Shi.) Throughout the volume, on multilevel journeys, his "loopings" are complex motions that spiral us from the bird of spring to the spring-bird of death:

> bird bone dust
> earth receiving
> itself

Or from the summer love bee with its usual buzzing "body language" to the stillness:

> the bee stops singing.
> we find
> who we are[172]

The life-death loopings in the autumn and winter sections of *Rabbit in the Moon* are even more frighteningly beautiful. Autumn's finale begins with a tribute to Pope Paul VI and ends with

---

172. The first-published version of this haiku appeared on *Modern Haiku* 14:2 (Summer 1983) with different line breaks: "the bee / stops singing. / we find who we are."

from my hand ...
winghold
on the void

In *The Still Point,* Roseliep celebrated the awesome suspension between life and death with haiku of *mu,* moving us to no handhold, no foothold. One of Roseliep's dedications to Nobuo Hirasawa drives home the precarious reality:

every thing
is
no thing

Haiku of *mu* are also everywhere in *Rabbit in the Moon,* but most noticeably in the winter section, inviting disappearance:

chimes
no
wind

fog
stairs find
sky

But the main motion of this poet, conscious as he was of death and life-in-death, is that of love. The most dazzling of the haiku sequences in the book deals with love. Out of the background of an almost over-whelming sequence of mother-love, Roseliep takes us to another kind of loving. On an earlier occasion we inquired about the identity of Roseliep's passionate "significant other." [173] Asking again would prob-ably yield nothing additional, since asking the question will always be part of the mystery of this sensuous priest-poet lover. Once the reader admits the intensity of the love expression in this sequence, all other haiku in *Rabbit in the Moon* remain bathed in a romantic, elusive and reflective moonlight; for example, consider the complexity of love ex-pressed in these haiku:

---

173. Bauerly, "Raymond Roseliep: 'Where Are You Going? Where Have You Been?'" 35.

your hair
bee gold
on the move

wildwood
where your hand
clings more

before love:
the meadowlark's
alarm note[174]

    mist
  on my mouth
air you touched

The "you" dominates in direct address and makes us wonder, as always, just who is that elusive "you": muse, lover, an idealized presence? The absence of the "you" in the "alarm note" of the meadowlark would seem to indicate the you is quite personal.

Even Roseliep's Henderson Award–winning haiku[175]

      horizon
  wild swan drifting through
    the woman's body

becomes more personalized when it is placed across the page spread from

leave the dream
in the sand
where we slept

Finally, readers might want to remain the objective critic, but as we turn to the Sobi-Shi poems it becomes clear that it is not possible. How easy to read them as farewells from our brother and friend. Consider these:

---

174. In the first-published version of this haiku, in *Modern Haiku* 14:1 (Winter–Spring 1983), line 1 read "before we love:".

175. First Place, Haiku Society of America Harold G. Henderson Award for Best Unpublished Haiku, 1982.

the firefly
acting like he knows
Sobi-Shi's swan song

never alone
Sobi-Shi and the big dog
in the southern sky

good eye closed,
Sobi-Shi views
the last leaves

gone through a moon
    Sobi-Shi still
        on "Hold"

Some of us wanted to cry "Hold" when our friend held precariously to life and breath and heartbeat. He would not have it so. Instead, Father Ray left us, perhaps leaving much more to us. In any time of year, but especially the Christmas season of the Word Incarnate, we have his words for life.

Thoreau watched a winter rabbit at Walden Pond, fearing that it had succumbed to the cold. Concerned about his own survival, Thoreau's heart leaped for joy when the rabbit scampered away over the frozen ground. So, too, Roseliep's Rabbit leaps with life.

Would we look for him? Whitman told us at the end of "Song of Myself,"

I bequeath myself to the dirt to grow from the grass I love,
If you want me again look for me under your boot soles.

Rabbit in the Moon ends/begins with a bravery of assertion about Roseliep's own dis-appearance:

what is
in light
is light:

I am
all around
me

We know now where to look.[176]

Of course, Father Ray shared his anticipation over the publication of *Rabbit in the Moon* with his friend Elizabeth Searle Lamb. On November 21, in his last comments to her, he wrote, "[LeRoy] Gorman is reviewing the RABBIT for Hal [Roth of *Wind Chimes*]. Donna [Bauerly] for [*Delta Epsilon Sigma Journal*], as I think I told you; she's not wild about the illustrations—my first dissenter. The Reillys[177] haven't commented on them, so I suspect they aren't thrilled—but I asked them to comment, and promised I would not be hurt in the least."[178] Roseliep later wrote to Elizabeth, "Your words on RABBIT make me so happy. It's always fun to know which haiku this friend and that will single out—and the takes certainly vary. The ones you cited were all favorites of Dayton, by the way." In her last letter to Roseliep, on December 4, Lamb replied, "Good news about *Rabbit* on the move."

Rabbit in the Moon was released in October 1983 and so was not widely reviewed before his death. However, Roseliep indicated, in a letter to Dayton on November 8, that he was well aware of a number of forthcoming reviews. He quoted words from a letter from Bob Spiess: "reviewed it myself, in fact—wanted to be sure it got its just desserts of appreciation. Just to pique your curiosity I'll mention that in the review I made analogies between you and the ancient Sanskrit grammarians and to the words of a Shaker hymn." Spiess actually wrote:

> The highly disciplined concision of Raymond Roseliep's haiku is well known to readers of contemporary American haiku. Some haiku poets have attempted to write in his "style," none has consistently achieved the inner depth and aesthetic qualities that Roseliep maintains by his insightful selection and use of words in his haiku. Each word is as it ought to be, none is superfluous, none other is necessary.... But it should go without saying that concision per se is not the primary objective in a Roseliep haiku. In some haiku the simplicity of expression capsules the moment

---

176. Donna Bauerly, *"Rabbit in the Moon," Delta Epsilon Sigma Journal* 29:1 (1984): 4–7. Reprinted in *Wind Chimes* 12 (1984): 10–15.

177. Cyril A. and Renée Travis Reilly, the photographers who collaborated with Roseliep on *The Earth We Swing On.*

178. This emotion would most probably have been impossible for Roseliep.

of a simple event-experience; in others the same virtue of succinct-
ness and directness creates, almost paradoxically, multivalent "felt-
meanings" in us. Or it might be said that the haiku lifts cover after
cover from our psyche.[179]

Spiess included a generous sampling of haiku with brief comments about
how they affected him.

> intensive care:
> high wire walking
> souls

> steeplejacks:
> souls too small
> to have names

"As a concluding word, it may be remarked that although these haiku reveal
that Raymond Roseliep is erudite and highly literate, they first and foremost
show that he has, in the words of the Shaker hymn, 'the gift to be simple.'"[180]
    Roseliep also mentioned reviews forthcoming from Rod Willmot
in *Frogpond* and letters from William Stafford and Geraldine C. Little.
In his last letter to Dayton on December 1, Roseliep also mentioned
another forthcoming review by LeRoy Gorman for *Wind Chimes* that
eventually appeared in the Roseliep memorial issue. Gorman wrote,

> To cite or discuss at length haiku in this collection might prove re-
> dundant in light of the body of criticism available on the poet, for
> *Rabbit in the Moon* is predictably Roseliep. He remains true to his
> mandate to present intensely perceptive moments of love through
> which the reader may enter and, by perceiving, love the poet in
> return. And the poet we learn to love? Simply, he is a devotional
> seer constantly nurturing the spirit thorough birth, growth, and
> re-births—all within the human and natural world.

Gorman highlighted certain typical "experiments" of Roseliep's, including minimalist haiku such as

> sleet
> hones
> farewell

---

179. Robert Spiess, "Rabbit in the Moon: Haiku by Raymond Roseliep," *Modern Haiku* 15:1
(Winter–Spring 1984), 35–37.
    180. Spiess, 37.

Gorman also remarked Roseliep's puns, triptychs (though Gorman disagreed with the inclusion of longer than three-haiku poems under the rubric of "triptych"), senryu (again, Gorman granted the distinction but probably would have disagreed with Roseliep about how to characterize any difference between haiku and senryu), haiku dedicated to friends, and aphoristic haiku, such as

> snow
> all's
> new

Gorman wrote that such very brief haiku often cannot stand alone and "seem trite." Gorman ended his review on a positive note, however, "In summary *Rabbit in the Moon* may be deemed the work of a master who willingly takes risks in experimenting and admits that he may even stoop to senryu. In spite of such 'weakness,' the reader cannot help but feel compelled to let Roseliep take him along on a journey ever closer to the light."[181]

For *Haiku Review '84,* Elizabeth Lamb contributed a substantial review, commenting,

> *Rabbit in the Moon* from Alembic Press came out only weeks before the poet's death.... It is a substantial work, containing 188 single haiku and 12 longer poems composed of what Roseliep spoke of as "haiku-stanzas" divided into four seasonal sections.... The poems here are honed to the essence and sometimes not readily accessible to the reader. The collection as a whole, however, is a testament to a mature haiku poet who has developed an individual style through which both his spiritually and his great human-ness shine.[182]

The last Roseliep haiku she quoted was

> you enter
> your shadow
> reborn

A 700-word review by Geraldine C. Little, then president of the Haiku Society of America, is included in Roseliep's files, though there is no mention of publication. Little wrote,

---

181. LeRoy Gorman, *Wind Chimes* 12 (1984), 8–10.
182. Elizabeth Searle Lamb, "A Rich Harvest: Haiku Books of 1982–1993," *Haiku Review '84,* 2–18.

For those who have not followed the haiku movement in the United States and Canada, it should be noted that Western haiku poets began writing strictly in the traditional 5–7–5 form. But syllable sounds in Japanese do not have the same time value as do English syllables. The 5–7–5- form, in English, began to sound wordy and padded. Poets working in the genre gradually have pared away, and away, to essence, so that some of the best English-language haiku are being written in about ten syllables, or less. Father Roseliep is one of the best parers in the poetry world. Consider this gem:

> snow:
> all's
> new

Three syllables capture a season and a world made over by a snow-fall. Inherent in the poem is humankind also made new by the same cleansing snow. There are echoes of the delight a child finds on a morning of snow which hadn't been there when he went to bed. The brevity itself reminds one of a single snowflake, light, exquisite, and singular.... Delight in:

> hole in my sock
> letting spring
> in

The dailiness of it, the homelinesss of it, the "trueness" of it! Don't we all have figurative holes in socks of our lives? What a sigh of relief we breathe when a puff of fresh air makes the hole seem not such a lonely place, typified by spring, the season of renewal.

Little ended her review by taking in the wider world of haiku: "This is a first class book in a genre rapidly gaining eminent stature in the West."[183]

The Earth We Swing On[184]

Roseliep's *The Earth We Swing On: Haiku* was published in 1984, the year after the poet's death. Critiquing this volume requires a different approach, because it was a true collaboration with photographer Cyril Reilly and his wife, artist and photographer Renée Travis Reilly; and, of course, Father Ray could not exercise his usual control over the final production. *The Earth We Swing On* was intended to be a gift book: the first page provides spaces for the purchaser to enter information "From," "To," and "On the occasion of."

---

183. LCARC 325, D:1:12.8. Roseliep often sent out copies of intended books, asking particularly astute critics to write reviews. Geraldine Little sent a typed copy of her intended review.

184. Cyril A. Reilly and Renée Travis Reilly, *The Earth We Swing On* (Minneapolis: Winston Press, 1984).

As evident from the correspondence between the principals,[185] the process was often circuitous and fraught with bumps. Each of the three was an artist, and each had a particular vision of this "earth we swing on." These long-time friends began to discuss the concept of the book as early as 1979, sometimes meeting in person at Holy Family Hall, but usually communicating through the mail. The cycle of seasons, a common motif for Roseliep, seemed always present in their conversations after Roseliep first proposed using four separate books in seasonal sequences. Winston Press, already reluctant to take a chance on a poetry book, quickly put a damper on that idea.

The collaborative process accelerated in late 1981. Roseliep sent the Reillys many haiku, seasonally arranged, which the photographers rearranged as they sought to match poems with photos from their portfolio or else sent pictures for the poet to ponder and perhaps create a new haiku. Sometimes Cyril Reilly even set out to look for a new scene to give a photographer's view of the poet's vision. For one group Renée Reilly typed in the margin, "Cy feels strongly about this arrangement—I guess I love the bum with 'broken things' myself."[186] Renée is referring to a four-page layout: a beggar walking near an old wall is pictured opposite a feral dog. Haiku from these two pages read:

> still life
> hound
> of ghost town

> no one
> owns
> the air

On the following two pages a lone haiku fills the page

> in light
> broken things
> break

opposite a photo of an old window with panes of glass missing.[187]

Roseliep and the Reillys often exchanged views about such details as the number of photos of children that should be included in each

---

185. Cyril A. Reilly file, LCARC 325, A:2.

186. Cyril A. Reilly file, LCARC 325, A:2.

187. Roseliep, *The Earth We Swing On*, 48–51.

section, color schemes for the various spreads, and how photos and haiku on facing pages would work with one another. For years the process had this back-and-forth motion.

Spring was represented in thirteen haiku, summer thirteen, autumn seventeen, and winter eight. It was autumn and a deepening atmosphere of loss and sadness that dominated *The Earth We Swing On,* and an autumnal hush seems to hang over every section. Spring is muted by such words as "doldrums," "wrong number," "silence," "shedding the clown," "alone," and "shadow" as well as a photo of a kite with a skull and crossbones tangled in a willow. A burgeoning fullness is in the summer section, but words and phrases sound a somber note: "cicadas sizzling," "the child is gone," "sleep comes slowly," "bubble ... don't break," "you catch my breath," and "closing the blind." Autumn deepens the sense of impending loss: "emptying space," "light flies," "swamp," "old man's heart," "both breaths flying," "still life," "ghost town," "broken things," "wild geese," "earth swings off its axis," and "rooted ... leaf and leaf falling." The winter series suggests even deeper loss: "frosty owl," "blue breath," "nightmare," and "cracked bowl."

The haiku echo of some of Roseliep's earliest and most powerful poetry. This winter haiku,

> the storyteller
> leads us children through woods
> making Wolf come true

resonates with "Vendor" from *The Small Rain*[188] in which the setting is frightening for the persona, a man on a train who sees what he perceives as a threatening man selling "gimmicks." This dark man and the children on that train come back to haunt him in a nightmare in which they follow a Pied Piper: "in single file / those children passed, the vendor leading them up the aisle."

Many haiku in *The Earth We Swing On* are reminiscent of Roseliep's Sobi-Shi haiku.[189] This winter offering brings us abruptly to his ambiguous other:

> in snow the whisper
> of my lover's footstep ...
> or a bird's

---

188. *See* pages 61–62 for the full text and a discussion of "Vendor."
189. *See* Chapter Seven.

Somber and muted photos add to the restrained tone of the book. The faces of the children in the book are sad or at least pensive, and one can only wonder whether this was the deliberate intention of the coauthors.

Correspondence and the exchange of comments on the choices of haiku and photographs between the Reillys and Roseliep continued until his death. A typical comment from Renée about this haiku,

> unlocking dawn
> and dream:
> what a key a bird is

read, "Light from sacrarium (we feel two slides of light patterns too many and maybe the "bird" too literal)." Roseliep penciled, "Agree." However, this haiku finally appeared in the published text as quoted above with the light pattern. The poet's

> in dawn
> your body
> transparent

appeared on the page opposite an image of light through sheer curtains.

Roseliep usually prevailed with his own must-haves, but in response to Renée's question about

> lovers
> emptying
> space

"should we put in autumn? Color doesn't work too well here," Roseliep penciled in "yes." About the same composition, Cy wrote, "We worked most of the afternoon on this little book of ours.... So we moved the lovers silhouetted on bench down to fall ... which had no lovers. Moreover, the orange color of the water makes this pic look fallish, and it fits in with the two preceding fall ones in color." That haiku, which Roseliep had previously marked "omit" in a marginal comment, appeared alone on a spread with a page-and-a-half full-color photo.

One can get lost in these details by reading around and into the making of such a composite book. You might, if you are a purist for haiku or photography, begin to wish that each of these artistic media came solo instead of paired. Just what happens inside our brains when they are presented with a haiku together with a photograph?

The title haiku and accompanying photograph mark the start of the summer section. If taken in very slowly they open a world of complex sense:

> sun beat
> on drum and the earth
> we swing on

Some might not approve of Roseliep's pun. Most of the left-hand page is empty of anything but the haiku; across the gutter is a photo of a boy in a Scottish outfit with a drum that reads "Decorah Kilties." The image of the boy in his woolen tam and the powerful deep sound of the drum; the tactile feel of the beating sun on your skin; the taste of one's own perspiration; the smell of humidity and the kinesthetic motion of the spinning earth in rotation; the riotous color red and various shades of blue; the smell of the woolen kilt; the taste and sounds of candy thrown from various floats; the child and all he connotes; Decorah, Iowa, and storefronts reflected; your memories, perhaps, of that particular small town and all parades ever seen. Synesthesia gone wild. Juxtaposition that puts us constantly in motion from reality to memory, to haiku, to photo and, eventually, to a whole that keeps refiguring as "we swing on."

Robert Spiess, in a *Modern Haiku* review in 1985, chose his own favorite haiku, one from each season.[190] For spring he chose

> the child called
> a wrong number:
> we talked all spring

and calls attention to the "slightly enigmatic" smile on the boy's face. For summer he chose

> the farmer talks corn,
> pointing where the corn
> is talking

remarking the "simple photograph of the silhouette of corn stalks against a deep yellow and orange sky." Spiess's autumn choice was

---

190. *Modern Haiku* 16:1 (Winter–Spring 1985), 67–68.

milkweed
light flies
spun

He seemed particularly taken by the photograph that "covers most of two pages. A couple of milkweed pods are silhouetted against a lavender-blue sky. They are releasing their seeds with their silvery white filaments that make a slightly cirrus cloud effect." And for winter,

cracked bowl
that washed
her face

"An oval porcelain or enameled basin, mostly in shadow, is on the wide window ledge inside an adobe house. Its rim picks up the light coming through a window that is covered with a slightly frayed, patterned lace curtain." Spiess did not mention that the action is curiously reversed in Roseliep's haiku, giving motion to the bowl instead of the woman.

Spiess concludes,

> As Raymond Roseliep selected these haiku with the knowledge that they would be accompanied by appropriate photographs, the haiku are more "concrete" than some of his other haiku.... Persons who have all, or most, of Raymond Roseliep's books of haiku will want to add this one to their collection — and persons who appreciate excellent photography and/or fine haiku will find *The Earth We Swing On* an admirable book to have.

Our other favorite choices might include from the Spring section

after our silence
dawn sound
is different

This haiku is coupled with a highly shadowed photo of a man sitting against a tree with his head bowed low; on the other side of the tree is a young woman sitting on a grazing horse, her own head slightly bowed. This couple, while together, seems deeply apart. Silence between them heightens the sound of early morning. The pairing of haiku and photo is exquisite; each art form is perfect. Oddly enough, Roseliep in his first draft marked this haiku "Omit."

An ambiguous summer haiku reads:

> odor of earth
> you catch
> my breath

At first it could be read that for the one experiencing, "you" means that the earth is the odor that catches his breath. Most of us know the loamy smell of rich blue-black earth, newly plowed. In her notes, however, Renée Reilly typed "love the haiku." Roseliep, nodding his head to his alter ego Sobi-Shi, penciled in, "We need a second pair of lovers." The photo that eventually filled the opposite page is just that, a pair of lovers seated on the ground, the man playing what seems to be a Native American flute, the young woman near him. At first glance, she might be thought to be gazing deeply into his eyes and be picking the strings of her violin while the bow remains by her side. All is muted by soft sunset light.

An astute viewer would find nuances: the gaze of these lovers is not actually engaged — they are looking off at something unseen, perhaps rapt in the sound of music. The man wears face paint, reinforcing the idea of a Native American flutist. Both lovers are costumed, with ribbons or beads. A shiny container, a bowl perhaps, is beside the flute player. Deep light prevails, lengthening the shadows of the trees in the background. These lovers, though deeply engaged, are also independent listeners who catch the "odor of the earth."

A poignant autumn haiku is accompanied by a single white egret along the river shore:

> learn the river
> my brother said ...
>   egret, call him[191]

Roseliep had marked this haiku and another about a brother to be omitted. Loss is implied in both haiku, and much of Roseliep's life can be read into these few words. The river of life overwhelmed Roseliep more than once. If only an egret could call for someone lost — brother or caller.[192]

---

191. This haiku originally appeared in *Modern Haiku* 12:2 (Summer 1981), but instead of "egret" the bird was a heron. Perhaps Roseliep changed the bird to fit the photo.

192. The most likely candidate to be this brother was Roseliep's half-brother Will, yet he was apparently not aware of this relative all his life — *see* Chapter One.

For the winter haiku that closes *The Earth We Swing On*, one might wish that the Reillys had caught a glimpse of that elusive lover, Sobi-Shi. What they gave us is a window with opened heavy drapes and sheers letting in a blue light, a single empty chair, and four lit candles:

> enough window
> to light
> where you were

Roseliep and the Reillys all loved light. They loved illuminating. Roseliep earlier asked us to *Listen to Light*; Renée and Cyril Reilly, through their cameras and visual artistry, brought light from all seasons and places to tell us where we are. *The Earth We Swing On* can be a pendulum for all of us, a timeless collaboration of constant insight and meaning.

The reader will have to decide, however, whether a collaboration of haiku and photos, particularly when the images are simply illustrations of the haiku, does a disservice to one or the other art. The bombardment of closely related images might seem irrelevant to the essence of haiku or overwhelm the subtlety not giving any further insights to deeper meanings. For example, when the haiku

> sun beat
> on drum and the earth
> we swing on

is illustrated by a photo of a boy beating a drum against the background of a clear blue sky, our thoughts might simply remain with the photo, learning nothing deeper about "the earth we swing on." Whatever you choose or decide about the cohesion of *The Earth We Swing On*, surely most readers will agree with Spiess, who endorsed "an admirable book to have."

A Roseliep Retrospective

How does one cease critical comments and insights for the life work of any author? In Roseliep's case, one might wish to revisit a book that was published three years before his death: *A Roseliep Retrospective*.[193] This compendium of materials by and about Roseliep was preceded by a beautiful poster-sized broadside advertisement for two books, *A Roseliep*

---

193. David Dayton, ed., *A Roseliep Retrospective: Poems & Other Words By & About Raymond Roseliep* (Ithaca, N.Y.: Alembic Press), 1980.

Retrospective and *Listen to Light,* both put out by David Dayton of Alembic Press in 1980. This sheet bore the marks of two creative and fussy men, and the stamp of their razor-eyed genius is everywhere: from the laid paper stock, fonts, and type sizes to the text, separated into two columns and adorned by a border of long-stemmed rose buds. This poster contained blurbs from a bevy of notables: Elizabeth Searle Lamb, Richard Eberhart, Eric W. Amann, X. J. Kennedy, William Stafford, A. R. Ammons, and Josephine Jacobsen.

Roseliep's life work was summed up as follows,

> Spanning four decades, Father Raymond Roseliep's career in poetry is a record of fascinating changes; from the verse on strictly religious themes he wrote as a young priest, through a period in which his poems on both secular and religious topics showed mastery of a remarkable variety of forms, to the succinct, lyrical free verse celebrating love and sensual delight and the pithy haiku of Zen 'mu' found in his most recent books.

The major contents of the book were laid out: a hefty anthology of poems (fifty-three pages) selected by the editor; critical reviews of Roseliep's work; his two most important essays, "Devilish Wine" and "This Haiku of Ours"; and prose works, interviews, reviews and dedicatory poems from a wide variety of friends, including Dennis Schmitz, Mark Doty, Thomas Reiter, William Stafford, Colette Inez, Sr. Mary Thomas Eulberg, John Judson (also an editor), Bill Pauly, and Donna Bauerly.

Then followed the panegyrics. Lamb commented, "*A Roseliep Retrospective* will furnish those who have known only the non-haiku poetry with a generous introduction to his haiku, its possibilities and its importance as an element of Western poetry which should not be written off lightly. For the many haiku poets and other readers who know Roseliep only by his haiku … this overview of his whole poetic range of accomplishment will astonish." Eberhart, a fellow poet, wrote, "I have enjoyed Raymond Roseliep's poems for a long time. I advocate reading his *Retrospective* not only for his fresh, sprightly, buoyant, deep, and joyful poems but also for a rich fare of prose commentaries and poems about his work in this life-and-love-giving book."[194]

---

194. Elizabeth Searle Lamb, flyer from Alembic Press and "Light Will Wheel to a Point Sharper than Rain: Commentary on *A Roseliep Retrospective. Delta Epsilon Sigma Bulletin* 25:4 (December 1980) 113–16.

Amann's comment read in full, "During the past five years Raymond Rose-liep has emerged as one of the major haiku poets in America. Single-hand-edly, he has created a style of haiku that is unique in form and content. No other writer has gone so far in using all the resources of Western poetry to make the English-language haiku truly English. Some feel that he has gone too far and that his poems are no longer true haiku. I disagree; what is essential about haiku is always found in Roseliep's work—extreme brevity of expression, subtle evocation of mood, intuitive rather than intellectual apperception of reality, and, above all, an implied unity that links even the most disparate elements of experience."[195]

William Stafford, a well-known poet, had included the following tribute, written in haiku form:

> small things of the world
> arc out far, touch, and brighten:
> we call them Roselieps

and went on, "Raymond Roseliep helps us find and cherish what might otherwise slip away in the rush of our days. Billions of dollars' worth of charm and serenity pour unnoticed over our land every day.... Reading the poems in *Listen to Light* helps us find our way toward deserving that kind of world."[196]

Roseliep made a note in red pencil on his copy of one review of *A Roseliep Retrospective*, "*Choice*, not overly thrilled." Other critics' comments on both books, however, were entirely positive. Diane C. Donovan in *Abraxas*[197] ended her reading, "The intermingling of religious and passionate personal imagery is startling; yet refreshing." Randy Brooks, writing in *High/Coo*,[198] began, "This handsomely produced book belongs in every poetry library. It is a tribute, a sampling, an introduction, a review, and an appreciation of Raymond Roseliep's immense achievement as a poet." From Donna Bauerly's essay in the book, Brooks extracted a quotation: "The progress in Roseliep's poetry has been from using nature as ornament or accompaniment to recognizing nature as essence."[199] Roseliep annotated the margin of his copy, "I second this."

---

195. Flyer from Alembic Press.

196. Flyer from Alembic Press.

197. Diane C. Donovan, Review of *A Roseliep Retrospective*, *Abraxas* 23/24 (1981), 129–31.

198. *High/Coo* 5:18 (1980).

199. Bauerly in "Raymond Roseliep: 'Where Are You Going? Where Have You Been?'" *A Roseliep Retrospective* 29–34.

Lamb remarked, "Raymond Roseliep has brought a wealth of poetic power from the mainstream of the American poetry world over into the haiku field, and this book is of extreme value in its delineation of a widely recognized American poet who has extended his range into the field of Western haiku and become one of its most provocative voices."[200]

Bob Boldman praised Roseliep too,

> Unlike countless literary figures, he becomes less pretentious and more exact, less diffusive and more consistent. He does not become possessed by words, but they are his possession. That in itself could be the definition of haiku.... *A Roseliep Retrospective* is not the place for beginners, but it is the place for anyone willing to learn more of the crafting of poems and of haiku in particular, more of the spiritual journey that is not an ascent, but a stripping to the bones."[201]

In *Muse-Pie*, R. W. Grandinetti Rader wrote,

> For those of us who know Raymond Roseliep through his haiku, to read *A Roseliep Retrospective* is like becoming aware of a new facet of a friend's personality.... Despite the beauty and style of many of his longer poems, Roseliep is at his best when he is striving for the 'wordless poem.' His capacity to exaggerate the eternal quality of an object or occurrence in, many times, less than seven words is a quality of finely tuned perception. [202]

And finally, Spiess in *Modern Haiku* said, "This volume is of value for those of us who not only would like to read some of Raymond Roseliep's non-haiku poetry, but also for the many aspects of analysis of his haiku and for insights into his own views of haiku that haiku poets may want to consider in their own writing."[203]

A Roseliep Retrospective will never be outdated. This text remains definitive.

---

200. *Delta Epsilon Sigma Bulletin* 25: 4 (1980), 116.

201. *Portals* 3:3 (1980), 27.

202. *Muse-Pie* 1:1 (1981), 38–41.

203. *Modern Haiku* 12:1 (Winter–Spring 1981), 34–35.

Chapter Six: Sensei

for my students

past

present

and to come

Dedication, Love Makes the Air Light

The basic idea of haiku that existed in mid-century America was of a short nature poem, often rhyming and titled, displayed in three lines of five, seven, and five syllables, and using a keyword to signify the season of the verse—but not much more. Such a definition did major injustice to the precision and beauty of the Japanese genre, of course. Raymond Roseliep was a major figure in the rejection of such an inadequate characterization and the adding of bone and sinew to American haiku from the 1960s onward.

"Devilish Wine" and "This Haiku of Ours": Roseliep's Ars Poetica

Roots in classic haiku

Roseliep rejected rigid received rules. Even so, he felt his work was well grounded in the Japanese haiku masters, especially Bashō, Buson, and Issa, and that it was in one way or another an extension of the classics. He delighted in pointing out the many Japanese *haijin* who had departed unabashedly from the poetic norms of their time and place.

For his own haiku Roseliep rejected strict structure, especially the 5–7–5 norm, and was ready to accept or employ any poetic figure of speech. He did not insist on having a season word; in fact his haiku were more about people—especially himself—than strictly about capital-N Nature. He agreed that immediacy is a necessary attribute of a haiku, but he roundly rejected other categorical do's and don'ts, especially those touted by some prominent critics of the day. In a series of essays published in leading haiku journals and other writings, he presented his views about form, content, and aesthetics for American haiku. And of course his own poems were constantly reshaping haiku as well.

Sometime around 1978,[1] Mark Doty, editor of *Blue Buildings*, contacted Roseliep by mail: "We've never met, but I've admired your work for a long time." Doty must have asked to interview Roseliep, particularly about haiku, and Roseliep's long answer, found in the priest's files but probably never published, is instructive:

> You asked me what drew me to haiku. Well, I've always admired reduction, brevity, Greek Anthology terseness, Emily Dickinson's gnomic compression. And I like the symmetry of the three lines, the challenge of getting the right thing in the right place. I was beginning to experiment with haiku in my second book, The Small Rain, and became more and more caught up in them. That was in the early sixties. I was reading the classical Japanese haiku poets then, Issa and the others — Issa's the master of the two natures, the human world and the natural world, combining them so suddenly and often startlingly, or <u>showing</u> us their connections....
>
> But about two years ago I began worrying, am I using haiku as a crutch or excuse instead of waiting for longer poems to come? I wrote about that doubt to Felix Stefanile....[2] Felix has faith in my marriage to haiku. He writes: "Besides the value of your creativity here, there is the superb cultural contribution you are making to a field that has far too long been the special bailiwick of the club ladies. In other words, you are almost single-handedly rescuing a genre.... I have no doubt that in due time your writings in the genre will attract some intelligent critic....
>
> I'm simply finding my own way into my own form, using many of the techniques sacred to Western poetry as a whole.... I make every effort to retain as much of the magical and indefinable spirit of Japanese haiku as I possibly can: not to do so would be to deny the existence of soul in haiku.[3]

He might well have quoted Bashō's advice in "Words by a Brushwood Gate," "Seek not the paths of the ancients; seek that which the ancients sought."

In "This Haiku of Ours," his 1976 letter to the editors of *Bonsai*,[4] Roseliep commented: "I've been working with haiku — reading Japanese

---

1. Mark Doty rarely dated his letters to Roseliep.

2. Felix and Selma Stefanile were editors of Vagrom Chap Books of Sparrow Press. They published Roseliep's *Flute Over Walden*, 1976.

3. Unpublished manuscript, titled "I Knew There Was a Haiku in That Doll in My Notebook: A Conversation with Raymond Roseliep," sent to Mark Doty, editor of *Blue Buildings*.

4. Raymond Roseliep, "This Haiku of Ours," *Bonsai* 1:3 (19 July 1976), 11–20.

haiku of all ages in translation as well as varieties of haiku by American and English writers, studying articles and books about this exquisite formation, and of course writing haiku, ranging from classical/traditional on through vastly experimental kinds."[5] In the final paragraph of that same essay he wrote that Bashō's definition of haiku as "simply what is happening in this place, at this moment" is the touchstone none of us should lose sight of.... Haiku happens fast: the bullet entering the deer, the owl nabbing the mouse, the knife cracking the egg. The end result of the scintillating thrust is the flexibility of meaning and emotion available to the beholder."[6]

Roseliep's open-minded if not iconoclastic approach to haiku composition also came out in his critiques of other poets' work. "The Sponsors Speak" in *Portals* showcased seven haiku by unnamed poets and comments by three critics. As an introduction, Associate Editor Doug Ingels wrote, "Our third T.S.S. panel brings back the articulate commentary of Raymond Roseliep, haiku poet extraordinaire, whose work can usually be read in just about any current haiku magazine." Two *Portals* editors, Edna G. Purviance and Ingels (both haiku poets themselves), completed the panel. Roseliep seemed ready to accept a wide variety of poetic devices and ingenuity while his co-commentators were sometimes less enthusiastic. One haiku and comment read:

> Blustery March wind.
> the cactus bloom blown apart,
> bares a bumble bee.

RR: Simplicity in presentation (fewer words, less alliteration with "b" is needed here. The experience is wonderful.)

EGP: The alliteration in this composition seems overdone. There should be no obvious use of poetic device in haiku.

DI: A delightful third line climax. The number of basic subjects treated (3) offer maximum interplay of ideas and resonance without cluttering. How about getting rid of that heavy full-stop period at Line 1's end, though, substituting, say, a colon?

Another haiku with comment read,

> beyond white fields
> white fields
> beyond.

---

5. "This Haiku of Ours," 11.
6. "This Haiku of Ours," 20.

RR: "This is a splendid haiku, the best of the group.... How exquisitely the white expresses this — white, the perfect color, the absorption of all colors. It takes me back to Dante and his Paradise."

EGP: "To me, this type of composition is playing with words, and cannot be called a haiku. Where is the significance? (Aside: Raymond has shown me the significance!)"

DI: "No comment."[7]

In "This Haiku of Ours" Roseliep wrote in a folksy manner, inviting the reader to sit down and join him for "some of my present thought." He admitted that "my theory and practice are both in a healthy state of flux." Yet he challenged English-speakers to "exploit our fabulous native tongue" and for subject matter "to dig into our own teeming country." He believed that everything was a valid subject for poetry, but "in haiku it is the affinity between the world of physical nature and the world of human nature that concerns us, and so we focus our images there. It's American images I'm advocating rather than Japanese." He called for "illuminated moments in a haiku framework of our own language ... a Western haiku all right. American haiku." As he had done, he urged us to read widely in classical Japanese haiku and find what we need, especially "from their deeper spirit."[8]

Roseliep again defended classic haiku in an essay in *Haiku Review '80*, titled "'News That Stays News': Five Classic Haiku."[9] He opened with this assertion: "For me a classic haiku is the Poundian assertion 'news that stays news.' Meriting permanent attentions, such a haiku is marked by individuality and universality, and, in the phrasing of F. L. Pattee, 'always somewhere in the great classic comes the stage direction, often implied: 'Enter the gods.'" Again Roseliep did not quote his own haiku as a defense of that belief in what is classic. Instead, among his five "classics" were those from Kevin Driscoll, at that time a student of Bill Pauly's at Loras College; another termed "eyeku" from Bill Pauly's famous cat on a fence concrete poem. Roseliep rounds out the five with haiku from Elizabeth Searle Lamb, Geraldine Little, and Ty Hadman.

---

7. *Portals* 1:2 (July 1978), 30–33.

8. "This Haiku of Ours," various excerpts.

9. Raymond Roseliep, "'News That Stays News': Five Classic Haiku," *Haiku Review '80* (Battle Ground, Ind.: High/Coo Press, 1980), 14–15.

Subject matter

Traditional Japanese haiku avoided strong images that were likely to upset the delicate sensitivities of poets and readers; subjects such as violence and sex, and even love and personal emotions were looked upon with suspicion in haiku circles. One of the entries in Jane Reichhold's collection of "Haiku Rules that Have Come and Gone," reads: "Use of lofty or uplifting images. (No war, blatant sex, or crime.)"[10] Roseliep was one of the pioneers in making such received wisdom about haiku a thing of the past.

This bawdy Roseliep haiku caught the attention of Cor van den Heuvel as well as Randy Brooks:

> the cat
> lowers his ears
> to the master's fart[11]

Roseliep was able to try out many variations of haiku with the support of publishers as bold and perceptive as the Brookses. No wonder Roseliep, after the words "final issue" of his personal copy of *High/Coo* 24 (May 1982), penned simply "Sigh!"

Roseliep kept no fences around poetic themes or issues. In his award-winning 1968 "Timothy" poem, he used the word "pubic," and the publisher was sure he meant "public" so, without checking with Roseliep, changed the word. Roseliep objected, asked for a reprint and got it in the next issue (*see* Chapter Four, note 111).

One of the darkest poems from *The Linen Bands*, is "Professor Nocturnal," which contains these lines:

> Dismissing bees and bookmen from
> *The Grumbling Hive,*
> he pads in April dusk, afraid
> to be alive....
>
> Near bat-time, to the safe indoors,
> where lamb chops warm,
> he hurries from his boyhood spectres
> of alarm.

---

10. Jane Reichhold, "Haiku Rules that Have Come and Gone," *AHA! Poetry* website, http://www.ahapoetry.com/h_t_rules_come.html; accessed March 30, 2014.

11. *High/Coo* 2:8 (May 1978); and Cor van den Heuvel, ed., *The Haiku Anthology,* rev. 2nd ed. (1986) and expanded 3rd ed. (1999), 186.

Brandied and lounged, he slackens fear
at pages numb
with Congreve jabs—till midnight—
punctual, THEY COME.

Bats loop from Collins' evening ode
on the calm shelf,
rip the planks his brier smoked
about a self; ...

squeak warnings of
a gloomier hole
than terra firma
to his soul.

Bed will be bitter,
tangly, damp,
small solace wick
his all-night lamp.

He bargains the Lord
his soul to keep.
But what if he start
eternal sleep,

caught at last
in a web of wing,
bit, sucked
by a blacker Thing?

Even though Roseliep had warned himself in "Travel": "Soul, I said, it is/ unworthy to spread/ your disturbance/ round,"[12] he continued throughout his life to address what many would consider "out of bounds" in any revelation, self or other. *Sun in His Belly*, the chapbook from which "Travel's" lines are quoted, contained in this sunny-seeming yellow-jacketed 48 pages, at least 22 or more dark or sensual haiku and haiku-like poems. Roseliep often used misdirection, though his sensuality flows through quite rampantly:

---

12. Raymond Roseliep, *Sun In His Belly* (West Lafayette, Ind.: High/Coo Press, 1977), 46.

> in white tulips
> the rooster's red head
>   flowering

Red was often Roseliep's color of choice to express passion, his own or his stand-ins'. The rooster, the subject of the first poem in the entirely sensual *Swish of Cow Tail*, is also known as a "cock" and noted for its behavior among his brood of hens. "Cock" in full erection is red and swollen. White tulips seems like an easy nature opening, but tu-lips are dangerous in connotation, connecting quite sensually and ironically sexual with deflowering.[13]

Nature, of course, is often at the center of Roseliep's poetry, but—again from the very beginning—nature is fraught with danger. A few lines from "Where Roots Tangle" underscore a typical Roseliep fear:

> Where roots tangle the ground before their plunge
> under, he hooks his heels
>
> ...
>
> But he must turn
> from his esthetic distances almost
> as sharply as he taught them to his will
> once he discovers roots lead down and burn.
> And he will mark the night, this light-heeled ghost.[14]

Even posthumously in *The Earth We Swing On*, nature is often tinged with deep sensuality:

> in dawn
> your body
> transparent[15]

Roseliep was ever the "man of art who loves the rose," with all its deep color and insinuations from bud to full flower.

---

13. Raymond Roseliep, *Swish of Cow Tail* (Amherst, Mass.: Swamp Press, 1982).

14. Roseliep, "Where Roots Tangle," *The Linen Bands*, 31.

15. Raymond Roseliep, *The Earth We Swing On* (Minneapolis: Winston Press, 1984), 8.

Form: overcoming 5–7–5

As we have seen above, Roseliep's haiku evolved gradually from his longer poems. His 1963 "Spider" (discussed on page 93) was perhaps the watershed poem in showing the impact haiku was having on the priest-poet.

SPIDER
To John Logan[16]

Tender footed, tip
toe in raveling harshlight,
young-body ardent.

Nothing's more uphill
than airing a small glory
while spending a self

for five pagan wits
of greybrain neighbors to thrum
(hard or tender), though

it's you they pick: guts
dirty; elegant; godly:
ripple crossed, and flown.

Kiting is costly
Arachne and Ovid sigh.
A poem takes time.[17]

"Spider" uses rigid three-line stanzas of five, seven, and five syllables, which causes unexpected line and stanza breaks that heighten the poet's angst. The three stanzas that end with a period can be read as haiku, the other two cannot. "Spider" is a sort of hybrid poem.

Until the early 1970s, Roseliep hewed closely to the 5–7–5–syllable norm for haiku, but thereafter, his near-haiku and haiku were written in any line and syllable count that he fancied, usually with lines shorter than the norm. In his *Bonsai* letter he was so bold as to quote a haiku by that journal's coeditor Mary Streif as an example of extremely condensed language:

---

16. Critic and friend of Roseliep's who wrote the Preface for *The Linen Bands*.

17. Raymond Roseliep, *The Small Rain* (Westminster, Md.: Newman Press, 1963), 70.

> the dog
> eating
> bone sounds[18]

Roseliep was not concerned that the content of his haiku be chopped into proper syntactical units, and he was a fan of using enjambment for poetical purposes. His daring won him both ardent admirers and caustic critics. No matter; he stood his ground and was well willing to put his haiku philosophy before the public. Roseliep, it seems, wanted to lay to rest any criticism of his wanderings from accepted practice. For example, in his *Bonsai* essay he quoted his own haiku to defend its use of enjambment:

> Smoke leafy air
> the boy drop-
> kicks the ball

Moreover, freedom in haiku for Roseliep sometimes meant using the visual or concrete to help illuminate his experience. Though "eyeku" was never his favorite form, he often played around with word placement to emphasize his meaning. Two examples:

> autumn crow
> voicing   the void
> in us all[19]

> bObOlink tumbling
> nOte Over nOte,
> white patch On his rump
> (for bOb bOldman)[20]

Also see his most famous concrete haiku, "Boy in a red cap" (printed on page 129).

In "This Haiku of Ours" Roseliep referenced an evening he had spent with W. H. Auden discussing haiku. "[Auden] was amused by my derring-do with the acrostic haiku/senryu, a form I must have invented

---

18. *Seer Ox* 5 (1976), 19.

19. *Modern Haiku* 12:1 (winter–spring 1981), 22; Raymond Roseliep, *Rabbit in the Moon* (Plainfield, Ind.: Alembic Press, 1983), 78.

20. From the sequence "Narcissus," *Wind Chimes* 6 (Fall 1982), 9.

for I've seen no others except a couple by a few friends to whom I taught it." The priest-poet gave two examples:

EPITAPH: To His Body[21]		FORM[22]	
R	ot	M	ind's
		A	
R	oots	R	are
O	f	I	ndoors.
S	ad	A	
E	arth	N	et
L	ov-	N	o
I	ng	E	ye
E	arth,	M	akes
P	ause	O	ut.
		O	
H	ere	R	
A	nd	E	ach
I	'll	S	lim
K	eep	G	irl
U	s	Y	ou
I	n	M	eet.
S	low		
T	ime.		

Roseliep added, "We both agreed that haiku form is a wide open field for roamers," and finished "As Auden said of the poem, no haiku is ever finished, it's only abandoned. The reader gets on where the poet got off."

Sometimes Roseliep got embroiled, particularly in haiku circles, in arguments about his poetic beliefs. In 1970, *Modern Haiku* Editor Kay Titus Mormino had already acknowledged that "Several letters have been received asking for explanation of the distinction between haiku and senryu.... No 'answer' by any one person could be satisfactory to a serious student of haiku and senryu." Mormino followed her statement with a list of book and magazine references.[23]

21. Originally published in *Shenandoah: The Washington and Lee University Review* 19:2 (Winter 1968); Roseliep, "This Haiku of Ours," 18.

22. Originally published in *Delta Epsilon Sigma Bulletin,* December 1968.

23. Kay Titus Mormino, "Across the Editor's Desk," *Modern Haiku* 1:4 (Autumn 1970), 3.

Roseliep tried to clarify his own position on the haiku/senryu discussion in a letter to Elizabeth Searle Lamb: "Yes, I guess I would call that Sobi-Shi haiku on my envelope to you last time a senryu. I usually don't stop to distinguish haiku from senryu. Sometimes I know they are neither! Or a combination: haiku-senryu."[24]

Haiku sequences

One important legacy of Roseliep's longer poems was his love for haiku sequences, which he was pioneering in the 1960s. The evolution of Roseliep's work from longer poems to haiku sequences is explored above beginning on page 90. Roseliep had found his own way to lengthen the poetic statement without sacrificing the brevity and consequent impact of the haiku form. He would continue this extended haiku expression to his very last published volume, *Rabbit in the Moon*. The dedication to Wanda Wallis, a frequent correspondent and faithful friend and admirer, reads:

> cloud
> over the dove
> mourning
>
> above the keys
> your fingers
> shadow too
>
> after music
> the silence of it[25]

At least ten other sequences, many of them with titles, grace the pages of *Rabbit in the Moon*, but many more sequences appear, widely spaced haiku on one page, such as the Sobi-Shi trio on page 24:

> clothesline
> Sobi-Shi's pajamas
> kicking the sun

---

24. Roseliep to Lamb, August 22, 1978.
25. Roseliep, *Rabbit in the Moon*, 7.

the firefly
acting like he knows
Sobi-Shi's swan song

never alone
Sobi-Shi and the big dog
in the southern sky

or the pairing of art and music on page 26 through allusion to Marcel Duchamps's "Nude Descending a Staircase" with Claude Debussy's faun:

two
descending a staircase:
the cat's suppler joints
>   (for X. J. Kennedy)

out of
the parlor window
Debussy's faun

Roseliep kept pushing boundaries to the very end.

Haiku and the Western literary tradition

In working out a system of aesthetics for his own poetry, Roseliep focused almost exclusively on Western aesthetics and poetics, casting his haiku, for example, in the mold of English, not Japanese, literary traditions. While other North American haiku poets of the 1960s and 1970s were struggling with issues like the importance in haiku of season words (*kigo*), the relevance of Zen, and whether aesthetic and poetic devices such as *sabi, wabi,* and *yūgen* should be ported over from Japanese and employed in place of Western notions of beauty and truth, Roseliep barely considered such debates and came down strongly on the side that haiku was simply another sort of Western poem and subject to the same governing principles. For example in "This Haiku of Ours," he dismisses the *kigo*, considered by most experts to be essential to a haiku: "To me the Oriental season-word is nothing other than symbol—and if you'll agree to that, then symbol abounds in Japanese haiku!" and goes on, apparently to justify his own inattention to seasonality, "many haiku today don't have a season-word, nor is the season expressed or implied."

The following passage from the same essay succinctly states Roseliep's acceptance of the Japanese philosophical and Zen point of view without making a huge point of it:

> Basho's definition of haiku as "simply what is happening in this place, at this moment" is the touchstone none of us should lose sight of. American haiku must continue to court the here and now, the thingness of things, the thusness and suchness of realities. It must record what our six (counting the kinesthetic) senses experience in our everyday world of physical nature and in the vaster world of human nature, while displaying the subtle, often imperceptible blending of those two spheres. A revelation of heightened awareness, our haiku should be wide-awake to the seasons in both worlds. As Dr. Amann[26] beautifully stresses, haiku's "wordless" attribute is its economy, and so our poets shouldn't wreck reality by overstating it or tainting it with (too many) words. Our writers must point out the unity underlying all things: presenting two apparently disparate images and showing how they "unite." We allow the tramp and the butterfly to become brothers under a common sun; we motion the reader into an intuitive rather than an intellectual perception of reality — or sometimes we offer our reader "thoughts and ideas of predominantly intellectual import."[27]

Metaphor

The compositional topic that Roseliep wrestled with most often was the relationship of metaphor to haiku. As his haiku emerged out of poems written in the Western tradition, metaphor was not something he wanted to relinquish. Indeed, a large number of his haiku employed metaphor in the same way his early poems did. For this transgression of the standard notion of haiku he often came under fire from critics and reviewers. Curiously, Roseliep was not a fan of simile: of his approximately 1,600 published haiku, only eight contained the word" like" and twenty-five "as":

> fish peddler
> handling them
> like babies[28]

---

26. Roseliep refers to Eric W. Amann, *The Wordless Poem: A Study of Zen in Haiku.* (Toronto: Haiku Publications, 1969), a special issue of *Haiku Magazine* 3:5.

27. R. H. Blyth, *Haiku, Vol. 1: Eastern Culture* (Tokyo: Hokuseido, 1949), xiii.

28. *Modern Haiku* 8:3 (August 1977), 19, and Roseliep, *Sailing Bones* (1978), 22.

LOVER

Innocent as ice
cream, his hand on the oval
of your white belly.[29]

In February 1978 Roseliep published an essay, "Cry, Windmill," in
High/Coo 2:7. He opened by quoting R. H. Blyth's translation of Issa's
metaphorical haiku

> A cicada is crying:
> It is precisely
> A red paper windmill

Roseliep continued:

> Flourishing on metaphor, this is one of the most stunning haiku in
> any language. Issa wrote it, and he proves indeed that metaphor can
> be an effective (and often dramatic) way of seizing and intensifying a
> moment from the here and now. If the reader approaches Issa's haiku
> with an agile and open mind to play upon the known factor of the
> poem—the cicada crying—he will gradually experience the sound,
> the form, and the color of the flimsy windmill as it applies to the
> insect. Besides that, the reader will feel the pleasure existing between
> the two interchangeable objects. Metaphor helps him, as it helped
> the author, to see and to see more intensely.

Roseliep went on to give a short history of what he calls "the basic poetic
figure." He brought in Quintilian as well as Kenneth Burke, who says:
"Man is the symbol using animal."

At the heart of his argument for metaphor, Roseliep asserted:

> While the haiku poet is sparing in his use of all figurative language,
> fearful that he might destroy the immediacy of the experience he
> is recording, he nonetheless will occasionally employ metaphor as
> the inevitable tool in building a sound haiku structure. He knew
> that to decorate haiku with metaphor is pure disaster, but to instill
> metaphor into haiku so that the figure becomes part of the essence
> of the poem's captured moment is simply being true to his vocation
> as poet." He also advocates that the haiku poet "inject functional
> metaphor that invigorates haiku bloodstream.

Roseliep called upon Bashō, another ancient authority, in Blyth's
translation, to showcase the use of functional metaphor:

---

29. From "Upon Cherry Blossoms," Roseliep, *Love Makes the Air Light* (1965), 85.

A flower unknown
To bird and butterfly, —
The sky of autumn[30]

Roseliep then cited a few moderns to stress his faith in the true use of metaphor: J. W. Hackett, Nick Virgilio, Charles Reznikoff, and Bill Pauly, who wrote:

vine
of your earthy eye
potato[31]

Roseliep did not often publicly enter into arguments about his haiku, but he could not resist parrying an assault from Canadian poet and critic Anna Vakar. In *Wind Chimes* 4 (spring 1982) she wrote trenchantly of a haiku of his that had won the grand prize in 1980 in the Shugyō Takaha Award from the Yuki Teikei Haiku Society of the United States and Canada. Vakar addressed the editor in "On Poetic Devices and Raymond Roseliep," claiming that his use of "treacherous poetic devices" encouraged other poets to "revert to the ridiculous." She was particularly offended by his use of metaphor (*see* haiku text following Denise Levertov's praise on page 210).

Vakar went so far as to call this use of metaphor "specious bull." Her attack became quite personal when she called Roseliep "self-indulgently romantic" as well as "self-deluding."

Roseliep responded to Vakar's letter in the following issue of *Wind Chimes,* pointing out that the haiku that so offended her had won an award. He might also have noted that David Andrews, the book editor for *Wind Chimes,* had written a review of *Listen to Light* in June 1981, in which he pointed out key qualities of Roseliep haiku (originality, brilliance, perception, sensitivity and humor) before discussing the campfire haiku, which had been reprinted in *Listen to Light.* Andrews called this haiku "pure Roseliep" and critiqued each line separately, concluding "this prize-winning haiku would seem to pass all the tests of believability."

In any event, in his riposte Roseliep told the editor, "It is obvious that her knowledge of outdoor domesticity is deficient," going on to clarify the image of campfire dishwater and ended: "It would be great if

---

30. Roseliep, "Cry Windmill," *High/Coo* 2 (February 1978), 2–3. Translator not identified.
31. Bill Pauly in Roseliep, "Cry Windmill."

one could wash dishes in a pan of lightning, but I do not advise Anna
Vakar to attempt it."[32]

Readers could not let this dialogue between Vakar and Roseliep end.
Wind Chimes Editor Hal Roth conducted his own experiment with soapy
water and stars and affirmed Roseliep's description with his own:

> even in dirty water
> the shimmering stars
> of a spring sky[33]

Roth tried to cap the dialogue with a comment in the next issue:

> But I feel you [Vakar] should know that ten of them [twelve per-
> sonal letters to Roth] are in strong disagreement with your com-
> ment, several being critical of me for publishing it.... The final letter
> contains the regret that the exchange has diminished us all a little.
> And so I shall bring to a close the now year-long debate which be-
> gan with the publication of Denise Levertov's statement in No 2:
> "Pinned on a wall where one sees it at odd times, a poem like this
> of Ray Roseliep's:
>
> > campfire extinguished,
> > the woman washing dishes
> > in a pan of stars
>
> can remind one of the whole woven tissue of gladness which, in
> these dark days, one struggles to preserve."[34]

Rhyme, onomatopoeia, etc.

Though Father Ray did not often resort to rhyme and other poetic
devices such as onomatopoeia and assonance, they always remained
tools available on his workbench, and he vigorously promoted the haiku
poet's right to use them. In "This Haiku of Ours" he wrote, again showing
his view that Western poems and haiku are woven on the same loom,
"Rime often sharpens, points up, acts out the experience; yet I don't press
haiku-writing friends to go searching for rime—I suggest they let it happen. Beloved by Emily Dickinson and Hopkins, myriad varieties of near
rhyme are also bracing, and these we should let happen also."

---

32. Raymond Roseliep, "Of Figures of Speech and Anna Vakar," *Wind Chimes* 5 (Summer
1982), 55–56.

33. Hal Roth, "Editor's Note," *Wind Chimes* 5 (Summer 1982), 56.

34. *Wind Chimes* 6 (Fall 1982), 69–70.

HSA Frogpond 1:1 published Roseliep's essay "A Time to Rime," which advanced a controversial position at a time when serious haiku poets in America were struggling to banish rhyme. He opened with an epigram from Samuel Butler: "For rhyme the rudder is of verses, / With which, like ships, they steer their courses."[35] Roseliep continued, "Yes, sometimes rime can be an amazing rudder for haiku, giving the poem a sure movement and direction.... Let me cite a handful of recent contemporary haiku possessing rimes and point out how effective they are in delivering the haiku moment." Roseliep drew examples from Cor van den Heuvel's *The Haiku Anthology* of 1974 and issues of *Modern Haiku* and *Outch*. He observed that rhyme can highlight balancing and struggling of motion as well as for irony, contrast of pace, or even nursery rhyme quality "appropriate when an adult talks to a garden snail."

> So slowly you come
> small-snail....   To you, how far
>   is the length of my thumb![36]

Roseliep ended his essay: "And the rime? Light breaks night."

Allusion and name-dropping

Sun in His Belly was also a touchstone for Roseliep's penchant for allusive name-dropping. The forty-eight poems contain references to twelve famous people of the past, predominantly poets: Samuel Taylor Coleridge, Lord Byron, Alfred Lord Tennyson, Ezra Pound, Robert Browning, and Edgar Degas, and several more modern: John Berryman, Theodore Roethke, W. H. Auden, Robert Frost, Virginia Woolf (and Edward Albee) as well as one of his very favorites, Marianne Moore. Katherine Anne Porter, with whom Roseliep often kept in touch by telephone, is the recipient of many references, though he later tempered his admiration for her (*see* the discussion on page 238).

Roseliep's name-dropping was noted by Thomas Reiter in one of his first letters to Roseliep after Reiter had just graduated with his BA from Loras College. Echoing a common criticism of Roseliep's poetry, Reiter wrote, "Mention of Plotinus in 'Reception' appears to be a bit stuffy, and

---

35. Raymond Roseliep, "A Time to Rime," *HSA Frogpond* 1:1 (February 1978), 18–20.

36. Ann Atwood in *HSA Frogpond* 1:1 (February 1978), 19.

borders on name-dropping. Do you agree?" Roseliep did not agree at all, and throughout his career he often wrote poems with names of prominent personalities from among the quick and the dead.[37]

Roseliep's urge to impress through association was also evident in a critical volume for his reentry into the world of poetry publication in 1973 after a long hiatus from 1965 with his essay, "Devilish Wine," reprinted in the *Voyages to the Inland Sea IV.* Eleven writers (classical and contemporary) are named on page one alone.

Perhaps Roseliep, who often felt extreme in his innovations, believed he needed to enlist both classical and modern literati to shore up his beliefs.

Condensed language: non–5–7–5

By using the word "Ours" in "This Haiku of Ours," Roseliep seems to be implying that others should find the same kind of freedom that he has found, not just created. But writers of haiku had already been arguing for a long time, detailing their own beliefs about the essence of haiku, and would certainly not be willing to accept Roseliep's declarative offering without debate.[38] In *Voyages to the Inland Sea IV,*[39] Roseliep also found ample room to put forth another set of poetic beliefs in his essay, "Devilish Wine."

Voyages to the Inland Sea was a showcase for Roseliep. In addition to his essay was a fine sampling of his poetry, some from his early books *The Linen Bands, The Small Rain,* and *Love Makes the Air Light* as well as many haiku from his future publication, *Flute Over Walden.* He also included a wide-ranging and comprehensive bibliography.

"Devilish Wine," which preceded the publication of "This Haiku of Ours," is not, per se, a defense of haiku, but an earlier definitive statement about Roseliep's broader poetic foundations. To substantiate his beliefs, he adduces evidence from well-known poets such as John Milton, Dylan Thomas, Arthur Rimbaud, Robert Frost, James Dickey, Ezra

---

37. *See* Chapter Eight for more about Roseliep's correspondence with Thomas Reiter.

38. For just one example, in 1976, Robert Spiess wrote his sixth essay on problem areas in American haiku. His first in the series, "The Problem of Originality," appeared in *Modern Haiku* 4:2, 1973.

39. John Judson, ed., *Voyages to the Inland Sea IV: Essays and Poems by Alvin Greenberg, George Chambers and Raymond Roseliep* (La Crosse, Wis: University of Wisconsin Center for Contemporary Poetry, 1974), 55–61. "Devilish Wine" was reprinted in a shorter form in David Dayton, ed., *A Roseliep Retrospective,* (Ithaca, N.Y.: Alembic Press, 1980), 16–17.

Pound, Ben Johnson, Andrew Marvell, Marianne Moore, and others, including some writers of prose.

The haiku from Roseliep's forthcoming collection constituted a sounding-out of his readers and clear indication of a direction for future publications. In the essay he titled the haiku "Walden Notes: Four Movements" and included five haiku from each of the four seasons.

The final section was a "Selected Bibliography," classified by sections "Poetry," "Prose," "Anthologies," "Recordings," "Periodicals" (subdivided into poetry and prose), and "About the Author" (subdivided into poems, articles, reviews and notices, and a brief biography). Perhaps Roseliep was more comprehensive than selective in this bibliography, but he was, in a sense, reintroducing himself to a broad range of readers. This was his first major publication since *Love Makes the Air Light* in 1965, almost a decade earlier. A flood of fifteen publications followed.

Roseliep's definition "A poet is an animal with the sun in his belly" became the title of a chapbook published by High/Coo Press in 1977. The title of the essay came from a student who translated Augustine's *vinum daemonum* as "devilish wine."[40]

Wordplay

Roseliep was a great fan of wordplay, especially punning, which, as we have seen, frequently put him at odds with his editors and reviewers. Roseliep chose the words of essayist Charles Lamb to open his essay "The Pun, a Haiku Tool": "A pun is a noble thing per se. It fills the mind; it is as perfect as a sonnet; better."[41] Roseliep contrasted Lamb's belief with Noah Webster's "Punning is a low species of wit." Appealing to yet one more authority, Roseliep further asserted: "The pun is frequently a dexterous tool of wit, and sometimes the pun will surprise with that 'fine excess' which Keats envisioned as the essence of poetry." Roseliep also told us: "It is not for me to say how skillful I am in handling this exquisite blade, but I should like to put on exhibit a dozen of my own haiku in which I pun, leaving the reader to judge the impact of lack of it in each illustration." The first reads:

> the jay's cry
> downs
> the blue

---

40. Roseliep, "Devilish Wine," 61.
41. Raymond Roseliep, "The Pun, a Haiku Tool." *High/Coo* 4:14 (November 1979), 2–5.

He commented about his own haiku: "I am asking the reader also to swallow my outrageous claim; if he does, he too should identify with sky and bird: and that is what haiku is all about."

Distancing himself a bit, Roseliep continued, "Sobi-Shi (my haiku name) wrote the following in the nine-syllable vertical form he has been cultivating lately:

> plum
> thoughts
> of
> you
> plumb
> dark
> in
> the
> snow

"Obviously, the effect desired is witty," Roseliep wrote in "The Pun, a Haiku Tool," and Sobi-Shi hopes also tender in its nostalgic summertime evocation during winter."

Father Ray's Legacy

Although Raymond Roseliep never joined or led any formal poetry groups, he lives on in the lives of many associates, students, and friends who were mentored by him. Many more throughout the literary world were influenced by the priest-poet. The main recipients of his inspiration and guidance were those who gave tribute to him in *A Roseliep Retrospective*: Colette Inez, William Stafford, Sr. Mary Thomas Eulberg, Sr. Mary Marguerite Schaul, Dennis Schmitz, Thomas Reiter, Donna Bauerly, Bill Pauly, and Jerry Kilbride. Editors including John McHale, Nobuo Hirasawa, David Dayton, John Judson, Mark R. Doty, Wade Van Dore, Jean Burden, Hal Roth, Randy Brooks, Ernest and Cis Stefanik, Robert Spiess, Frank Lehner, John Logan, Felix and Selma Stefanile, Robert Schuler, Jan and Mary Streif, and Edward Rayher often became friends through extended correspondence. Roseliep's influence was paramount with those who communicated with him over the years through numerous letters and tributes or with some other special friendship, including Elizabeth Searle Lamb, Rev. Daniel Rogers, Msgr. Robert Vogl,

Cyril and Renée Reilly, David Rabe, Denise Levertov, David Locher, Edward Rielly, Eve Triem, Katherine Anne Porter, Vincent and Denise Heinrichs, Margaret Carpenter, Wanda Wallis, John Vlakos, Jim Minor, and Marlene Morelock Wills (Marlene Mountain). Many other correspondents with Roseliep as well as an untold number of writers would echo their own tributes for his influence in their lives.

In large part owing to the influence of Raymond Roseliep, Dubuque, Iowa, became known as the "Haiku Capital of the Midwest." Many of Father Ray's associates and those he taught or mentored became top-rank haiku poets themselves. Here is a sampling of the haiku of a few of Roseliep's "literary heirs" that demonstrate his great influence:

Fr. Daniel J. Rogers, close friend of Roseliep's at Loras College.

> The dog-bark—
> cavern of my head
> this long summer night[42]

> fragrant
> crunchings,
> our step[43]

Donna Bauerly, student of Roseliep's from the 1950s and author of this biography.

> leaving you —
> lips at the winter
> pump[44]

> old country cemetery
> larger
> than its church[45]

42. Daniel J. Rogers, in *Modern Haiku* 24:1 (Winter–Spring 1993), 35.

43. Daniel J. Rogers, in *Modern Haiku* 24:3 (Fall 1993), 7.

44. Donna Bauerly, in *Wind Chimes* 12 (1984), 1.

45. Donna Bauerly, in Joseph Kirschner, Lidia Rozmus, and Charles Trumbull, eds., *A Travel-worn Satchel* (HSA Members' Anthology 2009), 52.

Sister Mary Thomas Eulberg, OSF, resident at Mount St. Francis, adjacent to Roseliep's rooms in Holy Family Hall, and was mentored by him.

> fields of corn stretching
> as far as the eye can see
> within   a lost child[46]

> early April rain
> that woman fills every jar,
> seals them forever[47]

Sister Mary Marguerite Schaul, OSF, long-time correspondent with Roseliep. Wrote and published many poems including haiku.

> a red rose
>   in his buttonhole
> he roams the streets[48]

> green blades of corn
> flap to the wind —
> the nuns' veils[49]

Barbara Ressler, popular teacher at Wahlert High School in Dubuque was president of the Haiku Society of America in 1996. Began writing haiku in Donna Bauerly's college class, continued with a Pauly/Minor Workshop in haiku. Self-taught from then on.

> broken ornament
> the child's face
> in pieces[50]

---

46. Sr. Mary Thomas Eulberg, Harold G. Henderson Awards 1980, Honorable Mention; published in Sister Mary Thomas Eulberg, *Far as the Eye Can See* (Glen Burnie, Md.: Wind Chimes Press, 1983).

47. Sr. Mary Thomas Eulberg, Harold G. Henderson Awards 1982, Honorable Mention; published in *Frogpond* 5:3 (1982), 28, and Eulberg, *Far as the Eye Can See.*

48. Sr. Mary Marguerite, in *HSA Frogpond* 1:1 (February 1978), 9.

49. Sr. Mary Marguerite, in *Modern Haiku* 9:3 (Autumn 1978), 5, Honorable Mention.

50. Randy M. Brooks and Lee Gurga, eds., *Midwest Haiku Anthology* (Decatur, Ill.: High/Coo Press, 1992).

teaching haiku
the poems
on their faces[51]

From 1989 through 2009, Ressler's students regularly swept the awards in the Nicholas Virgilio Haiku Contest (administered by the Haiku Society of America), and the Kay Titus Mormino Scholarship Award (from *Modern Haiku*), both for high school students. Two award-winners:

Robert E. Wild, student of Barbara Ressler's at Wahlert High School in Dubuque.

wind
rattling
the abandoned[52]

Nicole Grogan, student of Barbara Ressler's at Wahlert High School in Dubuque.

beep of the monitor
reminding me ...
to hope[53]

Edward J. Rielly, student of Father Ray's at Loras College and later professor of English at St. Joseph's College in Maine. Author of 25 books, 6 of them haiku.

the poet pausing
in his mass-saying —
rain rushes in[54]

---

51. Barbara Ressler, in *Frogpond* 19:1 (May 1996), 2.

52. Robert E. Wild, Kay Titus Mormino Memorial Scholarship 1989, winner; published in *Modern Haiku* 20:2 (Summer 1989), 9.

53. Nicole Grogan, Nicholas Virgilio Haiku Contest 2007, finalist; published in *Frogpond* 30:3 (Fall 2007), 89.

54. Edward J. Rielly, in *Frogpond* 7:3 (1984), 22.

honking, the geese
barely visible, invisible
my longing[55]

Bill Pauly, student of Roseliep's at Loras College, assistant professor (1976–2001), and taught a haiku class there (1986–2001).

Old woman,
rain in the eye
of her needle[56]

heart drawn in dust
by the old Indian ...
rain[57]

sound of her voice
carrying eggs
across the ice[58]

snowmelt ...
she enters
the earth on her knees[59]

Dan Burke, student of Pauly's at Loras College.

a single strand
of spider silk
stops her[60]

55. Edward J. Rielly, Kaji Aso Contest (Boston Haiku Society), 2003, Honorable Mention.

56. Bill Pauly, Harold G. Henderson Awards 1981, 1st Place; published in *Frogpond* 4:3 (1981), 28.

57. Bill Pauly, Harold G. Henderson Awards 1983, 1st Place; published in *Frogpond* 6:3 (1983), 44.

58. Bill Pauly, Harold G. Henderson Awards 1984, 2nd Place; published in *Frogpond* 7:4 (1984), 23.

59. Bill Pauly, Harold G. Henderson Awards 1991, 1st Place; published in *Frogpond* 14:3 (Autumn 1991), 42.

60. Dan Burke, Harold G. Henderson Awards 1988, 1st Place; published in *Frogpond* 11:4 (November 1988), 13.

Bill Pauly conducted an informal discussion group called Haiku Overview in his home between 2003 and 2011. These gatherings continue in Mineral Point, Wis., with Gayle Bull, Bill Pauly, Francine Banwarth, and others: A sampling of the work of this "third generation" of Father Ray's influence:

Becky Barnhart, member of Haiku Overview.

> after the funeral
> whiskers still
> in his razor[61]

Connie Meester, member of Haiku Overview.

> that Venus!
> leading the cupped moon
> through every turn of the road[62]

> opening night ...
> missing the entrance
> of the night-blooming cereus[63]

Marilyn Taylor, member of Haiku Overview.

> in a semi circle
> retired sisters watch
> "Wheel of Fortune"[64]

> naked at the ironing board
> concentrating
> on a crease[65]

61. Becky Barnhart, Harold G. Henderson Awards 2004, 2nd Place; published in *Frogpond* 28:1 (2005), 80.

62. Connie Meester, Harold G. Henderson Awards 1997, Honorable Mention; published in *Frogpond* 20:2 (September 1997), 66.

63. Connie Meester, Gerald M. Brady Awards 1995, 2nd Place; published in *Frogpond* 18:3 (Autumn 1995), 40

64. Marilyn Taylor, Gerald M. Brady Awards 1994, 1st, Honorable Mention; published in *Frogpond* 17:3 (Autumn 1994), 12.

65. Marilyn Taylor, Gerald M. Brady Awards 2002, Honorable Mention; published in *Frogpond* 26:1 (2003), 91.

Valorie Woerdehoff, graduate student in Pauly's Haiku Writing class; also in Haiku Overview group, 2006–2008.

> how long we sat together
> our teacups
> > empty[66]

> your fingers touch me …
> sunlight on the tree
> moves down the trunk[67]

Francine Banwarth, an officer of the Haiku Society of America and editor of the HSA journal, *Frogpond*, since 2012 to 2015. She is also widely published in haiku journals and anthologies and long-time member of Haiku Overview.

> child's wake
> the weight
> of rain[68]

> autumn light
> just this much
> to go on[69]

> the river freezes …
> silence is also
> an answer[70]

---

66. Valorie Woerdehoff, National League of American Pen Women—Palomar Branch International Poetry Contest 1996, Haiku Section, 1st Place; also published in Randy M. Brooks and Lee Gurga, eds., *A Solitary Leaf: 1996 Members Anthology, Haiku Society of America* (Decatur, Ill.: Brooks Books, 1997), 40.

67. Valorie Woerdehoff, Gerald M. Brady Awards 2000, Honorable Mention; published in *Frogpond* 24:1 (2001), 89.

68. Francine Banwarth, Harold G. Henderson Awards 2005, 1st Place; published in *Frogpond* 29:1 (Winter 2006), 83.

69. Francine Banwarth, The Betty Drevniok Award (Haiku Canada) 2009, 1st Place.

70. Francine Banwarth, 2nd HaikuNow! Contest (The Haiku Foundation), 2011, Contemporary Section, 1st Place.

turning again
to touch the red hibiscus[71]

Cynthia Cechota, student of Bill Pauly's at Loras College; also a member of Haiku Overview.

in his email his ego[72]

not a lick of a breeze sweet nothings[73]

Jayne Miller, attendee at Haiku Overview 2006–2010; good friend of Fr. Daniel Rogers.

dead of winter
making stock
from the bones[74]

river mud
the shape
of boys[75]

*****

Charles Trumbull has said, "Raymond Roseliep was about as close as we have in America to a Japanese haiku *sensei,* and his students and followers, for at least two generations, comprise a true haiku 'school' that carries his teachings forward."[76]

71. Francine Banwarth, Hawai'i Education Association International Haiku Writing Contest 2003, Hawaii Word Section, Honorable Mention.

72. Cynthia Cechota, in *Modern Haiku* 44:1 (Winter–Spring 2013), 15.

73. Cynthia Cechota, in *Modern Haiku* 41:1 (Winter–Spring 2010), 14.

74. Jayne Miller, in *Modern Haiku* 43:3 (Autumn 2012), 100, Favorite Haiku of Issue.

75. Jayne Miller, Harold G. Henderson Haiku Contest 2012, 2nd Place; published in *Frogpond* 36:1 (Winter 2013), 127.

76. Trumbull e-mails, April 2 and 17, 2014.

Chapter Seven: Raymundo,
Selected Correspondence

> His natural charm and warmth, his brilliance
> made it easy for me to name him the more
> theatrical Raymundo (world of Ray) and to
> share little drawings and confidences of a
> fellow lover of birds and haiku.

> — *Letter from Colette Inez, Jan. 22, 2015*

> I don't want to lose touch with you ever.
> Not ever.[1]

> — *Roseliep to Thomas Reiter*

Raymond Roseliep went to some length not to lose touch with his friends and professional contacts—not ever. His indexed letters at Loras College number almost 23,000 pieces. Roseliep's correspondents over the years included his close friends, of course, but also celebrities, especially writers such as Katherine Anne Porter, Marianne Moore, Denise Levertov, Richard Eberhart, and Thomas Merton, from whom he would often ask for signed photographs. He was particularly meticulous in his correspondence with editors, and they would be among the first to confirm Roseliep's fastidiousness in dealing with his poems. No incorrect comma or extra space went unnoticed. For certain correspondents, even among those editors, he also kept his personal voice and creative signature handy. He used a wide variety of signatures: Raymundo (a favorite), Spider, Rosy, The Rainmaker, Brother Francis, Poet-Man, and the Black Martin.[2]

---

1. Roseliep's last letter to Thomas Reiter, November 29, 1983.

2. Rosy, of course, is a diminutive. Spider refers to his lean frame and long slender fingers; Rainmaker is a reference to his text *The Small Rain*; Brother Francis made use of Roseliep's middle name and was a nod to the Franciscan sisters; the Black Martin was a name he gave himself, referring to his dark hair and quick, bird-like movements.

Editors: John McHale

Raymond Roseliep's correspondence with editors and publishers could comprise a book all its own. He was extremely fortunate in his choice of publishers, but even more so for the devoted attention of his editors. Topping the list was John McHale of Newman Press, which published *The Linen Bands* (1961) and *The Small Rain* (1963). McHale, an outstanding, responsive, and caring editor in the style of Maxwell Perkins,[3] remained exceptionally loyal to Roseliep, not only in connection with his writings, but also throughout some personally difficult years for the poet.

Roseliep's self-promoter persona was particularly evident in his correspondence. In his first letter to Newman Press, inquiring if they would be interested in a manuscript of fifty poems, he readily offered that John Logan's 2,000-word preface would be appearing in the *Chicago Review* along with a selection of Roseliep's poetry. He also informed McHale, "Since this is a first book, the MS would qualify for the Lamont Award (deadline June 1961, I believe); Mr. Logan has been encouraging me to try for that, if possible."[4]

The almost instantaneous response, typical of McHale, came on August 23, 1960. Though not totally without qualifications, McHale agreed to read the manuscript. From then on, however, the publication of *The Linen Band* moved at what we might now term "warp speed." By December, Roseliep had already gone through multiple proofs, given suggestions for colors and quality of the binding, specified the number of review copies that Newman would send, and commented on the availability of promotional fliers. Roseliep never totally trusted any publishers' projections of numbers of books that could be sold, and he felt he could be his own best publicist by writing in person to poetry editors or other potential reviewers.

Roseliep's engagement with Newman Press proved mutually beneficial. By September 1962, Newman had already sold 1,400 copies of *The Linen Bands*. McHale wrote, "[*The Linen Bands*] increased our prestige as quality publishers.... The percentage of people who reviewed *The Linen Bands* was the highest in our experience."[5] McHale also expressed interest in Roseliep's second book of poetry, *The Small Rain*. "Send it on," he

---

3. Maxwell Perkins (1884–1947) was Scribner's editor of F. Scott Fitzgerald, Ernest Hemingway, and Thomas Wolfe, among other greats.

4. Roseliep to John McHale, August 1960.

5. McHale to Roseliep, September 23, 1962.

wrote.[6] By November 23, McHale acknowledged receipt of the manuscript, and Roseliep's second book was released in 1963.

The path to publication of this book was not as smooth as that for *The Linen Bands,* however. Roseliep wanted a reproduction of a Rembrandt painting on the cover, but the cost was prohibitive, so a line drawing in gold by John Roseliep, Raymond's nephew, appeared instead in the upper right-hand quadrant of the dark-brown cover. Another of Roseliep's requests was honored, however: "I would also prefer not to have my picture on the jacket this time; the image of a priest in Roman collar doesn't seem just right now for the type of poem prevailing in the collection."[7]

Roseliep and his collaborator-friend John Logan faced a controversy over the text on the jacket flap, purportedly anonymous but which drew heavily from a forthcoming review by Harold Isbell in *The Catholic Worker.*[8] In letters to Roseliep and the publisher, Isbell objected strenuously to the unacknowledged use of his text: the first paragraph paraphrased and the third paragraph and a concluding sentence quoted verbatim. Eventually, some small recognition of Isbell's words on the book jacket appeared in introductory remarks to *The Catholic Worker* review: "Unsigned portions of this review appeared on the dust jacket of *The Small Rain.*" McHale sided with Roseliep throughout, but readers of the letters among the three men might be left with a bitter taste that smacked of self-promotion on Roseliep's part.

McHale and his daughter Jeanie met Roseliep in 1964 when he was in residence at Georgetown University. McHale's letters at this time were warm and friendly: "I can't tell you what a pleasure it was meeting you recently. Jeanie was certainly delighted at the opportunity to make your acquaintance."[9] Roseliep's letters, in return, usually promoted his poetry, though he did acknowledge a gift of cookies: "Indeed I did receive Jeanie's box of delights, and I have written her of my joy in this other art of hers. What a little lady she is. I look forward to seeing her again."[10]

In late 1964 and early 1965 letters between Roseliep and McHale were scarce. On November 26, 1965, McHale wrote to Roseliep, then in

---

6. Roseliep sent the manuscript for *The Small Rain* on November 19, 1962.

7. Roseliep to McHale, April 26, 1963. "Prevailing" poems in *The Small Rain* were often erotic love poems, and Roseliep did not escape serious questioning by church hierarchy for his choice of theme.

8. Harold Isbell, "The Small Rain," *The Catholic Worker* 30:4 (November 1963), 4–7.

9. McHale to Roseliep, September 17, 1964.

10. Roseliep to McHale, October 15, 1964.

the hospital, "It is certainly a wonderful pleasure to hear from you, but we are distressed to know that you have been ill. We only hope that your recovery is complete and speedy. Let us know if there is anything we can do for you during this period when you are recuperating. I wish I had known you were at Madison. I was out in Milwaukee a few weeks ago, and I would certainly have given you a call."[11]

In this same letter McHale wrote, "I was rather surprised that Norton is bringing out *Love Makes the Air Light*. I will be looking forward to seeing a copy. What I am curious about mostly is whether Norton will sell as many copies as we have of the first two books of poetry that we published." No details are to be found in any letters from Roseliep to McHale or to the poet's new editors at Norton as to why Roseliep did not continue publication with Newman Press or, for that matter, how McHale learned that his friend had decided to switch publishers.[12]

Apparently very few letters were exchanged between Roseliep and McHale thereafter. McHale did ask Roseliep to review a manuscript from another poet and acknowledged his quick response. McHale wrote in July 1966 that he was happy to hear of Roseliep's departure from St. Mary's Hospital and his appointment as chaplain at Holy Family Hall. He also informed Roseliep that he would be leaving Newman for Pflaum Press in Dayton, Ohio.[13]

The correspondence between Roseliep and McHale ended rather abruptly. McHale wrote a last letter from his new position on December 9, 1966: "It is wonderful news that your health has improved…. The memory of our association at Newman was one of the most pleasant experiences I had in all the years I was there."[14] No answering letter from Roseliep has survived.

---

11. McHale to Roseliep, November 26, 1965.

12. However, in a letter to Denise Levertov, June 9, 1964, Roseliep made it quite clear why he chose Norton for his third book, *Love Makes the Air Light*. "I plan on working on a manuscript for my third collection; and though the Newman Press has done well with my two books, I wonder if I shouldn't try to get a secular publisher for the next one—I am free to do so…. I'll get to meet John McHale when I am out East this summer and intend to ask him if I may desert him for the next book." Though Roseliep had met John McHale at an earlier time, there is no record in their exchange of letters that Roseliep did talk with McHale regarding moving his third volume to Norton. McHale wrote in November of 1965 that he had recently learned of Roseliep's decision. Denise Levertov published extensively with Norton and was influential in Roseliep's decision to publish with them.

13. McHale to Roseliep, July 25, 1966.

14. McHale to Roseliep, December 9, 1966.

Editors: W. W. Norton & Co.

Roseliep's association with W. W. Norton & Company began in late 1964. Peter Jacobsohn of Norton wrote on January 7, 1965, "I take great pleasure in sending you our contract for the publication of your poetry manuscript *Love Makes the Air Light*. We are delighted to have you as an author on our poetry list."[15] Most of the subsequent letters were quite businesslike until an assistant, Kelly Dammacco, wrote warmly, "Your April 30 letter arrived yesterday. It filled my Monday full of glow and brought a pleased smile to Mr. Brockway's face."[16]

On August 30, Roseliep wrote to George Brockway from St. Mary's Hospital, asking that all correspondence be directed to that address. "I am on leave of absence from Loras College and trying to catch my breath here—lots of rest and laziness is prescribed."[17] Roseliep, however, did not miss a beat in his directives for *Love Makes the Air Light*. He had read galleys and was ready for the page proofs and other publishing information. In a later letter Roseliep wrote, "I expect to be returning to Loras College, yes; probably for the second semester, though this is not definite yet—it depends on how much rest I get in before that time. But I see no need for your mentioning my sick leave from Loras; keep me identified with the College, please, as a faculty member."[18]

In February 1967 he wrote to Anne Gorman at Norton, who was seeking his participation in a project to have Norton poets read their poems to various audiences: "I keenly regret that at the present time I will be unable to express my willingness to participate—my health has been rugged, and I am still away from teaching duties at Loras College."[19]

On June 23, 1969, Roseliep wrote Brockway about a manuscript of poems, all haiku, for possible publication. The letter was long and went into great detail about this manuscript or the choice of another of his manuscripts in progress. The reply came two days later: "After much soul-searching we have drastically reduced our poetry program and are making no further commitments at this time. You can therefore take this

---

15. Peter Jacobsohn to Roseliep, January 7, 1965. McHale was not aware of Norton's publication of *Love Makes the Air Light* until November 1965.

16. Kelly Dammacco to Roseliep, May 4, 1965. George P. Brockway was president of W. W. Norton & Company.

17. Roseliep to Brockway, August 30, 1965.

18. Roseliep to Brockway, September 13, 1965.

19. Roseliep to Brockway, February 26, 1967.

letter as formal release from the option provision in the contract."[20] We can only wonder about the effect such a blow from this abrupt dismissal had on the poet. Roseliep continued publishing individual poems but did not engage with a book publisher again until 1974.

Editors: John Judson

In John Judson, Roseliep found another editor friend. Judson invited Roseliep to be one of three poets for the fourth volume of *Voyages to the Inland Sea,* a series he was editing, featuring contemporary Midwestern poetry.[21] Imagine the look on Roseliep's face and the joy in his heart when he opened Judson's letter of November 21, 1973: "We would like very much to feature your work in the next volume."[22] Only three poets were featured in each volume. Judson requested,

> In our series each poet is represented by: an essay of his own especially written for this volume on the topic of poetry (in general, his poetry, or Midwestern poetry, etc.); a series of poems (about twenty pages), half of which have been previously published and half of which are new, unpublished poems; a bibliography compiled by the poet which includes: a) a complete list or a check list of poems published, b) a list of prose pieces about poetry which each poet has written, and c) articles written about each poet and his work by people other than the poet.

Roseliep's cheer could probably have been heard all the way down to the mailbox he visited several times a day. *Voyages to the Inland Sea* would have been a showcase for any writer's work, and eventually for Roseliep it signified reentry into the world of book publishing.

Roseliep lost no time in answering. He replied to Judson, "Your offer and invitation as outlined in your kind letter of 21 November are attractive, and I am happy to sail your Inland Sea."[23] Roseliep learned that Alvin Greenberg and George Chambers were to be his poet co-journeyers.

Once again, letters flew furiously between poet and publisher. Roseliep was predictable: "You will, I am sure, allow me to read my own proofs, yes? Do your contributors get complimentary copies (like how

20. Brockway to Roseliep, June 25, 1969.

21. John Judson to Roseliep, November 21, 1973. The series *Voyages to the Inland Sea* was published by the Center for Contemporary Poetry, Murphy Library, Wisconsin State University at La Crosse, beginning in 1971. The university was renamed University of Wisconsin—La Crosse in that year.

22. Judson to Roseliep, November 21, 1973.

23. Roseliep to Judson, November 25, 1973.

many)?"[24] Ever the self-promoter, Roseliep wrote on January 31, 1974, "I know you will be limited as to the number of review copies for ISLANDS, coming up, but do let me give you a few suggestions—some of these no doubt will be on your limited list of 'musts.'"[25] Roseliep followed with a detailed list of ten magazines and editors that should receive free review copies. Judson reminded Roseliep in a follow-up letter that "we are working on a shoestring."[26] Judson's quick replies to Roseliep were all the more amazing in light of a glimpse that he provided into his life outside publishing, "Sorry to be so long in answering your last letter. I have 40 grade school kids in a class called 'Creativity,' and it has been a joy, a hell, and an incandescence I live with three days a week beyond my full university load this semester."[27]

Voyages to the Inland Sea IV was a handsome hardbound text, a capacious stage for Roseliep to present his essay "Devilish Wine," which contained his deepest thoughts about poetry and the poet. Roseliep's penchant for name-dropping was evident, with eleven writers (classical and contemporary) named on page one. Roseliep's third of *Voyages to the Inland Sea IV* featured eleven individual poems. He selected from his very best work, particularly "My Father's Trunk" and "Vendor," and included a group of "Thoreauhaiku" that would soon be published in *Flute Over Walden.*[28] The bibliography for Roseliep's writings was also impressive and certainly encouraged Judson to publish three more Roseliep chapbooks: *Walk in Love* (1976), *Light Footsteps* (1976), and *Sky in My Legs* (1979).[29]

Roseliep reached out to other small-press editors who continued to welcome this *haijin:* Felix Stefanile of *Sparrow* magazine for *Flute Over Walden* (1976); Ernest and Cis Stefanik of Rook Press for *A Beautiful*

---

24. Roseliep to Judson, November 25, 1973.

25. Roseliep to Judson, January 31, 1974.

26. Judson to Roseliep, February 6, 1974.

27. Judson to Roseliep, February 15, 1974.

28. Raymond Roseliep, *Flute Over Walden: Thoreauhaiku* (West Lafayette, Ind., Sparrow Press, 1976).

29. Roseliep received a surprise birthday gift from John Judson, the tiniest of chapbooks, *Light Footsteps*, a Juniper Special (1976). Just seven of Roseliep's haiku graced the pages of 250 hand-set and -printed copies. Roseliep wrote to Judson: "You took the wind out of me. A friend of stunning surprises. I am so moved, so impressed with your birthday gift…so downright delighted. Your fine taste and exquisite care are all here…. I will treasure this all my life as one of the most special things that has happened; it's the kind of joy only a poet understands." Roseliep to Judson, September 17, 1976.

Woman Moves with Grace (1976), *Step on the Rain* (1977), *Wake to the Bell* (1977), *A Day in the Life of Sobi-Shi* (1978), and *Sailing Bones* (1978); Randy and Shirley Brooks of High/Coo Press for the chapbooks *Sun in His Belly* (1977) and *Firefly in My Eyecup* (1979); Robert Schuler of *Uzzano* for *The Still Point* (1979); and Ed Rayher and Sarah Provost of Swamp Press for *Swish of Cow Tail* (1982).

Editors: David Dayton

In the 1980s Roseliep worked with Alembic Press on three hardback books: *A Roseliep Retrospective* (1980), *Listen to Light* (1980), and *Rabbit in the Moon* (1983). In David Dayton, Roseliep found one of his most attentive and devoted editor-friends. Their correspondence began in December 1977 and was halted only by Roseliep's death.[30]

The early exchanges between Dayton and Roseliep followed the established pattern. Dayton contacted Roseliep first. On December 19, 1977, he wrote, "William Pillin [poet] suggested I solicit some poems from you for *Alembic*. I took one of his for the first issue and asked if he knew of others I should be in touch with regarding the possibility of submitting."[31] Roseliep answered on December 31, "It was good of Bill Pillin to suggest me to you. I am working mostly in haiku these past months, but before sending you a MS I want to be sure you care for haiku — many editors don't." Dayton's reply was just as swift: "I wouldn't reject a haiku just because it was a haiku.... I'm interested to see what you have; there's nothing I'd like better than to publish as many good haiku as I can get hold of."[32] The long editor-poet friendship was launched.

Dayton was the kind of editor that Roseliep could only have dreamed of. If Roseliep was picky, Dayton was even pickier. Dayton began by printing a sequence of twenty-four Roseliep haiku in issue 2 of *Alembic,* his small-press poetry magazine. Roseliep did not take long before asking Dayton: "Wonder if you would like to do a book of my haiku?"[33] Then, after a series of specific instructions, Roseliep added: "I think you are going to hit me just right."

A query from Dayton, however, led first to the publication of *A Roseliep Retrospective: Poems and Other Words By & About Raymond Roseliep.*

---

30. Eight folders of letters between the Daytons and Roseliep; LCARC 325, C:3.
31. Dayton to Roseliep, December 19, 1977.
32. Dayton to Roseliep, January 9, 1978.
33. Roseliep to Dayton, June 22, 1979.

Dayton had asked, "Is there anybody sitting on an essay on your work? Anybody who's expressed an interest in writing one? This would be a good time to get such prose into print."[34] By December of that year, Dayton was writing to Roseliep about his philosophy of publishing poetry: "I want to put poetry I like before the public in a bigger way than *Alembic* will ever enable me to."

A Roseliep Retrospective, published in 1980, was soon followed by *Listen to Light*. Alacrity could have been the middle name of editor and poet in their collaboration. Both Dayton's and Roseliep's inexhaustible powers of scrutiny were tested in the endless round of permissions required to print and reprint Roseliep's poems and the writings of his admirers and critics. The idea of an all-haiku publication from Alembic was realized through a grant from the National Endowment for the Arts that Dayton received in 1980. He wrote Roseliep on March 31, "Plan on a haiku book for next fall." On June 28 Dayton wrote, "Let's start on the haiku book now; it wouldn't hurt to have it done and ready to see several months early." Roseliep responded on August 8: "Glad you like *Listen to Light*. I fully mean it to be my best collection of haiku."

Attention to detail never failed Dayton. When he wrote to Roseliep on September 20, about the proofs of *Listen to Light,* he inquired, "Anything else? Let me know if I've forgotten some important detail; otherwise hold the worries until the last moment; you'll be seeing everything before it goes to print, book, ad, etc., and if I forget something you tell me then, right now, I'd probably forget the small details anyhow—will use your letters as reminders when setting copy, though."

By January 7, 1982, Roseliep was proposing to collaborate again. "I do look forward to another haiku book with you come 1983." Despite the fact that Dayton and his wife Nancy had moved to Mexico and were expecting their first child, they collaborated on *Rabbit in the Moon*. All did not go smoothly this time, however. Dayton rejected the illustrations by Jon Vlakos that Roseliep had chosen. Vlakos had illustrated Roseliep's *Swish of Cow Tail* with images that most people considered intriguing, challenging, and highly erotic. Ed Rayher and Sarah Provost of Swamp Press, publishers of that chapbook, had used Vlakos as an illustrator before, and, though there was much back and forth between Rayher and

---

34. Donna Bauerly, "Raymond Roseliep: 'Where Are You Going? Where Have You Been?'" David Dayton, ed., *A Roseliep Retrospective* (Ithaca, N.Y.: Alembic Press, 1980), 29–44.

Roseliep, production of that book proceeded without fanfare. William Higginson in a review of *Swish of Cow Tail* in *Modern Haiku* had written: "On turning the 3×3 cover one discovers a carefully folded piece of Japanese paper that opens out to four feet in length, covered with beautifully sensual prints in a rainbow of colors.... These illustrations by Jon Vlakos are worth the price of the book."[35] Dayton insisted upon a different illustrator for *Rabbit in the Moon*, however, which caused Roseliep much anguish in telling Jon Vlakos about the rejection.[36] Rayher, when prompted by Roseliep, characterized the artist: "Vlakos—he's 1st generation Canadian, his parents are from Greece. He's a loner, studied anatomy for a while, paints—his main concern, and works just enough to get by—at the O'Keeffe Cultural Center in Toronto.... His paintings are very impressive—but definitely out of the mainstream. The figures are very realistic, tortured—almost medieval in that sense, and always tinged with sexuality."[37]

Roseliep yielded to Dayton's adamant rejection, eventually agreeing to illustrations by Teresa McNeil. In a letter to Thomas Reiter, Roseliep commented:

> David Dayton rejected the magnificent drawings by Jon Vlakos; they don't "illustrate" my haiku, quoth he, they are too much like Beardsley, and miss the point of the haiku overall. I was shocked at the rejection. I had presumed that I had the final word on the drawings. How wrong I was. Now Dayton is hiring another artist. So all production has stopped till we get the art. Nuts. The book still could come out in the fall if this gal works fast, and if she pleases us both."[38]

Rabbit in the Moon was published in late 1983 as Roseliep hoped, but some readers might have been disappointed by the literal treatment that McNeil gave to Roseliep's highly suggestive haiku.

Students and Friends: Thomas J. Reiter

Roseliep's correspondence extended far beyond editors and publishers. Many former students corresponded with their mentor, and one of the most important of these was Thomas J. Reiter, who began exchanging letters with Roseliep just after he graduated from Loras College in 1962.

---

35. *Modern Haiku* 13:2 (Summer 1982), 31–32.

36. Roseliep to Elizabeth Searle Lamb, May 21, 1983.

37. Ed Rayher to Roseliep, November 9, 1981.

38. Roseliep to Thomas Reiter, April 26, 1983.

His first letter, four handwritten pages in blue ballpoint pen, was a study in temerity. Just 22 years old and only recently mentored by Roseliep in a creative writing class, Reiter was replying to a set of poems that Roseliep was readying for *The Small Rain*. No wonder, Reiter relates, that Roseliep never answered this extensive critique of poems. What student dares tell his former teacher, "The things I liked very much about the poems vastly outnumbered the criticism on the other side of the ledger but as my time was short, and you will likely receive mostly praises anyway, the following remarks in the main touch upon areas of the poetry which I thought were weak, or could be made even stronger."[39] One could wonder about the position of Roseliep's eyebrows after reading that missive! Reiter commented further that "the quotes in stanza II of 'Wild Bells' perplex me; perhaps they get so 'personal' that the reader feels he's an outsider all of a sudden." In the next comment the young critic said, "Are you satisfied with 'mothering sea' in 'Green Bedroom?'" Then, "'appointed' in *Mutiny* version of 'My Mother Bought Me Red Things' seems more effective than 'was willing' in current version.'" Ultimately Roseliep decided upon "appointed," but he never informed Reiter of any changes suggested by his former student that he incorporated.

In a longer comment Reiter wrote, "a reader of the whole manuscript is struck by your propensity for constructions like 'The fingers were bough slender.' This appears to be a genuine part of your voice, and it nearly always succeeds." Reading between the words, Roseliep might have visibly winced. Then, echoing a common criticism of Roseliep's poetry, Reiter called him on his propensity for name-dropping (*see* page 212).

In yet another comment Reiter observed astutely, "1st two lines of 'Love Song When It's Snowing' strikes me as quite ineffectual and 'precious': the image of the robe of snow seems to be mainly expression for its own clever sake." Roseliep would eventually read many more comments from readers about his bent for cleverness and his capacity for being "precious." Perhaps it was after reading Reiter's comment that Roseliep changed the first two lines to "Your face in the snow is virginal / as snow catching its hem on the ground."

About another set of poems Reiter wrote, "the 'Wish for Paolo' segments are among the weakest; yet I realize that *Poetry* took them (or at

---

39. Reiter to Roseliep. December 31, 1962.

least one of them)." This Reiter comment could make any reader chuckle, and one could wonder if Roseliep had a laugh or two himself. Reiter also gave his overall interpretation:

> The book's tone, even more so than in your first book, is intensely personal. A definite soul is behind these poems and one finds out more about it (because it tells him more and more as he reads) than it is customary to discover about the writer of a volume of poems in this century of Eliot. The voice grows firm, insistent, self-conscious, delicate, moody, and confessional. It puts a sometimes embarrassing burden to the reader when he realizes that someone trusts him enough with his previous human experience. I, myself, sometimes wince at the burden. But perhaps I do this because your work produces a tension in me: I cannot deny nor exclude the validity of your raw experiences and its artistic usage; it is your sacrament. Yet, as Eliot maintains, the fact that my expression of experience now differs from yours, I tend to look with some doubts on poetry not agreeing largely within my norms of creation. This, then, is the basic mental framework within which the book was read and reactions occurred.

Reiter's parting comment read, "I suppose you realize it, but one of your favorite constructions uses 'or' between two nouns, verbs, etc. It occurs more frequently at the book's beginning, and hence anticipation is set up in the reader's mind. This comment is neither pro nor con, but just an observation."

No other letters from Reiter ever delved into his mentor's poems quite as deeply. Perhaps the young critic was intimidated because Roseliep had never responded in any way. In a recollection many years later Reiter wrote, "I'm sure Ray did not respond to my effusions. Nor did he or I ever bring up the subject later. I see now that he almost completely ignored my suggestions. He never sent me a copy of *The Small Rain,* so my mother bought me one. Unfortunately, Newman printed it on acid paper, so it's brittle and yellowed now." [40]

However, the two men—perhaps not as equals but as fellow poets—did begin communicating again by letter in 1977. Reiter traveled back to Dubuque, his hometown, and made a personal visit to Roseliep at Holy Family Hall. During the fifteen-year period from 1962 to 1977, Roseliep was active in publishing books and from 1966 to 1979 softcover chapbooks. For his part Reiter explained, "the lapse between 12/31/62 and 9/10/77 was due to a number of factors: Ray's silence at my comments in that handwritten letter that might have seemed to him

---

40. E-mail from Reiter, November 8, 2010.

like a betrayal; my hesitance to write fearing I wouldn't get a response; and my launching out into graduate work, teaching, raising a family, etc. But my mother [who lived in Dubuque and was interested in their careers], kept the both of us informed of the other's activities."[41]

In his first letter to Roseliep after that 1962 commentary, Reiter told his former mentor of his own literary success, the publication in 1977 of his *River Route,* which might have elevated him in Roseliep's eyes to the status of fellow writer.[42]

The years of correspondence between Roseliep and Reiter were distinguished by a sharing of that important world of publishing poetry. Reiter often sent copies of recent poems to Roseliep, asking for critical responses and often receiving praise from his mentor. These two poets, with a deep and abiding love of nature, eventually seemed worlds apart in form. In his later years Roseliep confined himself to writing haiku, even lamenting, "[I] long to write something beyond a haiku, which is all I write anymore. This is a challenge I need.... I need some push to get out of this haiku rut."[43] Reiter, on the other hand, was always committed to a longer line and a strong narrative strain.[44]

Roseliep and Reiter not only shared their views of the externals of publishing but also sometimes delved into their internal personal struggles as well. Reiter was more open about the quotidian aspects of his life, especially the abandonment by his muse resulting from what he termed his "funks" or "the vapors." In a letter of March 23, 1980, Reiter

---

41. E-mail from Reiter, April 4, 2011.

42. Reiter's success was recognized in a 2009 article in *Sewanee Review* 119:1 (Winter 2011): "Thomas Reiter's *Catchment* abounds with stories brought to life. From memory, myth, and imagination comes a faith in the power of poetry to bear witness. Here we find a variety of personae engaged in dutiful labor ranging from gardening to tomb repair. The lore of occupations centers these narratives and dramatic lyrics, and the texts range widely in time and place, with settings in the Caribbean islands, with their colonial and postcolonial realities, their multiform history, culture, and topography; the Midwest of the pioneer era as well as of the poet's own childhood; and the New Jersey Pine Barrens.

"These poems, inclusive of so many perspectives and voices, enter wide sweeps and strong currents of history, not to generalize or point a moral but rather to render moments in the lives of people caught in the effects of time's passing. Reiter is drawn to portray those who hold their lives together in spite of adversity, even calamity, who — simply, profoundly — go on. Passionate, authoritative in tone and detail, *Catchment* embodies a vision in which art comes out of a necessity to repair the world."

43. Roseliep to Reiter, April 6, 1979.

44. See this interview with Thomas Reiter: http://connotationpress.com/poetry/802-thomas-reiter-poetry.

began to voice what became a refrain: "This weekend has seen me struggle mightily against a funk that's had me in hip boots for about a month. I'm apparently feeling the gathered force of deferred frosh papers and of intimate contact with illness."[45] Later Reiter reiterates, "I wish I could say this summer has been full of poems, but alas I've been failing to adequately finish anything — my closures don't close, or maybe they close what hasn't yet been opened; I've been pushing, straining, rearing back and throwing smoke. I've got to relax and speak more softly. Every one of my recent poems wears a truss."[46]

Roseliep was more reticent about sharing inner troubles with Reiter. The first stanza of a poem titled "Travel" might explain his hesitation: "Soul, I said, it is / unworthy to spread / your disturbance / round."[47] Roseliep did not often comment on Reiter's revelations but kept his letters tuned to praise of his former student's poems and of his own satisfaction with his publication success.

The poets often shared memories of Loras College and recalled the successes of such writers as David Rabe[48] and Dennis Schmitz.[49] Reiter also often shared his love of the outdoors and expressed his longing to take Roseliep with him on a trek to a wildlife preserve. Roseliep demurred in a variety of ways, since he dreaded leaving his snug quarters in Holy Family Hall. Reiter rebuked his mentor in a letter of February 4, 1980: "I don't believe you responded to my suggestion that we spend a couple unpublic hours at the E. B. Lyons Preserve. That adventure would mean a great deal to me — the sharing of various odds and ends of plant info I've gleaned toward poems."[50]

---

45. Reiter to Roseliep, March 3, 1980. The "intimate contact with illness" refers to the extended illness and death of his wife JoNell's mother.

46. Reiter to Roseliep, July 30, 1980. Reiter was in a kind of funk after the publication of *River Route*.

47. Roseliep, "Travel," *Sun In His Belly*. 1977, 46.

48. David Rabe was Reiter's classmate and also visited Roseliep on occasions when he returned to Dubuque to visit his parents.

49. Dennis Schmitz, a highly successful poet, was a senior at Loras College when Reiter and Rabe were first-year students. Schmitz was not particularly communicative with either Reiter or Roseliep.

50. Reiter to Roseliep, February 2, 1980. Reiter finally coaxed Roseliep to the nature preserve. In a letter dated October 19, 1980, he refers to a "chigger haiku" that Roseliep wrote about their trek. In remembering more than one outing, Reiter wrote: "While there we playfully showed off our botanical lore to each other, and even located the openings to some of the Mines of Spain." Reiter also took Roseliep to Eagle Point Park on various occasions. Reiter e-mail, June 1, 2011.

Sometimes, Reiter allowed months to go by without writing, invoking Roseliep's rebuke. On December 12, 1981, Reiter wrote: "Months of silence, then this halting letter—what are we to make of me? At the turn of the year a return to energy, a sloughing off of teaching skin yielding to naked nerves for poems before the second semester skin grows."[51] Then Roseliep's brief comment five days later: "Now I can enter Christmas in peace. I know that you are alive." Roseliep also commented about his friend's venture as editor of the *New Jersey Poetry Journal* and said he was "very proud to be one of your first contributors." As always, Roseliep added advice about whom Reiter should ask to submit—for example, William Stafford—and to "Feel free to drop my name; he [Stafford] really likes me."[52]

In 1982 Roseliep gave high praise to Reiter for his poetry, calling it "a bountiful year for TJR." In the same letter Roseliep revealed how difficult it was for him to refuse invitations to read his poetry. He had been requested by the president of the Haiku Society of America to come to New York to read. Roseliep told Reiter: "Wish I could. In September. How I hate getting these invitations; they only make me aware of how frightened I am to move away from my cave. There is enough light here."[53]

Correspondence between Reiter and Roseliep peaked in 1982 and 1983. Roseliep even wrote, "I told you when you were here that I had transferred my Reiter preciosa from my vertical file to my horizontal one. Well, as proof positive, you will see me on the photo before my cherry-wood, rope handled horizontal file with an open box before me labeled 'Thomas Reiter Correspondence.'"[54]

Roseliep's letter to Reiter in January 1983 was a cornucopia of good news and bad. The good news had to do with the publication of Reiter's *Starting from Bloodroot* and Roseliep's elation over the planning of his Winston book of haiku with the Reillys as well as his ideas for *Rabbit in the Moon*. Balanced against the good news, perhaps even overwhelmed for a time by it, was Roseliep's reaction to Joan Givner's biography of

---

51. Reiter to Roseliep, December 18, 1981.

52. Roseliep to Reiter, December 23, 1981.

53. Roseliep to Reiter, 1982. Date not specified.

54. Roseliep to Reiter, September 3, 1982. Roseliep had his coffin created by a local craftsman, James P. Fabricius. He kept that coffin in his rooms at Holy Family Hall, and eventually used it as his "horizontal file" for papers and manuscripts.

Katherine Anne Porter. "It's been rough going for me. I was hard hit by
the early reviews of the KAP biography, then stunned when I read the
book." According to Roseliep,

> Givner turned on her subject. Evidently she is getting her revenge on
> KAP, who threw her overboard — though she did indeed pick her for
> her biographer.... Something changed [Givner's] mind on me, or
> someone did, and I was amazed to see how little of the material I had
> fed her over four years was actually used.... She sent me an inscribed
> copy of her book, expressing appreciation for the big part I had in
> it. And I hardly appeared.... So it would seem that she has tossed
> me out, having used me. I thought we were such dear friends. It's all
> such a confusing mess, and I am heartsick and sick about it all....
> How I wanted the facts of KAP's last days recorded — I gave Givner
> enough on those — from those telephone conversations I had with
> KAP, which Givner never was able to have....[55] It would have killed
> me had she [Porter] thrown me out as she did so many others."

In a final typed note on the far right horizontal side of the letter, Roseliep
asked Reiter to send any reviews that Reiter sees about the Givner biography. "I am keeping a special file on these."[56]

Roseliep had shared with the biographer much about his own personal relationship with Porter, including notes he had taken from their
phone conversations. He had expected to find that friendship honored
with great detail in Givner's biography. That did not happen. Instead,
searching the index, Roseliep found just four short references to their
relationship. One described a time when he was poet-in-residence at
Georgetown University in 1964. Givner wrote about a large emerald ring
Porter bought for herself, one that Roseliep put on his own finger at the
time of his visit with Porter, "wore ... the entire time and mentioned it
frequently in the poems he wrote to her."[57] Roseliep had been criticized
before for name-dropping in his poems, so this reference might have hurt
him since he mentioned it frequently in the poems he wrote to her.

More irksome, however, were Givner's detailed references to David
Locher, a former student and friend of Roseliep's, who had introduced
Roseliep to Porter. Locher had taken classes from Porter in Minnesota
in 1953 and kept in touch with her. Roseliep not only requested an introduction but also asked his young friend for Porter's private telephone

---

55. Roseliep kept a transcript of those phone calls. *See* Porter file, LCARC 325, A:2.

56. Roseliep to Reiter, January 22, 1983.

57. Roseliep to Reiter, January 22, 1983, quoting from Joan Givner, *Katherine Anne Porter: A
Life* (New York: Simon and Schuster, 1982), 448.

number, which, he said, Locher gave "reluctantly." Locher asserted that Roseliep "took over the friendship" with Porter and that she "turned on him at one time "when he got too possessive and demanding.""[58]

Though Roseliep wrote to Reiter that 1982 was a "bountiful year" for the latter, it was during that year and 1983 that Reiter often wrote of his "vapors, or what Holly Golightly in *Breakfast at Tiffany's* calls the 'mean reds.'"

Roseliep opened his April 1983 letter to Reiter with these encouraging words: "'Piney' is all the assurance I need that your powers are not declining." Roseliep also mentioned his own problems: "My *Rabbit in the Moon* is delayed."

In the last months of their correspondence, Roseliep was both humorous and startling. He wrote Reiter: "My god, what will I do if they change the keyboards on our typewriters? At my age, with my non-mechanical mind, I would never be able to relearn how to type. It is also now announced that after this year no more manual typewriters will be manufactured by any company! Big Brother is looking over our shoulder." And, later, he added: "Our tulip tree is in full bloom. I managed to pick one, with a hoe...." He included this haiku:

> lighting a lantern
> in the tulip tree
> old moon.[59]

Roseliep's August news was surprising: "I can't believe this myself, but tomorrow Vince and Denise Heinrichs[60] are coming for Mass at 6:45, then after breakfast we drive to Chicago to see the Vatican art exhibit at the Art Institute. Will stay overnight at friends of theirs, quiet like, and return Friday p.m. The hermit leaves his hermitage. I am just like [Thomas Merton]."[61]

Roseliep's last two letters to Reiter were filled with praise for Reiter's poems "Mulberry" and "Q and A" as well as his own excitement over

---

58. Interview with David Locher, February 27, 2003.

59. Roseliep to Reiter, June 14, 1983. The haiku was later published in *Wind Chimes* 11 (1984), 12.

60. Vincent Heinrichs was a student of Roseliep's at Loras College. He graduated in 1959. He and his wife Denise remained lifelong friends of Roseliep's. Vincent was one of the pallbearers at Roseliep's funeral.

61. Roseliep to Reiter, August 17, 1983.

the final arrangements for his new book: "The soft cover of my *Rabbit* came on 21 October, and the hardbound on 28 November—I am much pleased with the hardbound in every way.... I really appreciate all you wrote about my book; you are one of the few friends I can count on for that important kind of response." Then, the true ending to this correspondence, though neither Roseliep nor Reiter realized how final these words would be: "Try to get me a letter before Christmas. I don't want to lose touch with you ever. Not ever."[62]

Reiter's last letters to Roseliep were typed under the letterhead *The New Jersey Poetry Journal,* marking an exciting excursion into editing for him. He wrote, "no lit news of upbeat note." But Reiter was always quick to praise Roseliep, especially for *Rabbit in the Moon*: "I understand your 'panic' building till you actually hold the new book in hand and count its fingers & toes. Can't wait to celebrate it."[63] And he did in his last letter to Roseliep: "*Rabbit in the Moon* arrived perfecto about a week ago & since then I've been carving away at a new poem,[64] to be able to respond in kind (if with a minor grace note only) to your great gift. *Rabbit* is without doubt the finest production of your haiku to date.... Beautiful format & graphics: reminds me of the last line of an ars poetica poem by Robert Wallace[65] that the poem is finally something "beautiful, surrounded, shining, and stopped." Reiter's final words to Roseliep: "Love from my 'winghold / on the void.'"[66] Roseliep printed at the bottom of Reiter's letter: "vade mecum—a go-with-me."[67] Reiter had done so in his transition from a student to a colleague and poet of Roseliep's.

Students and Friends: Elizabeth Searle Lamb[68]

"The postal authorities won't go out of business while you and I are alive and healthy," Elizabeth Lamb assured Father Ray.[69]

---

62. Roseliep's last letter to Reiter, November 29, 1983.

63. Reiter to Roseliep, October 27, 1983.

64. Reiter's poem, "Q &A," was included in his last letter to Roseliep. He had printed on the copy enclosed, "Does the title work?" Roseliep penned on that copy, "Absolutely!" Roseliep also added these words in his final letter to Reiter: "The best compliment my book [*Rabbit in the Moon*] will ever get is the "Q & A" that came out of your reading."

65. Robert Wallace, American poet, 1932–1999.

66. Roseliep haiku in the autumn section of *Rabbit in the Moon*, 93.

67. Reiter to Roseliep, November 14, 1983.

68. This author's conversations with Elizabeth Searle Lamb proved especially rich in detail about Roseliep's life and art.

69. Lamb to Roseliep, September 27, 1981.

In his bulging files of letters to and from friends—many of whom are poets and many quite famous—Roseliep the self-promoter is never far distant. Friendship begins to emerge more prominently, particularly if the letter writing continued for years. Such was the case of the correspondence between Elizabeth Searle Lamb and Raymond Roseliep. The two poets never met nor even spoke on the telephone, but they exchanged many long letters and shared their views about their own and each other's writings and on the world of haiku. In this way they came to a deep understanding of one another through their poetry and the concentric ripples from their impact on a larger world.

In 1980 Roseliep dedicated *Listen to Light* to "Elizabeth Searle Lamb, First Lady of Haiku." By that time they sometimes exchanged letters as often as three times a week. Lamb may have been peripherally aware of Roseliep as early as 1962, attested by her letter to him of March 3, 1978: "Yesterday I got some boxes of papers ready for storing in an outside closet … and found *The Minnesota Review,* Spring '62—with your 3 absolutely stunning poems!!!! I've been given a gift."[70] These poems were highly structured, but they were not haiku; and since Roseliep's name appears prominently on the cover of *The Minnesota Review,* it is possible this reading in 1978 was her first contact with Roseliep's earlier, longer poems. Lamb was certainly aware of Roseliep's haiku work in November 1969, when she reported having spotted a two-page spread of Roseliep's haiku in *The Catholic World.* [71]

Their correspondence is the best witness to a Roseliep almost devoid of his multifaceted persona. He wrote without shading about his daily life, including his eating habits and bodily disorders, his vast collection of Santa Claus cards, his thoughts and observations about the Sisters of St. Francis, his hermitic ways and happiness with the silence of his black desk telephone, his insights into haiku, gossip about writers and critics, ongoing angst over publication, and the vagaries of various publishers.

---

70. Lamb to Roseliep, May 3, 1978. Actually four poems eventually published in *The Small Rain.*

71. Bauerly interview with Elizabeth Searle Lamb, May 11, 2004. Though Lamb said that she read Roseliep's haiku and wrote to him, no record of this earliest correspondence exists in the Roseliep files at Loras or in the Lamb papers at the American Haiku Archive. Roseliep did not save Lamb's letters until 1978. Then correspondence between them ballooned. Some 819 letters dated 1976 to 1983 are on file at Loras College. See http://libguides.loras.edu /roseliep for a full catalogue of all Roseliep's letter correspondence.

Haiku was the core of their friendship, but from this poetic center ripples emitted that reached to the far shores of their souls. With Lamb, Roseliep seemed more at ease than with anyone else. On May 5, 1983, he wrote her: "I sound really gossipy today; but am in such a good mood—it's just that it's fun sharing a few emotions with understanding YOU." In a 1981 letter Lamb had already written: "This is all magnificently unimportant, of course. Now I've given you the gossip … and must to work."

Their letters and cards were often themed to a season or some celebration. Colors of typing paper were carefully chosen, and the two shared a love of commemorative stamps and how they should be canceled and saved. When the post office issued series of bird or state stamps, Roseliep and Lamb had a contest to see who could get them all first. On May 7, 1982, he wrote, "Sure, let's give progress reports on the birds in our race," and on May 17, "Your addition of Massachusetts to my stamps brings my count to 27. Better not send me any more of your duplicates until our 'contest' is over—it isn't fair that you should help me get ahead of you." Finally, on July 7, 1982, Lamb conceded to: "the Rose-lieping Cat who ate the canary and other birds and flowers on a whole 50 stamps in record time. Congratulations and Salutations From: the Beaten Lamb." Obviously, this race to see who could collect all 50 states first concerned more than stamps. Both poets were highly competitive, and 50 states was an outward sign of a comprehensive array of correspondence from friends, admirers, and publishers.

Both poets were born in 1917, but their lives were quite different. Roseliep's life could be summed up, perhaps too neatly, in the chapter titles of this biography: son, scholar, priest, poet, *haijin*, *sensei*, letters, and Sobi-Shi. Roseliep resided in Farley and Dubuque, Iowa; and except for studies in Washington, D.C., and Notre Dame, Ind., he rarely left the Dubuque area. Lamb, on the other hand, traveled widely and lived in exotic locales, from Topeka, Kan.; to Trinidad, Brazil, Guatemala, Costa Rica, Honduras, Puerto Rico, Panama, Colombia, and New York City finally settling in Santa Fe, N.M., where she died in 2005.

The interests of the two were much more parallel. Lamb originally trained as a harpist, and though she always retained a love of music, her focus turned to writing. She said she became a writer "out of necessity" from an inner urging."[72] She began writing children's stories, puzzles and

---

72. Lamb interview.

reference-book entries, and especially short spiritual pieces and poems. She discovered haiku in the late 1950s; the first dated haiku composition of hers is January 6, 1960. She soon met Harold G. Henderson and Leroy Kanterman, cofounders of the Haiku Society of America. Lamb was a charter member of the society and served as its president in 1971 as well as editor of the HSA journal, *Frogpond*, for several years.[73] Her first two published haiku appeared in the second issue (1963) of *American Haiku*, the pioneer English-language haiku journal, published by James and Gayle Bull. She also placed her early haiku in Eric Amann's journal *Haiku* and Kay Titus Mormino's *Modern Haiku*. Three of her haiku appeared in Mormino's 1968 *Haiku Anthology*.[74]

Roseliep, as detailed in former chapters, began writing and publishing poetry in grade school; continued throughout all his days in high school, college and years after until the time of his death in 1983. At first, he favored classical forms, but often introduced variations such as a fourteen-word sonnet. He began focusing on haiku about 1967.

Lamb's first letter to Roseliep was dated August 8, 1976, and sent from Topeka: "I have wanted to send a word of appreciation for your article in *New Catholic World* … now your fine thinking-out-loud letter about haiku to Jan and Mary Streif.[75] Perhaps a copy of my book will serve to say thank you for these, and other poems including haiku & senryu which I have seen and enjoyed. All best wishes."[76]

By December 1976 Lamb had begun to share personal comments: "My husband and I have just found and bought a wonderful 'funky' old adobe house in Santa Fe—will not be able to move before summer.… I hope to begin to add some of your books to my shelves—what (that is available) is most real haiku? I am interested in *Sun in His Belly*." On February 13, 1977, she added,

---

73. Lamb's illustrious career and ongoing involvement with the world of haiku is outlined in Miriam Sagan's "Introduction" to *Across the Windharp, Collected and New Haiku* by Elizabeth Searle Lamb (Albuquerque, N.M.: La Alameda Press, 1999).

74. Kay Titus Mormino, ed., *Haiku Anthology: 1968* (Danbury, Conn.: T.N.P.C. [The Nutmegger Poetry Club], no date [1968]).

75. Roseliep to Jan and Mary Streif. The letter was printed as "This Haiku of Ours" in *Bonsai* 1:3 (July 19, 1976), 11–20, and in David Dayton, ed., *A Roseliep Retrospective* (Ithaca, N.Y.: Alembic Press, 1980), 19–22.

76. Lamb to Roseliep, August 25, 1976. Lamb's book, though not named in her letter, was most likely *In this Blaze of Sun* (Paterson, N.J.: From Here Press, 1975).

> This two year interim in my old home of Topeka has been good
> for us, as a kind of breathing space after New York. It came about
> because Bruce wished to take early retirement ... we planned to live
> here and care for my Mother for as long as she needed us (or perhaps
> take her to Santa Fe—we were already thinking Santa Fe). However,
> her death came shortly after we got here and it has been really good
> that we were here to manage things until her estate is settled, since
> my brother and sister both live outside of Kansas.

In a letter dated June 6, 1977, Lamb added more about her family's
home in Topeka, "The property here—house and 5.27 acres of a beautiful hilltop with old trees and landscaping etc.—is now on the market and
is being shown. It is all that is left of what was my Father's 160 acre dairy
farm when I and my younger brother and sister were growing up. It is
now one of the few remaining loose ends of my Mother's estate of which
I am the executor." In this same letter she wrote about the Harold G.
Henderson haiku contest that she had judged for the Haiku Society of
America that year. She fretted that the awards listing had been late because
someone in charge did not make plans early enough. Roseliep and Lamb
often exchanged opinions about the HSA and its politics and peculiari-
ties. Lamb signed this letter: "and lovejoypeacepraisehealthstrengthlife
also ever, Elizabeth." The word "love" appears for the first time in their
correspondence.

Lamb wrote "Dear Ray," for the first time shortening his first name,
on July 17, 1977. She was eager to tell more about the Henderson awards
and made it quite clear that she had judged the competition blind, i.e.,
not knowing which poets had submitted haiku nor knowing which poet
wrote which haiku. In her next letter, however, she was free to rejoice
with Roseliep over his tie for first place honors in the contest. His prize-
winning haiku read

> reaching into sky
> the girl breaks the wish-
> bone of geese[77]

Providing more detail about her real estate sale, Lamb wrote:

> Things are moving here—negotiations for the sale, friends to move
> into house till matters are settled, and it appears Bruce & I may be
> able to leave for Santa Fe 1st or 2nd week in August. No, no heart-
> aches over this move—our 2 yrs. here are happy and productive and

---

77. Roseliep included the haiku in *Sailing Bones* (1978), 25.

a gift I could make to my Mother and Father <u>and</u> to my brother and sister. But now it IS time to go—and we will accomplish the last chores and confusions with joy.... A real answer, dear friend, to your good letter when I am able. This, just to keep in touch and thank you for prayers, poetry, affection. Love, Elizabeth.

A hiatus of two months, a short time, but seeming like forever between these correspondents, occasioned Lamb's opening burst in her "trio of rabbits on the front" note of September 9, 1977: "We are here! We are happy! We are home! I have thought this word to you many times since we arrived, a month ago now, but it somehow has not gotten onto the paper." Lamb wrote about her choice of cards and special stamps, responding to Roseliep's choices as well:

how do you happen to have always these special no-longer-available [stamps] on hand. I have a feeling that you take almost as much pleasure in the card for itself as in the fact it will bring pleasure to the one who gets it. Are we kindred spirits in this? I sometimes think my delight in writing notes/letters on cards that give *me* pleasure is almost a selfish kind of thing. At any rate, I enjoy the writing to friends—it's a special part of my life—almost as much as the hearing from them.... The coming of the mail was always an important part of the day.

Lamb's letter of October 5, 1977, opened "Dear Friend-in-Iowa." She again commented on the state of the HSA, observing that only four members had been present at the recent meeting and that there had been talk of disbanding. A month later she wrote to thank Roseliep for including a poem of hers in a collection he edited titled *Into the Round Air.* "Medieval Tapestry" was a set of two memory poems, one for a remembered "thousand threads" tapestry; the other recalling her harp: "of a sudden my fingers smooth / the folds of a flowing gown / and reach to strum the silent strings / of the pear-shaped lute I hold.... To what music, then, I wake."[78] As Christmas 1977 neared, Lamb wrote "Bruce now home from Peru and we are looking forward to our first Christmas in Santa Fe.... But, as always, I become itchy for the holiday to be over and the back-to-the-poetry, haiku, essays and so on."[79] At times she turned a full typed page sideways to type more text in the margins.

---

78. Lamb to Roseliep, November 9, 1977. Roseliep edited *Into the Round Air* (Derry, Pa.: Thistle Publications, 1977), a collection that included well-known poets: Richard Eberhart, Ted Kooser, John Logan, Vassar Miller, May Sarton, William Stafford, and a few Loras-connected poets: Francis Lehner, James Minor, Bill Pauly, Daniel J. Rogers, and Dennis Schmitz.

79. Lamb to Roseliep, December 12, 1977.

For quite some time Lamb had been urging her Iowa friend to join in a renga by post,[80] but he never succumbed. She finally wrote, on January 9, 1978: "And of course I am not mad—this is not a thing to make any difference in our friendship, it's just a perfectly reasonably 'being honest' response, and it adds to my respect and understanding.... Must stop but want you to know friendship does not hang on renga." Collaborative work was never Father Ray's métier, and perhaps he did not like to give up any kind of control in the creation of poetry. In 1978 Roseliep began saving copies of some of his letters to his friend in Santa Fe. He opened his first letter of that year "My dear Elizabeth" and commented at length about haiku, especially the one-line form, as well as renga. He mentioned his "sacred rules" of never going beyond 17 syllables. He was much the editor in this letter, commenting on Lamb's longer one-liners and the fact that they wouldn't fit on a normal page. He rewrote some of her lines and gave her directions for typing. Typical of many Roseliep letters, he commented about food, "I had mustard greens (cooked) for lunch this noon, first time; I do not recommend them. I'm fond of all vegetables, but this is one for omitting. (I love spinach, beet tops, all other greens—even as a kid.)" He signs off, "Love from my snowy hill."[81]

In a quick answer to Roseliep's 17-syllable rule, Lamb queried, "Just a comment—your no-more-than-17 syllables. If one accepts a 17-syllable norm, then how do you rationalize a shorter count without also accepting a slightly over-17 count? Grin. I agree with you that probably 17 syllables is as long as one should go, generally speaking, but I think there would be exceptions."[82] Lamb's letters implied that she always had Roseliep's letters nearby as she typed, and she never failed to thank for the many stamps, cards, and inserts that he sent.

Another common theme was the weather. On February 12 Lamb inquired, "Does the sun shine on you today? And does snow lie underfoot? We continue to be most fortunate ... several inches of new snow

---

80. Renga, a linked poem, began over seven hundred years ago in Japan as a sort of literary party game. Poets worked in pairs or small groups, taking turns composing the alternating three-line and two-line stanzas. Renga were sometimes hundreds of stanzas long, though the favored length was a 36-line form called *kasen*. Several centuries after its inception, the opening stanza of renga gave rise to the haiku. From "The Academy of American Poets," online. Composing renga by mail and later by e-mail has been a popular pastime among haiku poets.

81. Roseliep to Lamb, January 12, 1978.

82. Lamb to Roseliep. January 19, 1978. The interjection "grin" was often used in letters by Lamb to soften a criticism, much as we might use an emoticon in an e-mail.

yesterday and last night, but no wind with it, and this morning the sun is bright. I know I have not properly answered your last letters. Forgive me.... Do you find that often the poems which seem the most 'right' to you are the ones that languish unpublished?"[83] Ten days later she wrote that Bob Spiess, editor of *Modern Haiku*, had asked her to review Roseliep's *Step on the Rain*.[84] They often traded editorial suggestions about each other's work, such as Lamb's rebuff of notes Roseliep had penciled in to her longer poem, "Mission Ruins." "I want a certain 'proseiness' of the conversation of the Franciscan Brother ... talking."[85]

That closeness of friendship is underscored in a letter that Lamb sent to Roseliep on April 30, 1978: "You know, I had really been feeling something not right with you[86]—it is strange how close haiku/poet friends can become ... there is a wavelength ... a pathway ... on which many of us travel together (well, perhaps not so *very* many)." But, in a letter on May 3, 1978, Lamb is, as always, the independent critic of haiku, sharing her observations about haiku in general and even specifically about Roseliep's. "The others [haiku], to be honest, I find tell me too much and usually by way of metaphor, which is not (for me) necessary. I would prefer not to have the poet tell me the corn kernels were 'jewels' for instance. But then—you already know I am not taken, usually, with metaphor. It's the plain speech that strikes me to the marrow of the bone! A literal statement—not figurative."

The poets also shared opinions about haiku magazines and editors. At times, both Lamb and Roseliep were invited "pre-editors" of various submissions for *Modern Haiku*. However, when his favorites were rejected by the editor, Roseliep reacted by saying, "That's his way of keeping us 'down, boy, down.'"

On July 20, 1978, Lamb wrote,

> I have wonderfully exciting good news to share with you: I have received word from Cor [van den Heuvel, president of the HSA] that I have won the Henderson Award (Check enclosed—grin). I entered 3, including my "Topeka—last day." "leaving all the morning

---

83. Lamb to Roseliep, February 12, 1978.

84. Lamb to Roseliep, February 12, 1978. Original copies of most magazines or books mentioned in the correspondence between Lamb and Roseliep are located in the Loras College Academic Resources Center, Room 315. The texts are arranged similarly to the location in Roseliep's room at Holy Family Hall. Lamb's review appeared in *Modern Haiku* 9:2 (Summer 1978).

85. Lamb to Roseliep, March 11, 1978.

86. Roseliep often discussed his gastric problems with Lamb, and we can assume he had another flare-up after a recent surgery. Yogurt became a staple in the diets of both poets.

glories closed." Anyway the recognition of the Henderson Award
gives me a new impetus—not that I've been discouraged, but it is
true that I have not yet found haiku friends here and I miss the New
York City contacts in that respect. The correspondence you and I
carry on has been one of the great helps in taking up the slack, dear
friend Raymond. I send love, Elizabeth.

Roseliep answered on July 24, 1978, "Such joyful news! I cannot tell
you how happy I am that you, the judge of last year, should be the winner
of the coveted Henderson Award." Roseliep did not remind her that he
had been the winner of the previous year's Henderson Award chosen by
Lamb. But, typical of a rather haughty side, Roseliep offered a suggestion
that she change the text

leaving   all the morning glories   closed

to "leaving the morning glory closed." What Roseliep did not see is the
way her sole first word leads to a kind of enjambment for the next words.
"Leaving," then, stands alone as motion away from, but can also be read
"leaving all the morning glories," substituting in a way for a line change.
Roseliep was often critical of one-line haiku. In a later letter on August
20, 1978, he picked up his criticism: "I wouldn't object to one-line haiku
for the format if they were shorter than your prize poem."

When the reclusive Roseliep was vexed by Janice Bostok, an Australian
haikuist who planned a trip in the U.S. and asked to meet him, he confided
to Lamb, who was also on the woman's itinerary, "I had written, in my most
gentlemanly way, that I would be unable to see her when she came to the
States, for health reasons. Then she began to probe what the health reasons
were. Finally, I had to be a little more detailed than I care to be in this extremely
personal (and sensitive) area; and I told her that I had had a breakdown some
years ago, and as a result I have lived a hermitlike existence." Bostok had
already written to a sister at Holy Family Hall, where Roseliep was chaplain, to
see if she could "come and stand outside the gate and see the buildings in which
I live."[87] Eventually, Bostok did not stop in Dubuque, but the ever-gracious
Lamb made every effort to entertain her in New Mexico, picking her up at the
Albuquerque airport, driving her to their home an hour away, touring the
area, and even taking her with them to their favorite mountain village of
Chimayó. Lamb also sought to give Roseliep some deeper understanding of
this visitor.

---

87. Roseliep to Lamb, August 18, 1978.

Lamb was curious about Roseliep's adoption of the haiku pen name "Sobi-Shi," and had asked him for an explanation.[88] No direct answer can be found in Roseliep's files, but in a letter dated August 22, 1978, he wrote, "Yes, I guess I would call that Sobi-Shi haiku on my envelope to you last time a senryu. I usually don't stop to distinguish haiku from senryu. Sometimes I know they are neither! Or a combination: haiku-senryu."[89] Lamb's response a few days later, "Haiku, thank heaven, is a growing developing thing"[90] and a month later, "*A Day in the Life of Sobi-Shi* is beautiful and I thank you for it!" "How your poetic gifts are flowering and coming into the light.... You very much enrich my life.... My favorite [of all Roseliep's haiku thus far] remains: inside / my day / the budding rain."[91]

Lamb was grappling with her own troubles at this time, "And since I am in one of my quite-rare days of depression, I respond especially to the 'shoulders droop with shadow.'"[92] She writes of many rejections of late—of trying to place her books in local bookstores and of her haiku being rejected by the editor of *Haiku.* "I walk around in irritation." In a week, however, she writes again: "I hasten to let you know the clouds have indeed lifted ... in fact, as you will also understand, the act of writing it out had already, just by the doing, begun the lifting of the weight of depression. So, I am in sunshine again!"

Roseliep, contrary to his usual schedule, wrote on October 24, 1978: "Unable to sleep I got up at 5:00, showered and shaved, and am at my IBM until time for offering Mass at 7:00. This is a bit unusual, as I am not very alert most of the morning! Let me try it, just for the hell of it, and see if I can make sense. I had a good night's sleep, however, and had taken a two-mile walk around 10:00 before retiring—the air was crisp & halloweeny."

Roseliep and Lamb corresponded at length about the new pope, John Paul II. Father Ray wrote also of his hopes for Givner's forthcoming biography of Katherine Anne Porter. Obviously Roseliep interrupted this letter, ending with, "Now I'm back from Mass, had breakfast, and will write another letter and then hit the sack until the morning mail comes. I enjoyed my visit, and hope it sounds like I am alive this bright day—oh such a sun coming through our maple."

---

88. *See* Chapter Seven.
89. Roseliep to Lamb, August 22, 1978.
90. Lamb to Roseliep, August 26, 1978.
91. Lamb to Roseliep, September 26, 1978.
92. Lamb to Roseliep, October 10, 1978.

In a typical pitch from Roseliep, he wrote to Lamb on November 7, 1978, about his ongoing passion for Christmas cards, especially those featuring St. Nicholas or the modern Santa Claus in any form. "So you might keep my hobby in mind. You get around so much, and may chance upon some in an antique shop, garage sale, and the like." Eventually, Roseliep collected over a thousand of these cards, which he carefully enclosed in plastic sleeves and placed in special boxes.[93] Lamb shared this love for Christmas. Her papers are filled with Christmas cards; she loved to make decorative Nativity scenes, especially using Southwestern figurines, and wrote some two dozen haiku using the word "Christmas."

Lamb was still struggling personally. "Forgive me! I've been somehow unable to do letters ... not depression, just confusements and confoundments ... grin."[94] She went on to praise Roseliep's *Sailing Bones* and listed her favorite haiku from the book: "The Sobi-Shi haiku, too, although I am not always sure of this 'other man of the rose' — but still, when he writes the one ending 'the frog said it' how can I help but be enchanted." And later she assured Roseliep that she would watch for Santa cards: "I do love to poke."[95]

In a few letters before Christmas, a very busy time for both of them, Lamb wrote about a trip that she and Bruce would soon take to South America with their daughter Carolyn. They planned to sail down the 2,000 miles of the Amazon from Peru to Belém, Brazil. "Bruce and I both rather hate to miss Christmas in Santa Fe. We do love it here. But tropical Christmases are in our blood, too. I have had the best of all possible worlds in my lifetime." The difference from Roseliep's lifetime could hardly be greater. He answered: "How good to hear of your exciting trip; but I couldn't imagine myself away from home at Christmas — not even if I had a wife.... Christmas is my favorite time, once ahead even of gay-sad autumn."[96]

By January 1979, after the throes of Christmas were over for both of them, Lamb regaled Roseliep with descriptions of their Amazon travels.

On March 7, 1979, Roseliep commented on a review of *Sailing Bones*, by Robert Spiess in *Modern Haiku:*

93. The collection is now with Roseliep's papers at Loras College.

94. Lamb to Roseliep, November 9, 1978.

95. Lamb to Roseliep, November 14, 1978.

96. Roseliep to Lamb, November 25, 1978.

What do you think of his review of me? My only reservation, if that's the word, is that Robert must remember that I too have my own concept of what haiku is and what it isn't. And *Sailing Bones*—more steady and less experiment (than [*Step on the Rain*])—is my statement of the way I want my own haiku to go, at least for the moment, and my belief in what I think American haiku is…. A man should be able to demonstrate what is really stunning in this elusive form when he writes his own haiku…. I find so much that is trite, flat, calendar artish.

Lamb answered with a few comments about *Modern Haiku* and Spiess's review, including plans for finishing her essay, "A History of Western Haiku," eventually published in *Cicada*.

While Lamb placed haiku in many magazines during the years between 1979 and 1982, she published only one full collection, the chapbook *39 Blossoms* (High/Coo Press, 1982). Roseliep, however, was at his most productive in these years, and Lamb was always ready to give him due recognition. In 1979 alone Roseliep published three books and chapbooks and was negotiating for *A Roseliep Retrospective*. In an unusually long letter dated January 1, 1980, Lamb detailed her hopes for publication of a chapbook as well as her plans to contribute to the *Haiku Review*, a new biennial publication by Randy Brooks at High/Coo Press.[97] On January 22, 1980, Lamb wrote of receiving her copy of *The Still Point*: "You've done it—seen clear into the intangible essences of the tangibles—'mosquito song/brings all my eyes/to the stone's core' and 'Braque's grapes/beyond/these' and 'glass/goes into the light/it gives'—these are beautiful, evocative, haunting. Some I do not yet see into and I must await enlightenment to come from within. Of course, I have a personal affection for 'a frog to sit with/and not say/a word'."

On February 3, 1980, Lamb sent Roseliep a long excerpt from *Haiku Review '80*, "Thoughts on the 1979 Haiku Books and Related Matters." She had included mention of Roseliep's 1979 trio of haiku books as well as a reference to recent publications of *Light Footsteps*, *Step on the Rain*, *A Day in the Life of Sobi-Shi*, and *Sailing Bones,* commenting, "he is now with publication of these new works clearly established as one of the strongest voices of the English-language haiku world." She then went into detail about each of the three texts, focusing on *The Still Point*. She closed her "Thoughts" with this nonpareil praise: "There has been no book of western haiku like this one! If I were permitted to have only

---

one haiku book from the 1979 list, *The Still Point* would be my choice."
When Lamb reminded Roseliep that "not too many people know that
we are warm and close friends! But I simply wrote my beliefs," he let her
know that he had shared Lamb's thoughts with another friend: "He has
known of our friendship for a long time, and is also a dear and precious
friend. But I will not mention it to another soul, never fear. Not that
there's anything wrong in our sharing, but we wouldn't want people to
think that friendship was a deciding factor. I think it's great when friends
can support friends honestly, anyway. I try never to overpraise or in fact
give any praise to a friend whose work is mediocre. We do have integrity
to maintain.... End of homily. Grin, yourself!"[98]

Now that the pressure of the haiku overview was past, on February 8,
1980, Lamb wrote of her next haiku ventures:

> I have the *39 Blossoms* book of haiku all put together as I want it ...
> the leaving New York City haiku, then Kansas haiku, a middle sec-
> tion of some return to New York haiku plus the one-line Nigerian
> series; and *All Night Singing* is a full book, too. Then I certainly have
> a chapbook of non-haiku poems I'd like published: *Readings from a
> Double Compass*; and another inspirational one similar in a tone to
> *Today and Every Day*, this is *Let the Banners Fly*. When things let up
> a bit I must see what I can do.

On July 23, Roseliep wrote to Lamb: "*A Roseliep Retrospective* coming in a couple of days—softbound copies.... I save everything you send
me; your file overfloweth. I am going to get a new drawer for you, that is
start a second drawer." Later, on July 30, he added: "My salary remains
at a standstill: $310 per mo! I got off all the copies of ARR (softbound),
and now will be watching for the 150 copies of hard bounds. For signing.
50 I return to Dayton—the others are ordered. He seemed pleased with
the ms. Of *Listen to Light*, my 200 haiku."

Lamb received her softbound copy on August 3, 1980, and wrote
on August 8, "Today the beautiful hardcover of *A Roseliep Retrospective* is
here and I am delighted to have No. 77—surely that is a most propitious
number."

Another triumph and a tribute to Elizabeth Searle Lamb came with
Roseliep's letter of September 8, 1980: "I have been keeping a secret.
Suddenly, almost impulsively, after getting your goldy September morn-
ing letter today, I have decided to break my silence, unseal my lips, and

---

98. Roseliep to Lamb, February 8, 1980.

tell you the secret. I have dedicated *Listen to Light* to you." Roseliep's dedication called his friend "First Lady of Haiku."

Typically rejoicing over the accomplishments of others even as she struggled to publish herself, Lamb wrote on September 12, 1980: "What happiness you give me, dear poet-friend—not only in this latest gift, but in the joy of sharing haiku and senryu and poetry and the trivia of the haiku world and the 'here and now' of two rather different external worlds. I am enriched and renewed in many ways." She also wrote this of the preface intended for *Listen to Light:* "It is a marvelously succinct, informative, intriguing essay. You have done an unbelievable feat in so capturing the 'essence' for the uninitiated and still giving the haiku poet also some new insights from your provocative quotations. I think it is a marvel!" The 1980 December issue of the *Delta Epsilon Sigma Bulletin* featured a comprehensive review of *Listen to Light* by Elizabeth Searle Lamb as well as three haiku of Roseliep's in honor of his long-time friend Katherine Anne Porter who died on September 18.[99]

By January 1981, Roseliep wrote of receiving the hardback copies of *Listen to Light:* "So I've had a busy weekend, inscribing and mailing. Yours went off first as I promised." Later Lamb wrote that her copy was defective, and Roseliep, of course, was horrified at her "freak copy" and mailed a replacement immediately. Publisher Dayton signed off a letter to Roseliep about the error: "Wearing the hairshirt of imperfection."

In June 1981, Roseliep wrote about his collaboration with the Reillys for *The Earth We Swing On.*[100] On August 14, 1982, he continued, "There's a big letter from Cyril Reilly too, with all kinds of questions about our book. He's given me a lot of behind-the-scenes information. Things are looking hopeful for both a hardbound and softbound, but I am afraid our material will be cut, which disappoints me. We had about 50 haiku and 50 photographs. How drastic the cut, I don't know yet." In the event, however, 51 haiku and multiple photos filled the pages when the book appeared after Roseliep's death. On the back cover the Reillys wrote, "It is an honor to have our photos paired with the haiku of our dear friend Raymond Roseliep (1917–1983), 'one of the best haiku poets in America' (W. H. Auden) and 'one of the world's outstanding practitioners of haiku' (*Yankee Magazine*)."

99. *Delta Epsilon Sigma Bulletin* 25:4. Roseliep's haiku, 113. Lamb's review, 113–16. A note following Roseliep's haiku states: "Raymond Roseliep's poems on his friend's ninetieth birthday appeared in our October issue less than a month after Katherine Anne Porter's death."

100. Roseliep, *The Earth We Swing On.* photos by Cyril A. Reilly and Renée Travis Reilly.

Lamb's haiku output was not as voluminous as Roseliep's, but she was far more active than he in writing critiques and other evaluations of haiku. One shining star was her monumental essay "A History of Western Haiku," published in 1979–80 in four consecutive issues of *Cicada*.[101] Roseliep's letter of February 28, 1982, after she had asked for his editorial input, began: "I have just finished re-reading, with great joy again, your History. Not having at my command your library or your knowledge of historical facts, I am not going to be helpful in correcting any errors you may have made.... Here are a few random things I jotted down as I reread, however, which may be of some wee help." The remainder of this lengthy letter gave Lamb numerous places for correction, reconsideration, or addition.

By September 4, 1982, Roseliep was well into planning his next collection. He wrote to Lamb: "Going through my unpublished haiku, I came upon this one: 'rabbit in the moon / in our broccoli / small buddha voices.' Rabbit in the Moon. For a book title?" He went on to tell about The Jakata, a massive collection of Buddhist tales "dealing with the 550 states of existence, as animal or human, of the Buddha prior to his final birth as Gautama. In one of these earlier incarnations, the Buddha is a rabbit in the moon." Roseliep continued,

> I would like to hope, though, that the poem will stand on its own
> without the note. Even though a reader may not know the legend,
> do you think the haiku is accessible enough, appealing enough? I
> want to think it is. Will be anxious for your reaction both to the hai-
> ku and the possible book title. Thanks pal.... Dayton is pleased to
> know I am consulting you — and I hope I won't be a bother. Dayton
> is fully convinced that we must not rely wholly upon our own judg-
> ments, and I know he is right.

Lamb's reply came swiftly. "Rabbit in the Moon is absolutely perfect! Even Bruce, who seldom comments on haiku things, said spontaneously as he was reading your letter 'A great title!' or something like that. I do think

---

101. Elizabeth Searle Lamb, "A History of Western Haiku (I)." *Cicada* 3:1 (1979), 3–9; "(II) Growth In the 1960's." *Cicada* 3:2 (1979), 3–9; "(III) Period of Expansion." *Cicada* 3:3 (1979), 3–10; "(IV)." *Cicada* 4:1 (1980). When Charles Trumbull published his version of haiku history, "The American Haiku Movement," in *Modern Haiku* 36:3 [Autumn 2005] and 37:1 [Winter–Spring 2006], he wrote, "Much of the material in this paper is a reworking and updating of the authoritative study, "A History of Western Haiku," written by Elizabeth Searle Lamb.... She declined to be named as a coauthor, but I am very much in her debt for allowing her materials to be altered and reused in this way." Trumbull dedicated his essay to her.

you've got it! I love the haiku; it seems appropriate to have the title haiku come complete with a bit of explanation. For me, certainly, the haiku does stand on its own! Yes, I believe 'our' in second line does add."[102]

Nonetheless Roseliep kept asking others for suggestions for a title other than "Rabbit in the Moon." Ty Hadman, a haiku friend, weighed in positively on another possibility Roseliep had offered: "Your title *Drink the Moon* is superb." Lamb's letter had not yet arrived before Roseliep offered her many more titles from various haiku he had written, adding "I will appreciate hearing your thoughts, preferences for title and haiku. And do you like anything here better than *Drink the Moon* or *Rabbit in the Moon*? (I still haven't heard from you on the latter.)" When Lamb's letter did arrive, Roseliep replied: "Thanks so much for commenting on *Rabbit in the Moon*. Again, you make my thinking shift…. I will eventually tell all this to Dayton, though I am sure he will want me to make the final choice."[103]

Roseliep's final choice, of course, was "Rabbit in the Moon." Much of the two friends' correspondence for the remainder of 1982 and 1983 centered on that book's preparation, publishing, and critical success. A particularly poignant letter from Roseliep on January 4, 1983, referred ironically to a dental visit: "Forgive brevity and unanswered matters. I will squeeze in a note here and there as I work away [Rabbit editing]. Must take out time for a visit to my dentist at high noon today—for a cap on an upper back tooth, drat."

Both Roseliep and Lamb endured much suffering at this time. Roseliep's was mostly mental, this time occasioned by his reading of Givner's biography of *Katherine Anne Porter*:[104]

> I've read all but 50 pages of the KAP biography. It's a revelation, to say the least. The 'affairs' she had, endless; and her disregard for the truth in life—she lived her fiction. A world of fantasy. I am so amazed that I know not what to say. Yes, there are several references to me in the book; most of my contribution, though, is buried and doesn't even show in footnotes. How strange it is to learn the life of a friend you thought you knew. All I knew, I guess, was her writing, the many things she shared with me … and above all, her love, which was pure and undefiled…. My sense of shock is my own private affair, one I will have to cope with, and resolve, as I will in time. But I have suffered, and I can tell you that, you as my dear

---

102. Lamb to Roseliep, September 9, 1982.

103. Roseliep to Lamb, September 13, 1982.

104. Joan Givner. *Katherine Anne Porter: A Life* (New York: Simon and Schuster, 1982).

and trusted friend. This is all making my Christmas preparations so
rough, and I am hoping Christmas will help me work myself into
the joy I want to carry in me and to others.[105]

Lamb did not fail Roseliep in his time of crisis. The salutation in her
letter of December 4, was "Dear, dear Raymond." She continued, "Your
30 November letter here yesterday and I am so distressed at your report
on the KAP book. I do hope that soon you can resolve your way out of
the shock of learning of the 'other KAP' and can remember only your
friend as you knew her. And take comfort in the knowledge that you
gave her a love, a relationship, which she undoubtedly got nowhere else
and which she must have desperately needed!" In a later paragraph from
Lamb about faith, Roseliep penned a red-ink remark in the margin of her
letter: "my blessed friend."[106]

On December 18, Roseliep wrote: "Christmas is falling into place,
more or less.... I am trying to keep my spirits, but am really not feeling
that well. The emotional upset has thrown brother body off; and I feel so
lacking in pep. And feel so sad, really; but am TRYING not to feel sorry
for myself. So offer some hours of pain for me—this is such good prayer;
and I know I will return to myself."

Lamb's sufferings at this time included mental anguish, but she was
suffering physically as well. She underwent serious surgery followed by
radiation. Lamb wrote on December 7, 1982: "I do know our prayers
are linked—yours for my health, mine for the ease of your heart's pain
over the KAP book." She elaborated about her health on December 18:
"I am dictating this to Carolyn [Lamb's daughter]. The surgery yesterday
was fine without any complications. The only problem now is that I feel
slightly as if they had an elephant tramping on my stomach, but in a
little while I'm going to sit up and on my feet (if I can make it) and the
doctors think I can." On December 30 she added: "I was limp as a rag
when we got home—130 miles roundtrip [to Albuquerque and back]
of driving/riding plus the emotional drain. I wept some tears driving
back ... which I needed to do, the only tears I have shed since I began to
learn of all this."

Lamb was more concerned about Roseliep's pain than he was of hers.
In an earlier letter she wrote: "You know that I am open to many avenues

of religious belief, but I am basically a Protestant Christian, and though some of my writing has been published in Catholic and 'orthodox' protestant places, I have written a lot for the 'new thought' magazines, especially *Unity*. All this as preliminary to saying I am sending the *December Daily Word* with my Christmas Chant—because I so want the whole wonderful magic of Christ to come back 'into the winter of your heart.' It will, very soon, I know."[107]

In 1983 communication between Elizabeth Searle Lamb and Raymond Roseliep became even more intense. The last year of Roseliep's life was fulfilling. He could look back on placing second in 1982 in the Henderson Awards, and he could be happy for Lamb's third place win that same year. He could also rejoice in the 1983 Henderson awards in which Bill Pauly, one of his former students, won both first place and an honorable mention. The blind judge for this contest, unknown to Roseliep, had again been Lamb, but he was aware only from Pauly himself that she had chosen his haiku. Roseliep wrote to Lamb on September 3, 1983:

> Must tell you how I found out the Henderson results. Yesterday Donna [Bauerly] left a package and a letter at my door; and in her letter she casually mentioned Bill Pauly's "Henderson awards." So I phoned Bill at the college to congratulate him, and he said he had just mailed out a copy of the page Alexis [Rotella] had sent him—it came this morning. Strange, but [Sr. Mary Thomas Eulberg] and I, who sent SASE's, did not get this page of results. I guess maybe Alexis sent them only to those who won—it is dated August 20th. Bill is terribly happy, of course, and was so appreciative of my warm and hearty congratulations.... I told Bill that SM Thomas and I thought you might enjoy having us identify our anonymous entries now that the contest is over. And he thought it would be a fun thing all right. I know if I had been the judge, I'd like to see exactly what you had entered, and what of yours I shuffled to the top of, hopefully, or just slightly lower, in the deck! Anyhow, I enclose our six entries, GRIN.

Lamb had not saved the entry cards but had already sent them on for publication in the HSA journal *Frogpond* and so couldn't share her selections. Roseliep would surely have thought himself to be the best judge of haiku and which ones truly deserved awards.

On January 1, 1983, Roseliep wrote to Lamb,

> The very first letter of the Year goes to you. Happy New Year to you and Bruce and Carolyn and Martha Mitchell [Carolyn's cat]. I hope

---

107. Lamb to Roseliep, December 4, 1982.

this finds you much, much improved. My eagle eyes watch for the mailman with a postmark from Santa Fe. Thursday, I began work on *Rabbit*, and feel good about that. It is pleasant work, and I am enjoying it; and it is helping keep my mind from what has saddened me so greatly [the Porter biography].

Roseliep also sent haiku news and descriptions of Christmas gifts he received. Four days later he wrote about the manuscript of *Rabbit in the Moon*,

Making progress. Have Spring, Summer, Autumn, on a paste-up. Winter today. Then I must study over my work to see if it adds up to a book. I think I am not going to keep the 200 as a "sacred" number; that round number was meant to keep me from going overboard. But this time, my pattern seems to dictate that I exceed the 200 by about a dozen or two dozen—can't tell till I see what winter does. But I am running out of "musts" and so won't put in a single one I consider filler.

Lamb wrote frequently of her progress from surgery and radiation

1) I am bored with having to tell so many of my illness, esp. friends, who call, not knowing, (long distance) and 2) I dislike having to pay so much attention to every twinge of body. But I am stronger each day. Trip Wed. to Albuquerque was easy and we are convinced I must go there for the 20 days of proton beam radiation.... I am praying and visualizing that the possible side effects both long and short term will not touch me.[108]

Roseliep was deeply occupied in all details of the forthcoming publication of his book. He wrote to Lamb on July 22,

It's so frustrating to work with a man in Mexico, a man in New Jersey, a company in Michigan, a mother in Indiana; and the delay of mail between here and Mexico, the awful waits. So I don't know how the book can be ready by September 9 [the month Dayton's first baby was due]. But I feel sure it will be a fall title, and will know the book is out when I have it in hand. 1,250 is a lot of copies; 500 of those hardcover.

Christmas was always an absorbing time for Roseliep, and a comment to Lamb on November 11 underscores his preoccupation that year: "My RABBIT is going to run right into my Christmas, I fear. But I'm going to love all the excitement and rush-dash of it all." By November 18, Roseliep had a sample copy in hand.

In his final letter to Lamb, Roseliep again wrote about the book and its likely reviewers. Her last letter to him, dated December 4, said, "Hardbound Rabbit on the move. That's such good news and I am so

---

108. Lamb to Roseliep, January 7, 1983.

eager to see it.... It's the end of a long day and I must stop. Stay warm and be well. Love E&B."

Quite possibly Roseliep never lived to read her note. He was busy signing copies of Rabbit in the Moon on the day of his death, December 6, 1983.

Emily Dickinson wrote a poem that began,

> The Way I read a Letter's — this —
> 'Tis first — I lock the Door —
> And push it with my fingers — next —
> For transport it be sure —
>
> And then I go the furthest off
> To counteract a knock —
> Then draw my little Letter forth
> And slowly pick the lock — [109]

Dickinson and Roseliep shared many personality traits — their penchant for a hermit-like existence as well as concise and pithy ways of expression. They could have competed with one another for daily and intense writing of poems and letters. Roseliep often walked from his Dubuque apartment in Holy Family Hall down the hill, sometimes more than once a day, to post his letters. We know that Dickinson often delivered letters personally, especially to her brother Austin's wife Susan who was, perhaps, Emily's greatest love. As the priest-poet did, Emily Dickinson might well have uttered the words, "I do not want to lose touch with you ever. Not ever."

109. Emily Dickinson, Poem 636. *The Poems of Emily Dickinson*, edited by Thomas H. Johnson. Cambridge, Mass.: The Belknap Press of Harvard University Press, Copyright © 1951,

Epilogue: Sobi-Shi

I am not always sure of this "other man of the rose"[1]

— Elizabeth Searle Lamb

Just who was Sobi-Shi? After many years of correspondence with Raymond Roseliep, Elizabeth Searle Lamb expressed the conundrum of Sobi-Shi. This response, quoted above, from her in 1978 after she first encountered his *haigō*—and never answered specifically by Father Ray—might have been the central question of his own life: who am I?

Many philosophers and poets have asked this question, perhaps none better than the Irish writer John O'Donohue, who writes in *Anam Cara* that, to take one example, in performing a play an actor is able to absorb a character entirely such that the character fully inhabits him. The actor's body houses and expresses that character's voice, mind, and action. Moreover, O'Donohue maintains, this essence of a thing or its soul has no fixed form or shape, but rather has its unique "fluency and energy" that that cannot be strictly contained.[2]

Roseliep was always well aware of his own inner fluidity. His 1957 poem "The Linen Bands" was rife with Roseliep's equation of himself with such famous "others" as the apostles James or Paul, King David, or "a man struck dumb." That poem from 1957 also addressed the growth of his angst over identity. Central lines evoked the ever-present question of his passion:

> or why, when sometimes touching other flesh
> they want to yield: and yet they do not break....

---

1. Elizabeth Searle Lamb to Raymond Roseliep, November 7, 1978.
2. John O'Donohue, *Anam Cara* (New York: HarperCollins, 1997), 45, 51.

261

and mind regirds the will with strips of white
that have the burning quality of snow."[3]

The Linen Bands contains narrative poems that use a variety of standard poetic forms and techniques such as syllabic verse. Roseliep often
recalled someone's childhood memories, most probably a variant of
his own, especially in those poems in which he was grappling with the
thought that "roots lead down and burn,"[4] or that "Childhood is over,
and we shove/ ourselves to manhood, linking arm with those/ who feign
a forward motion."[5] Throughout all of his writings, Roseliep was the
shapeshifter, assuming many roles, often through memory and recollection, and the reader seeking a particular referent for the "I" was kept off
balance.

Seeking the self through the past can be tricky, however, even for the
self-aware Roseliep. He might have remembered the words of Heraclitus:
"No man ever steps in the same river twice, for it's not the same river and
he's not the same man."[6]

When in the late 1970s Roseliep began searching for a *haigō*—in
order to give a specific name to one of his personae, *haijin*—he turned
to his Japanese friend Nobuo Hirasawa, who proposed "Sobi-Shi" (*see*
pp. 115–16). The first poems by Sobi-Shi to appear in print were those
in 1978 among the "50 Haiku" that *Uzzano* published in 1978 (*see* the
text and discussionon page 145), later appearing separately as *A Day
in the Life of Sobi-Shi*. A note accompanying that collection gave more
information about the *haigō*:

> [Hirasawa and Roseliep] both thought it would be meaningful if
> they could come up with a name for this other-self based upon Ray's
> Germanic surname. (Roseliep originally as Roselieb: "rose/ love," or
> "lover of the rose.").... Now christened, Sobi-Shi is a "rose man of
> art," or "a man of art who loves the rose."[7]

Sobi-Shi was precisely "this other man" who created a kind of
uneasiness in Elizabeth Lamb. That same uneasiness for Sobi-Shi or other

---

3. Raymond Roseliep, "The Linen Bands," *The Linen Bands* (Westminster, Md.: The Newman
Press, 1961), 3–5, lines 55–56 and 63–64. "Strips of white" refers to the ordination ritual in which
at one point in the ceremony the man to be ordained has his hands bound with cloth.

4. Roseliep, "Where Roots Tangle," *The Linen Bands*, 31.

5. Roseliep, "Some Men a Forward Motion Love," *The Linen Bands*, 38.

6. Found online at http://www.iep.utm.edu/heraclit/.

7. *Uzzano* 9/10 (1978), 3.

personae of Roseliep's occasioned more than one written inquiry and/ or visit from his priestly superiors concerned about this often erotic and explicit first-person narrator.

Roseliep usually sidestepped questions as to just who he was, particularly in his poetic expressions. He often used the concept of a muse for his love attentions, or the acceptable idea that he was entering into the persona of an ardent adolescent. Sometimes he clearly adopted his own youth or imaginative variants for such love adventures. Roseliep was not particularly happy with the often repeated characterization "priest-poet." He did not want his photograph — certainly not one showing him in his clerical cassock and white collar — to appear on the jackets of his books as had been done with *The Linen Bands*. The blurb in *A Roseliep Retrospective* still identified him as "Father Raymond Roseliep," but all mentions of him in *Listen to Light* omitted the clerical references; he was "Raymond Roseliep," "Ray Roseliep," or "Roseliep."

He probably concurred with O'Donohue's philosophy of self: "Individuality is never simple or one-dimensional. Often it seems as if there is a crowd within the individual heart.... At the deepest level of the human heart, there is no simple, singular self. Deep within, there is a gallery of different selves."[8] Long before he named one of his selves Sobi-Shi, Roseliep would have acknowledged and accepted this inner "gallery." He was used to adopting a variety of personae even in his student days — whether in an acting role or the role of an older-but-not-necessarily-wiser poet expressing sentimental views of religious posturing.[9]

Roseliep, the struggling grown-up, evolved into a man of deep passion. His passion and fierce inner battle, denoted by his favorite color, red, was early shown in his 1963 poem "My Mother Bought Me Red Things," published in 1963:

My Mother Bought Me Red Things

My mother bought me red things, innocently enough:
an elegiac bear with sunset eyes that could blink
on and off at button touch, a small filling station
having "Danger / Inflammable" printed on each tank,
a fire engine to pedal with my bare summer feet,

---

8. O'Donohue, 113–14.

9. *See* Chapter Two for one of Roseliep's poems written while he was in high school.

a wagon the copy of our maple in autumn,
then a bicycle matching the lunch bucket apple;
and later, some cuff links of ruby glass echoing
the soft thud I heard (shamefully astir) in my blood.

Now I am older, my mother is gone. I have drawn
the drapery across the window to stop her hand
from heaping coals on my bed. Maybe tonight I can
clamber past boyhood and the growing years to meet these
abusive tears, violent as the red
velvet shroud she appointed to hang over my head.[10]

The young Roseliep who wrote "My Mother Bought Me Red Things"
would have recognized the future Sobi-Shi. The poem is red throughout—from a bear's eyes, to filling station labels, to a pedal car, to an
autumn maple tree, to a wagon, to a bicycle, to a lunch-bucket apple,
to ruby cuff links—all these while his mother was still alive to gift him
"innocently enough" with red. But even after her death, Roseliep credited
his mother with an ability to "heap coals on his bed" and appoint a "red
velvet shroud" to hang over his head.

What should readers learn from this autobiographical, complex, and
ambiguous poem? One who has read a good deal of Roseliep's early work
would know that he was, often uneasily, a passionate red-boy becoming
a red-man. In a wide variety of poems, haiku included, Roseliep gave us
a pastiche of his passion couched in red: mulberry skies, wine, tanagers,
burgundy carpets, clover, poppies, and plums—every volume of Roseliep's
poetry paid tribute in shades of red to the vitality and the anguish of his
loving.

> unable
> to get hibiscus red
> the artist eats the flower[11]

A double quatrain from *Sun in His Belly* was aptly titled "Variation
on a Theme" (*see* page 150). It reads: "house aflame/house aflame/
rembrandt on the wall/tomcat in the hall/what to save/what to save/oil
fur   fire/I chose a lyre" Roseliep was this "house aflame," but he told

10. Roseliep, "My Mother Bought Me Red Things," *The Small Rain* (1963) 14.

11. Roseliep, *Step on the Rain* (1977), 27. This haiku first appeared in *Light Footsteps* (1976).

the reader in this simple poem how he survived and what he saved: he *knew* the extent and the incredible gift of his passion; irony and wit and experiential wisdom gave him the way through the flame—the "lyre" of song, poetry. The double entendre of "lyre/liar" is entirely fitting for any poet who can "tell all the truth but tell it slant."

From the youthful passion of the red-boy who discovered "roots lead down and burn"[12] to one of his darkest musings as the mature red-man, who as an almost terrified "Professor Nocturnal" cried out:

> Near bat-time, to the safe indoors,
> where lamb chops warm,
> he hurries from his boyhood spectres
> of alarm ...
>
> caught at last
> in a web of wing,
> bit, sucked
> by a blacker Thing?[13]

And, finally, to one of the very last unpublished haiku, found on the table by his bedside:

> of berry
> nip
> you dissolve[14]

Sobi-Shi should never have been a surprise for readers. He was coming for years, waiting for a specific name. What one might always question would be Roseliep's own stance about his passion and the real life struggles it cost him, internally and externally.

In his essay "The Love Haiku of Raymond Roseliep"[15] Randy M. Brooks set out "to examine how Roseliep explored the possibilities of writing love haiku, employing that same spirit of the maker or creator."[16]

---

12. Roseliep, "Where Roots Tangle," *The Linen Bands*, 31.

13. Roseliep, *The Linen Bands*, 17–18, lines 13–16 and 45–48.

14. Roseliep, last page of his final notebook by his bedside, labeled: "Raymond Roseliep 30 October 1983 to +"

15. Randy Brooks, "The Love Poetry of Raymond Roseliep," *Modern Haiku* 40:3 (Autumn 2009), 23–38.

16. Brooks refers to his earlier essay, "A Spiritual Quest Through the Haiku of Raymond

Brooks carefully crafts his argument: "In this exploration of Roseliep's love haiku, I will present the haiku not as biographical instances but as creations of a talented literary artist — a haiku poet capable of remembering feelings of attraction, imagining young lovers or newlyweds, and appreciating the long-lasting love of an old couple sitting on the porch with nothing to say."

Brooks employed Roseliep's own stance toward the first-person pronoun from the essay "This Haiku of Ours" in which he averred, "The first-person singular — in spite of constant war against it by our more conservative haiku writers and editors — is prevalent in the work of the best Japanese artists. I shudder to think of Issa without the very personal self in those whimsies of his."[17] Roseliep went on to "favor the perpendicular pronoun when we can somehow universalize the experience."

Distance, probably for a variety of reasons, was safely called to order by both Roseliep and Brooks. What might be questioned is the cost of such distancing for both poet and critic. Surely, a reader of Roseliep's erotic haiku, aware that he was an anointed priest, might need the cover of *agape* or the universal experience. How else to take in:

> waiting for my love.
> the incurled
> apple bud[18]

Yes, one could hold up the fig leaf of the "apple bud," but apple was quite lost in the suggested readiness of the female lover. Roseliep intended the full stop after the first line, using an unusual period for lingering. Perhaps the waiting lover needed a breath of fresh air from a real or imagined orchard.

One might also take notice of many haiku that Brooks quoted from *Sailing Bones*, also published in 1978, the year Sobi-Shi first appeared in print. Clearly, Roseliep had gone much deeper into causing his readers to question the speaker, just as Elizabeth Searle Lamb had done. Sobi-Shi appeared by name in fifteen of the haiku in *Sailing Bones*. Most were highly erotic.

Roseliep," *Bottle Rockets* 9:3 (February 2008), 74–86, in which he explored the spiritual basis of Roseliep's haiku poetics.

17. *Bonsai* 1:3 (July 1976), 13.

18. Roseliep, *Sailing Bones* (1978), 8.

One triptych from *Sailing Bones* that was not discussed in Brooks's essay celebrated Sobi-Shi and could certainly deepen our wonder:

NIGHT PIECE

i

bumping in the dusk
    Sobi-Shi promises
    no power blackout

ii

taking flame
from Sobi-Shi's candle
    the beauty sighs

iii

from Beauty's bedroom
    Sobi-Shi brings the moon
back to his own[19]

Surely, we know the place, we know the act, we know the lasting effect when Sobi-Shi returned to his own bedroom.

Brooks also gave one plenty to ponder in culling love poetry from six of Roseliep's texts and quoting from "50 Haiku"—fifty haiku, including a triptych titled "after dusk." Brooks crafted his belief in the necessary but poetic distancing, coming to a full crescendo in his ending:

> [Roseliep] writes erotic haiku as natural celebrations of the power of love to bond lovers intimately together. His haiku celebrate soul mates who find life-long companionship and the accompanying joys of sharing a lifetime of love. Throughout his literary creations and with all of his personae and many haiku narrators, Roseliep celebrated the Creator and His abundance of love. The spark of creativity—compassion and love—shines through as a celebratory gift of light from God in Raymond Roseliep's love haiku."[20]

Readers cannot really quarrel with Brooks's argument. Many critics have also believed in such distancing. Readers and critics confronting "masks" in writing often believe in the same necessary distancing evoking personae, a muse or the universal "I."

---

19. Roseliep, *Sailing Bones*, 14.
20. Brooks, "Love Haiku," 9.

But what if you don't believe? What if your own beliefs are close to a Celtic oneness, "not to be caged within any fixed form?" What if Roseliep, despite his avowals of a safe distance, agreed with O'Donohue's philosophy: "At the deepest level of the human heart, there is no simple, singular self. Deep within, there is a gallery of different selves."[21] One's reading, then, of Roseliep's entire oeuvre would be simultaneously simpler and more difficult. One would no longer be torn between priest and poet. There would just be Roseliep. But you would need to grapple with his deep passions and, perhaps, his choice of haiku as his sole form of expression in his later years. You might wonder, as did Thomas Reiter:

> It's sensible to say that "erotic" haiku celebrate love, but to have spent so much time doing that. I have a notion — I claim no profundity — that writing of "erotic" love in haiku not only exploits the native suggestiveness of the form but also allows Raymond Roseliep to "automatically" hold back from the full exposure of sexuality that writing in a narrative form might have encouraged. Sparks and fireflies rather than conflagration; touch and go."[22]

We know that Roseliep, despite his own warning,

> Soul, I said, it is
> unworthy to spread
> your disturbance
> round[23]

wrote deeply and disturbingly in longer poems about the effect of his nervous illness and his hospital stay. The poems "Calico June," "Field Cricket," "In Extremis," "At My Mother's Grave," "In the Dry Light," "Walk in Woods," and "On His Return" appeared in an unpublished manuscript titled "Tip the Earth," but could also be read in "A Roseliep Anthology" in *A Roseliep Retrospective*, 86–99.

Cogent and powerful lines from some of those longer poems can make readers wonder about Roseliep's eventual choice to write almost solely in the haiku form:

> Now,
> she [his Calico cat] is studying my face.

21. O'Donohue, 113–14.

22. Thomas Reiter e-mail, April 3, 2013.

23. Raymond Roseliep, "Travel," *Sun in His Belly* (1977), 46.

What can she unearth
beyond the comfortable mask?
The parade of pain's inside
catacombs of brain,
and I'll not let her tangle
in the daisychain of happenings,
where dream is mixed up
with real, weather is weighty,
and the Slough of Despond
is a strange little flicker
of candle bidding the traveler in.

Roseliep opened the next stanza with this observation: "I'm heavy company for myself/ sometimes."[24]

In "Field Cricket," Roseliep mused: "Pocket companion, darkheaded/ shadow of my boyhood." He ended with this regret: "And I keep shedding my body/ forever saying goodbye/ to the departing boy." In the powerful poem "Extremis," remembering the anointing of Extreme Unction for his mother at her death, he also recalled, perhaps, the red gifts from his mother: "On the nostrils (mother, breathe/ loudly) this ancient olive/ sweetening flesh from my flesh/ drives like an exquisite wave." In "At My Mother's Grave," Roseliep willed: "I give short shrift/ to the boy in me/ asking how do I cope with a ghost." Then, in "In the Dry Light" he regretted: "A boy's made man too soon" and "a priest hangs/ on the edge of nothing/ with his fingers buttered." In "Walk in Woods" he promised to "check a cavern of self/ unbothered by existence."

Emerging from his year of recovery in a hospital, Roseliep proclaimed in "On His Return":

Holy ghost of a moth
ricochets over head,
my sleeper's breath gone,
doors opening and shutting
in psyche's island.
Heaven works of itself.

---

24. Roseliep, "Calico June," David Dayton, ed., *A Roseliep Retrospective* (1980), 87.

Tho here's a green hand,
sir death,
on your blueprint.
Flesh decks my bones,
I tip the earth.[25]

What followed these soul-wrenching poems in that anthology was a chronology of sorts from his best published haiku and a few in forthcoming all-haiku texts. One haiku echoed his old theme and longing:

child voice calling
    my shadow grows
      heavier[26]

Readers might well ask, "What if Roseliep, in his later years, had not almost totally abandoned all forms except haiku, banishing or walling out other poetic form and voices from that inner crowd he housed within?" Are these words of a former student and well-published poet, prophetic? After Dennis Schmitz read some unpublished work in "Tip the Earth," he believed the longer poems in that manuscript were less continuous than earlier long poems, more broken. Schmitz also believed that haiku became a kind of retreat for Roseliep when he lived at Holy Family Hall. "There, and through haiku, he staked out a territory for himself—a safe haven—and, for haiku, in a small enough duration."[27]

Was Sobi-Shi the watchful guardian of that safe haven? Did Roseliep/Sobi-Shi, as Robert Frost was said to do, walk up to the chasm, look over and walk away? Or in Louise Bogan's words concerning Frost: "He stopped exploring the frightening outside—and the heights and depths come into his later work only in a repressed, and therefore in a negative and melancholy, way."[28]

No matter how often you plumb the depths of the poet Roseliep, you will always have to wrestle with his chosen alter ego, Sobi-Shi. If you accept that there is a oneness of his true identity, from boyhood until his

25. "On His Return," *A Roseliep Retrospective*, 97–99.

26. Roseliep, "New Haiku: 'As the Swift Seasons Roll,'" *A Roseliep Retrospective*, 108. The haiku also appeared in *The Earth We Swing On* (1984), 18.

27. Interview with Dennis Schmitz, September 9, 2007.

28. Louise Bogan, *Achievement in American Poetry, 1900–1950* (Chicago: H. Regnery Co., Gateway Editions, Inc. 1951), 47.

last goodbye in *Rabbit in the Moon,* you may have a long journey of reading or rereading and pondering ahead.

> before the Star was lit
> there was a light   that left
>   singing[29]

> leaving you—
> lips at the winter
> pump[30]

29. Elizabeth Searle Lamb, "In Memoriam, Raymond Roseliep," *Wind Chimes* 12 (1984), 1.

30. Donna Bauerly, "In Memoriam, Raymond Roseliep," *Wind Chimes* 12 (1984), 1.

A Roseliep Bibliography

1. Works by Raymond Roseliep

Books and chapbooks

Roseliep, Raymond. *A Beautiful Woman Moves with Grace.* Derry, Pa.: Rook Press, 1976. Includes 2 haiku-like sequences, "Winter Wedding" and "Variations on a Theme." The poem "Bloodroot" discussed in our text.

———. *A Day in the Life of Sobi-Shi.* Ruffsdale, Pa.: Rook Press, 1978. Includes 2 haiku. "Night Piece" discussed in text.

———. *Dusk and Ocean.* No place [Derry, Pa.]: Rook Society, 1977.

———. *The Earth We Swing On: Haiku.* Minneapolis. Minn.: Winston Press, 1984. 52 haiku, 16 discussed in text.

———. *Firefly in My Eyecup.* West Lafayette, Ind.: High/Coo Press, 1979. 16 haiku, one discussed in text.

———. *Flute Over Walden: Thoreauhaiku.* West Lafayette, Ind.: Vagrom Chap Books/Sparrow Press, 1976. 61 haiku; 9 discussed in text.

———. *Light Footsteps: Haiku.* La Crosse, Wis.: Juniper Press, 1976; 2nd ed., 1978. 7 haiku, one discussed in text.

———. *The Linen Bands.* Westminster, Md.: The Newman Press, 1961. Preface by John Logan. 50 longer poems, including the following discussed in text: "The Linen Bands," 3–5 (first published in *The Commonweal,* January 17, 1958); "A Short Letter to Dr. Johnson," 6; "No Laughing Matter," 7; "Picasso's 'Boy with a Pipe,'" 9; "From His Study Window," 10; "Satire of Circumstance," 21; "Where Roots Tangle," 31; "Some Men a Forward Motion Love," 38; "The Yellow Christ," 50; "For a Seventy Fifth Birthday," 58; "The Day My Father Died," 59; "Ragman," 60; "The Scissors Grinder," 61.

———. *Listen to Light: Haiku.* Ithaca, N.Y.: Alembic Press, 1980. 188 haiku and 9 3-haiku/stanza sequences: "After Dusk," "Firefly," "Intimations of Immortality," "From Recollections of Early Sky Gazing, "'Mu' Triptych: A Primary Color," "Pool," "Seascape," "Sobi-Shi Writes His Epitaph," and "Toward Evening." 28 haiku (some in sequences) discussed in text.

———. *Love Makes the Air Light.* New York: W. W. Norton & Co., 1965. Includes 87 longer poems, including these discussed in text: "My Father's Trunk," 15–16; "May Song," 17; "English Sonnet," 20; "Italian Sonnet," 21; "Red Hair," 22; "To His Dark Lady," 24.; "Platonic Lover," 27; "Invitation to a Promontory Over the Mississippi," 28; "When Lutes Be Old," 32; The Barbara poems: "For Barbara, by Mistletoe," 34; "Note, with Glove," 35–36; "The Singing Lesson," 37, "First Communion," 38; and "For Barbara, Eight," 39; Haiku: "Priest to Inquirer," 41. At least

273

100 haiku are included in *Love Makes the Air Light* as well as a few other sequences of 4-line haiku-like poems.

————. *Rabbit in the Moon: Haiku.* Plainfield, Ind.: Alembic Press, 1983. 221 haiku and 2 3-haiku/stanza sequences: "Firefly" and "Wild Geese." 26 haiku discussed in text.

————. *Sailing Bones: Haiku.* Ruffsdale, Pa.: Rook Press, 1978. 131 haiku and the 3-haiku/stanza sequence "The Morning-Glory." One triptych, 2 other haiku discussed in text.

————. *Sky in My Legs.* La Crosse, Wis.: Juniper Press, 1979. 38 haiku and the 3-haiku/stanza poem "Mise en Scène." One haiku discussed in text.

————. *The Small Rain: New Poems.* Westminster, Md.: Newman Press, 1963. 56 longer poems, 6 of them looking like haiku sequences and 6 4-line linked stanzas looking like haiku sequences. The following are discussed in text: "The Vendor," 3–4; "Ways of My Exile," 10 "My Mother Bought Me Red Things," 14; "Priest's Diary: Two Entries," 36; "Hospital Visit," 49; "The Hunter," 65; "Leaving Through July, 66; "Elegy for Edward," 68; "No Horn in August," 72; "This Singular Moment," 73.

————. *Step on the Rain: Haiku.* Derry, Pa.: Rook Press, 1977. 120 haiku, 5 discussed in text.

————. *The Still Point: Haiku of "Mu."* Menomonie, Wis.: Uzzano, 1980. 54 haiku, 13 discussed in text.

————. *Sun in His Belly.* West Lafayette, Ind.: High/Coo Press, 1977. 27 haiku and concrete poems, 2 haiku discussed in text. Also includes these longer poems discussed in text: "Travel," 46, and "Variation on a Theme," 27.

————. *Swish of Cow Tail.* Amherst, Mass.: Swamp Press, 1982. 7 haiku, 4 discussed in text.

————. "Tip the Earth." Uncollected poems, unpublished manuscript. 2 poems discussed in text: "Calico June," 86–87 and "Walk in Woods," 95–96.

————. *Wake to the Bell: A Garland of Christmas Poems.* Derry, Pa.: Rook Press, 1977.

————. *Walk in Love.* La Crosse, Wis.: Juniper Press, 1976. Includes one haiku. 2 longer poems discussed in text: "Lorenzo's Bridge," and "Re-entry."

Broadsheets and ephemera

Roseliep, Raymond. *Bard Cards (1–8).* Derry, Pa.: Rook Press, 1976. Poemcards.

————. *The Morning-Glory.* New York: Poetry in Public Places, ©1978 by Yankee magazine. Broadsheet.

————. *Only the Attentive, People Who Care, Sharing Stillness,* and *Tonight,* Poemcards made by Sr. Iva Halbur, OSF. Dubuque, Iowa: The Prefest I, no date.

————. "Permanent Record and Memorandum." A notebook in which Roseliep kept odd information such as remembered lists of his grade school graduation class or "The Cathedral Gang."

Award-winning poems and haiku

Loras College verse and essay contest, 1939:

"Jonathan" [poem] and "Poet and Critic" [essay] *The Lorian* 15 (May 19, 1939), 1 and 5. First Place awards.

Yankee Award for best-in-year: 1970 "Christmas," 1981 "Birthday Poem for Peggy," and 1982 "Low Tide."

Bonsai Quarterly Award:

"fish / swallowing / the moon." *Bonsai* 1:4 (1976), 11.

"in the window." *Bonsai* 1:2 (1976), 14.

"Boy in a red cap." *Bonsai* 1:3 (1976), 21.

Modern Haiku Special Mention:

"by the autumn hill." *Modern Haiku* 8:1 (February 1977), 5.

"the black hen." *Modern Haiku* 8:2 (May 1977), 5.

"night window." *Modern Haiku* 13:1 (Winter–Spring 1982), 6.

"my sins told," *Modern Haiku* 14:3 (Autumn 1983), 4.

Modern Haiku Kay Titus Mormino Award:

7 individual haiku and 2 haiku sequences, "Wild Geese" and "Winter Set." *Modern Haiku* 14:2 (Summer 1983), 6–8.

Harold G. Henderson Award for Best Unpublished Haiku (Haiku Society of America)

"reaching into sky." First Place (tie), 1977; published among "50 Haiku by Raymond Roseliep," *Uzzano* 9/10 (spring–summer 1978).

"never expecting." Honorable Mention, 1979. *HSA Frogpond* 2:3–4 (November 1979), 5.

"horizon." First Place, 1982. *Frogpond* 5:3 (1982), 26.

Cicada Award:

10 haiku and 3 3-haiku/stanza poems. Presented in Eric Amann, "In Praise of Roseliep" in the special section of *Cicada* (Toronto) 4:3 (1980).

Yuki Teikei Haiku Society Contest:

"campfire extinguished." First Place, 1980. Published in *Listen to Light* (1980), 62.

Hawai'i Education Association Annual Contest:

"No wave today." First Place, Season Word Section, 1981. Published in Darold D. Braida, comp. *Na Pua'oli puke'ekolu: The Anthology of Hawaii Education Association Haiku Award Winners, 1981–83.* 1983.

Periodicals in which Roseliep's work was published
Including titles of works mentioned in text

Alembic (supplement to *The Cornell Daily Sun*) 7 (December 4, 1980): "From a December Daybook" 7-haiku sequence; "Butcher, Baker, Candlestick Maker," 4-haiku sequence; and "EROS / Four Seasons," a 4-haiku sequence.

America.

Annals of Iowa.

Approach.

Art Journal.

The American Ecclesiastical Review.

The Antigonish Review (Canada).

Arts in Society (University of Wisconsin) 4:3 (Fall–Winter 1967), 526: 1 poem; 5:3 (Fall–Winter 1968), 478–84: "Troll" poems 11:2 (Summer/Fall 1974), 338; "Walden Prints," 3 haiku; 12:1 (Spring–Summer 1975), 133–34: review of William Pillin's poetry.

August Derleth Society Newsletter.

The Beloit Poetry Journal.

Bits.

Blackfriars (Cambridge, England).

Blue Buildings.

The Blue Canary.

Blue Cloud Quarterly.

The Blue Hotel.

Blue Unicorn 1:2 (1977), 16: "Mise en Scène," 3-haiku sequence.

Bonsai 1:1 (1976)–2:24 (1978). 22 haiku, including 4 in the essay "This Haiku of Ours" in 1:3 (July 19, 1976): "Three for Anthony," haiku sequence in 1:2 (April 19, 1976), 11–22.

Brussels Sprout 2:4 (1982)–3:1 (1983): 61 haiku, including 9 in David Andrews's review of *Listen to Light*, 3:2 (June 1981); 11 in the sequence "Whisper Song," 2:3 (1982); and 16 in "Rose Anthology," 2:4 (1982); and 6 in 3:1 (1983).

The Carolina Quarterly.

Catfancy.

The Catholic Worker.

The Catholic World, November 1969, 62–63: "O Western Wind: A Sheaf of Haiku," 8 haiku with illustrations by Martin Charlot.

The Cee-Ay. "The lily, pure and white." Poet's Corner, 11:9 (March 10, 1934), 18.

Charlatan.

Chicago Review.

Chicory. 7 haiku and the 3-haiku/stanza sequence "Night Piece," 1 (1978), 16.

Choice.

The Christian Century.

Cicada (Toronto). 120 haiku in issues 1:1 (1977)–5:4 (1981).

College English.

The Colorado Quarterly.

The Commonweal, January 17, 1958. "The Linen Bands."

Counter /Measures.

The Critic.

Delta Epsilon Sigma Bulletin (renamed *Delta Epsilon Sigma Journal* in 1982). Roseliep poems included in this biography are: "Spider" and "Flight" 7:3 (October 1962); his haiku include: "A Scale of Haiku," 9:4 (December 1964); "For Her Biography" [Katherine Anne Porter] and "Clown," 24:1 (March 1979), 14–15; "For Her Ninetieth Birthday," 5 haiku sequences for Katherine Anne Porter, 25: 3 (October 1980), 68–70; haiku sequence "The Eighteen of September (Katherine Anne Porter: 1890–1980)," 25:4 (December 1980).

Elizabeth.

Encore.

The Dubliner (Ireland).

The Echo.

The English Journal.

Esquire. One haiku criticizing a W. H. Auden article: "Meeting the moon, eyes / speak the first words and nothing/ beyond double O." 22:3 (September 1969), 8. 2 4-line haiku reacting to a previous article about Auden, 23:4 (April 1970), 24.

Fragments.

Frogpond (initially *HSA Frogpond*) 1:1 (February 1978)–15:2 (Autumn–Winter 1992): 170 haiku, including those reprinted in essays and reviews and including the following sequences: "Waking," 4:3 (1981), 4; "On the Green Earth," 4:4 (1981), 10; "Woodsman," 5:1 (1982), 26; "Cityscape," 5:1 (1982), 27; "Housewife," 6:2 (1983), 35; "Greentime to White," 6:3 (1983), 24; "Firefly Sequence," 7:1 (1984), 28; "A Collection of Haiku by Raymond Roseliep" (34 haiku), 7:1 (1984), 43–48.

Gallery Series.

The Georgia Review.
The Gorey Detail (Ireland).
Gravida.
Green Revolution.
Green's Magazine.
Guts & Grace.
Hai Hakkosho (Japan).
Haiku Byways (England).
Haiku Journal.
Haiku Magazine (Toronto). 4 haiku.
Haiku Spotlight (Japan).
The Hartford Courant.
Hartwick Review.
Hawk & Whippoorwill.
Hawk & Whippoorwill Recalled.
High/Coo. 51 haiku in issues 1:2 (September 1976) through 6:24 (May 1982), including the sequence "Vines" in issue 2:7 (February 1978).
The Hollins Critic.
The Honolulu Advertiser.
Images.
The Indian P.E.N. (Bombay, India).
The Journal of Freshwater.
John Berryman Studies.
The Lake Superior Review.
Landfall (New Zealand).
The Literary Review. One haiku titled "Roethke," 9:4 (Summer 1966), 550. 5 longer poems, 547–50.
The Lorian 15 (May 19, 1939), 1 and 5. "Jonathan" [poem] and "Poet and Critic. Lionel Johnson, Catholic Poet" [essay]. Both won first place awards in the verse and essay contests.
Manhattan Review.
The Massachusetts Review.
Michigan's Voices.
Midwest Poetry Review.
Milkweed Chronicle.
The Minnesota Review.
Modern Age, Spring 1958. "Where Roots Tangle."
Modern Haiku. 261 haiku in issues 1:2 (Spring 1970) through 24:1 (Winter–Spring 1993), including those reprinted in reviews and essays and the following sequences: "The T'ang Dynasty," 12:2 (Summer 1981), 64, and "Four Poems," 12:3 (Autumn 1981), 43.
Monks Pond.
Muse-Pie.
Mutiny.
The Nation. 10 poems, 1964–1969. 4 poems in the May 1965 issue, 538. One 4-line haiku-like sequence titled "Wheels," October 26, 1964, 283.
New Catholic World.
The New Jersey Poetry.
New Letters.
The New Orleans Poetry Journal.

The New Salt Creek Reader.
New World Haiku.
The New York Times.
The New York Herald Tribune.
North Country Anvil.
Northeast.
Outch (Japan).
Pikestaff Review.
Pikestaff Forum.
Pilgrimage.
Poet (India).
Poetry. 16 poems, including "Where Roots Tangle," February 1960; 14 haiku; and 4
    reviews by Roseliep of a varying number of poetry texts in each review. One adver-
    tisement for *Listen to Light* on the back cover of 127:2 (1980). 13 issues ranging
    from 1960 to 1980.
"Poetry in Public Places." "The Morning-Glory" (3-haiku sequence), poems selected for
    display on New York City buses, 1980.
Poetry Nippon (Japan).
Poetry Northwest.
Poetry Now.
Poetry Venture.
Portals.
Prairie Schooner.
Ramparts.
River Quarterly.
Shaman.
Shenandoah. 11 poems, 5 haiku plus a 4-stanza haiku sequence, 19:2 (Winter 1968) to
    26:4 (Summer 1975).
Slow Loris Reader.
South Dakota Review.
The Southborough Villager.
Sparrow.
Spectrum: The Richmond Tri-Annual Review.
The Spoon.
Still (U.K.). 9 haiku reprinted in volumes 1 (1997) through 3 (1999).
Studia Mystica. "Love Poem," 2:3 (fall 1979), 21.
The Tablet (London).
Third Coast Archives.
Thoreau Journal Quarterly 5:4 (October 1973), 13–14. 16 "Thoreauhaiku."
The University of Kansas City Review.
Time.
Transatlantic Review.
Tribune Magazine.
Tweed (Australia).
Unaka Range.
Uzzano. "50 Haiku." Issues 9 and 10 (Spring–Summer, 1978), 3–13. Review by Bill
    Pauly of *Step on the Rain*, 14.
The Waterloo Review (Canada).

Voyages.
West Hills Review: A Walt Whitman Journal.
Wind Chimes. 145 haiku in issues 1 (1981) through 15 (1985).
The Windless Orchard.
The Wormwood Review.
Wind Magazine.
World.
Yankee. 59 haiku in 12 sequences.
Yukuharu (Japan).

Anthologies and critical works
containing individual poems and haiku of Roseliep's

Aikins, Suezan, ed. *Cicada: A Selection from Volume 2, Nos. 1 & 2.* Haiku Canada, 1978. One haiku.

Banwarth, Francine, comp. *Plugging in the Moon.* No place [Dubuque, Iowa]: self-published, 2008. One haiku.

Briley, Alice, ed. *Encore! Encore!: A Selection of Poetry from Encore, a Quarterly of Verse and Poetic Arts.* Corry, Pa.: Allegheny Press, 1976.

Brooks, Randy M., and Lee Gurga, ed. *Midwest Haiku Anthology.* Decatur, Ill: High/Coo Press, 1992. 4 haiku.

Brunini, John Gilland, ed. *Invitation to the City: Selected Poems, 1954–1959.* New York: Catholic Poetry Society of America, 1960.

———. *Sealed Unto the Day: Selected Poems from Spirit, A Magazine of Poetry, 1949–1954.* New York: Catholic Poetry Society of America, 1955.

Burden, Jean, ed. *A Celebration of Cats.* New York: Paul S. Eriksson, Inc., 1974; paperback, New York: Popular Library, 1976.

Burns, Allan, selector. "The Haiku Capital of the Midwest." *Montage* [Web] (week of August 9, 2009). http://thehaikufoundation.org/montage/HaikuCapitalMidwest2009_08_09.pdf; and Allan Burns, ed. "The Haiku Capital of the Midwest," Gallery Thirty-Three, August 7–13." *Montage: The Book.* Winchester, Va.: The Haiku Foundation, 2010. 7 haiku.

Clausen, Tom, selector. Cornell University Mann Library's Daily Haiku [Web]. http://haiku.mannlib.cornell.edu/category/author/raymond-roseliep/. 31 haiku, one posted each day during August 2006.

Derleth, August, ed. *Fire and Sleet and Candlelight.* Sauk City, Wis.: Arkham House, 1961.

Drevniok, Betty, ed. *Aware—A Haiku Primer.* Bellingham, Wash.: Portals Publications, 1981.

Gildner, Gary, and Judith Gildner, ed. *Out of This World: Poems from the Hawkeye State.* Ames: Iowa State University Press, 1975.

Glikes, Erwin A., and Paul Schwaber, ed. *Of Poetry and Power: Poems Occasioned by the Presidency and by the Death of John F. Kennedy.* New York: Basic Books, 1964.

Gregory, Robin, ed. *Ipso Facto: An International Poetry Society Anthology.* Derbyshire, England: Hub Publications Ltd., 1975.

Hardy, Jackie, ed. *Haiku: Poetry Ancient & Modern.* London: MQ Publications, 2002; Rutland, Vt., and Tokyo: Charles E. Tuttle, 2002, 82. Also French and German editions. One haiku.

Harris, Marguerite, ed. *A Tumult for John Berryman.* San Francisco: Dryad Press, 1976.

———. *Emily Dickinson: Letters from the World.* New York: Corinth Books, 1970.

Hazo, Samuel, ed. *A Selection of Contemporary Religious Poetry.* Glen Rock, N.J.: Paulist Press, 1963.

Higginson, William J., with Penny Harter. *The Haiku Handbook: How to Write, Share, and Teach Haiku.* Tokyo: Kodansha, 1985. 2 haiku.

Joyce Kilmer's Anthology of Catholic Poets. Revised edition. New York: Doubleday Image Books, 1955.

Judson, John, ed. *Voyages to the Inland Sea, IV. Essays & Poems.* Center for Contemporary Poetry, University of Wisconsin—La Crosse, 1974.

Kacian, Jim, Philip Rowland, and Allan Burns, ed. *Haiku in English: The First Hundred Years.* Introduction by Billy Collins. New York and London: W. W. Norton & Co., 2013. 13 haiku.

Kennedy, X. J., ed. *An Introduction to Poetry.* 4th edition. Little, Brown and Company, 1978 5th ed., 1982.

———. *Literature: An Introduction to Fiction, Poetry, and Drama.* 2nd ed. Boston: Little, Brown, 1978; 3rd ed., 1982. 2 haiku.

Kooser, Ted, ed. *The Windflower Home Almanac of Poetry.* Lincoln, Neb.: Windflower Press, 1980.

Lee, Lawrence, & Mildred Durham, ed. *Cathedral Poets II: New Poetry,* Pittsburgh: Boxwood Press, 1976.

LeMaster, J. R., comp. and ed. *Poets of the Midwest.* Appalachia, Va.: Young Publications, 1966.

Lentfoehr, Sr. Mary Therese, ed. *I Sing of a Maiden: A Mary Book of Verse.* New York: Macmillan, 1947. Includes poem "Maiden Eyes."

Levertov, Denise, ed. *War Resisters' League Engagement Calendar--Out of War Shadow.* 1967.

McGovern, Robert, & Richard Snyder, ed. *70 on the 70's: A Decades History in Verse.* Ashland, Ohio: Ashland Poetry Press, 1976.

Novak, Robert, ed. *Haiku from the Windless Orchard.* West Lafayette, Ind.: Indiana University–Purdue University, 1977.

Pichaske, David R., ed. *Beowulf to Beatles & Beyond: The Varieties of Poetry.* New York: Macmillan, 1981.

Ray, David, ed. *From A to Z: 200 Contemporary American Poets: 200 Poets from New Letters Magazine.* Chicago: Swallow Press/Athens: Ohio University Press, 1981.

Religion Teacher's Class Record & Planner: 1978–79 School Year. Minneapolis: Winston Press, 1978.

Ross, Bruce, ed. *Haiku Moment: An Anthology of Contemporary North American Haiku.* Boston, Rutland, Vt., and Tokyo: Charles E. Tuttle Co., 1993. 3 haiku.

Rotella, Alexis, comp. *Butterfly Breezes: A One Time Anthology.* Mountain Lakes, N.J.: A. K. Rotella (Jade Mountain), 1981. 24 haiku.

Schott, Webster, & Robert J. Myers, ed. *American Christmas.* 2nd ed. Kansas City, Mo.: Hallmark Cards, 1967.

Stefanik, Ernest & Cis, ed. *Once in a Sycamore: A Garland for John Berryman.* Ruffsdale, Pa.: Rook Press, 1976.

———. *The Sound of a Few Leaves.* Ruffsdale, Pa.: Rook Press, 1977.

Streif, Jan and Mary, ed. *The Best of Bonsai: Haiku, #1.* Prepared for publication in 1977 but probably never printed.

Stryk, Lucien, ed. *Heartland: Poets of the Midwest.* DeKalb: Northern Illinois Press, 1967.

Swede, George, and Eric Amann. "Toward a Definition of the Modern English Haiku." *Cicada* (Toronto), 4:4 (1980), 8. 2 haiku.

Swede, George, and Randy Brooks, ed. *Global Haiku: Twenty-five Poets World-wide.* Northumberland, England / Oakville, Ont.–Niagara Falls, N.Y.: Iron Press / Mosaic Press, 2000. 24 haiku.

Tobin, James Edward, ed. *The Second America Book of Verse (1930–1955).* New York: America Press, 1956.

van den Heuvel, Cor, ed. *The Haiku Anthology: Haiku and Senryu in English.* New York, etc.: Simon & Schuster Touchstone, 1986. Revised [2nd] ed., 1986. 25 haiku and the 3-stanza sequence "The Morning Glory."

———. *The Haiku Anthology: Haiku and Senryu in English.* New York and London: W. W. Norton & Co., 1999. Expanded [3rd] edition. 24 haiku.

Vas Dias, Robert, ed. *Inside Outer Space: New Poems of the Space Age.* Garden City, N.Y.: Anchor Books, 1970.

Weil, James L., ed. *My Music Bent.* New Rochelle, N.Y.: Elizabeth Press, 1973.

———. *Of Poem.* New Rochelle, N.Y.: Elizabeth Press, 1966.

Willmot, Rod, ed. *Erotic Haiku: An Anthology.* Windsor, Ont.: Black Moss Press, 1983. 2 haiku and 2 3-haiku sequences: "3 Ages of Man" and "After Solomon."

Winke, Jeffrey, and Charles Rossiter, ed. *Third Coast Haiku Anthology.* Milwaukee, Wis.: House of Words, 1978. 2 haiku.

Essays, reviews, and interviews

Hayes, Dennis. "Magic and the Magician," interview with Raymond Roseliep. *Today* 19:1 (October 1963), 18.

Roseliep, Raymond. "By What Is Not the World." *Poetry* 107:6 (March 1966), 394–96.

———. "Commentary" [on a triptych of haiku by Satoshi Hirasawa and a haiku by Sr. Mary Thomas Eulberg]. *Outch* 5:1 (Spring 1980).

———. "Cry, Windmill: Haiku and Metaphor." *High/Coo* 2:7 (February 1978), 2–3. Reprinted in *HSA Frogpond* 1:2 (May 1, 1978).

———. "Devilish Wine." John Judson, ed. *Voyages to the Inland Sea IV: Essays and Poems by Alvin Greenberg, George Chambers and Raymond Roseliep.* Center for Contemporary Poetry (La Crosse, Wis:, Murphy Library, University of Wisconsin, 1974). Reprinted in a shorter form in David Dayton, ed., *A Roseliep Retrospective* (1980), 16–17.

———. "From Woodcarver to Wordcarver." *Poetry* 107:5 (February 1966), 326–30.

———. "The Haiku Moment." *Thoreau Journal Quarterly* 10:2 (April 1978), 34.

———. "I Celebrate Myself." *High/Coo* 3:9 (August 1978), 3.

———. Interview. *The Witness* (Dubuque archdiocesan newspaper), November 28, 1963, 10–11. No interviewer is listed.

———. "Michael Dudley, through the green fuse." *Wind Chimes* 9 (1983), 58–59.

———. "'News That Stays News': Five Classic Haiku." *Haiku Review '80.* Battle Ground, Ind.: High/Coo Press 1980, 14–15.

———. "On a Rhyming Planet." *Cicada* 3:1 (1979), 30–33.

———. "On Figures of Speech and Anna Vakar. The Forum—Comment/Commentary." *Wind Chimes* 5 (summer 1982), 55–56.

———. "Our Land & Our Sea & Hallelujah." *Poetry* 111:3 (December 1967), 189–95.

———. "A Poet's Belief, *The Catholic World,* 219:1 (January/February 1976), 41–43.

———. "The Pun, a Haiku Tool." *High/Coo* 4:14 (November 1979), 2–5.

———. "Raptures and Roses." *Cicada* 4:2/3 (autumn 1979), 1–5.

———. "This Haiku of Ours." *Bonsai* 1:3 (19 July 1976), 11–20.

———. "A Time to Rime." *HSA Frogpond* 1:1 (February 1978), 18–20.

———. "Tree, Lake, Moon: and Man." *Poetry* 108:1 (April 1966), 54–57.

———. "Under My Japanese Yew." *Cicada* (Toronto) 3:1 (spring 1978), 1–5.

Roseliep, Raymond, and M.R. Doty. "In Memory: The Inner Light of Raymond Rose-liep," Haiku Society of America Twentieth Anniversary Book Committee, ed. *A Haiku Path: The Haiku Society of America 1968–1988.* New York: Haiku Society of America, 1994. Reprints of Roseliep's essays "Devilish Wine" and "The Haiku of Ours," from Dayton, ed., *A Roseliep Retrospective.*

Roseliep, Raymond, and Robert Spiess. "Downpour: Author and Reader," essays on "downpour/ my 'I-Thou'/ T-shirt." *Modern Haiku* 14:2 (Summer 1983: Memorial Issue for Kay Titus Mormino), 34–35.

———. "'Monarch Drying': Author and Reader," *Modern Haiku* 14:2 (Autumn 1983), 19.

Roseliep, Raymond, Edna G. Purviance, and Doug Ingels. "The Sponsors Speak." *Portals* 1:2 (July 1978), 30–33. Panel discussion of haiku by 7 unidentified poets.

"Raymond Roseliep, Priest, Poet and Teacher" [interview with an unnamed reporter]. *Telegraph Herald*, February 24, 1963, 17 and 24.

Edited works

Lloyd, David. *Snowman: Haiku.* Pilot Light Editions/The Rook Press, 1978.

Roseliep, Raymond, ed. "Some Letters of Lionel Johnson." PhD dissertation, University of Notre Dame, 1954.

———. *Into the Round Air.* Derry, Pa.: Thistle Publications, 1977.

2. WORKS ABOUT RAYMOND ROSELIEP

Essays and reviews

Andrews, David. "Listen to Light." *Brussels Sprout* 3:2 (1981).

Bauerly, Donna. "Flute Over Walden: A Review." *Delta Epsilon Sigma Journal* 21:3 (October 1976), 98–101.

———. "One More Roseliep," *Studia Mystica* 7:2 (Summer 1984), 3–12.

———. "*Rabbit in the Moon,* by Raymond Roseliep." *Wind Chimes* 12 (1984), 10–15. Reprinted from *Delta Epsilon Sigma Journal* 29:1 (March 1984), 4–7.

———. "*Rabbit in the Moon.*" *Delta Epsilon Sigma Journal* 29:1 (March 1984), 4–7. Reprinted in *Wind Chimes* 12 (1984), 10–15.

———. "Raymond Roseliep: Where Are You Going? Where Have You Been?" *A Roseliep Retrospective,* 29–44.

———. "*Swish:* A Review." *Delta Epsilon Sigma Bulletin* 27:2 (May 1982), 61–62.

———. "*The Still Point:* A Review." *Delta Epsilon Sigma Bulletin* 25:2 (May 1980), 59–62.

Berrigan, Daniel. "The Season of Youth." *Today,* May 1964, 29–30.

Boldman, Bob. "Book Review: *The Still Point.*" *Portals* 3.2 (1980), 9.

———. "Book Review: *A Roseliep Retrospective,* David Dayton, ed." *Portals* 3:3 (1980), 27.

Bostok, Jan. "Review: *Flute Over Walden: Thoreauhaiku* by Raymond Roseliep." *Tweed* 5:2, 36–38.

Bradley, Sam. "Four Poets Take Note," *Mutiny* 4:1 (1961), 19–26.

Brickley, Chuck. "*The Still Point: Haiku of 'Mu.'*" *Modern Haiku* 11:2 (Summer 1980), 32.

———. "*Listen to Light.*" *Modern Haiku* 12:2 (Summer 1981), 32–34.

———. *"Firefly in My Eyecup."* *Modern Haiku* 10:3 (Autumn 1979), 38–39.

———. *"Sky in My Legs."* *Modern Haiku* 10:3 (Autumn 1979), 52–53.

Books Received [*Flute Over Walden*]. *John Berryman Studies* 2:3 (1976).

Books Received, *Sun in His Belly*/Raymond Roseliep." *Bonsai* 2:1 (April 19, 1977), 32.

Brooks, Randy. "Contemporary Haiku: Focus Midwest." *The Old Northwest* 6:1 (Spring 1980).

———. "Haiku, Poetry of Being." *Cicada* (Toronto) 4:1 (1980), 3–9.

———. "Raymond Roseliep's Contribution to Haiku in English: A Bibliography." *Haiku Review '82*, 32–34.

———. "The Haiku Communication Process." *Muse Pie* 1:1 (May 1981), 10–19.

———. "The Love Poetry of Raymond Roseliep." *Modern Haiku* 40:3 (Autumn 2009), 22–37.

———. "A Spiritual Quest Through the Haiku of Raymond Roseliep." Paper delivered at the Midwest—The Cradle of American Haiku Conference, Mineral Point, Wis., August 24, 2008. Published in *Bottle Rockets* 18 (2008), 74–86.

Cargas, Harry. "Raymond Roseliep: Poet-Priest." *The Catholic World*, 49:5 (December 1977), 228–29.

Cotter, James Finn. *"Flute Over Walden: Thoreauhaiku."* *America* 135:6 (1976), 129–30.

Donovan, Diane C. *"A Roseliep Retrospective."* *Abraxas* 23/24 (1981), 129–31.

———. *"Firefly in My Eyecup."* *Modern Haiku* 10:3 (Autumn 1979), 38–39.

———. *"Flute Over Walden."* *Conservation Call* [San Diego, Calif.]. November–December 1976, 37.

———. *"Flute Over Walden."* *Modern Haiku* 7:3 (Fall 1976), 47.

———. "Human Love and Happy Anguish." *The North American Mentor* 2:1 (Spring 1965), 9–10.

Eulberg, Sr. Mary Thomas. "Poet of Finespun Filaments: Raymond Roseliep." *A Roseliep Retrospective*, 11–15.

Geisler, Pete. "Fr. Raymond Roseliep Caught in 'Small Rain.'" *The Lorian*, October 13, 1963, 3.

Goldstein, Sanford. *"Listen to Light."* *High/Coo* 5:20 (1981).

Gorman, LeRoy. *"Rabbit in the Moon,* by Raymond Roseliep." *Wind Chimes* 12 (1984), 8–10.

Harr, Lorraine Ellis. *"Flute Over Walden."* *Dragonfly* 4:3 (July 1976), 20, 66.

Hayes, Dennis. "Conversation with a Poet: The Method and the Art of Father Ray Roseliep, the Famous Priest/poet. *Acorns & Oaks* (Davenport, Iowa) 5:2 (June 5, 1964), 4–12.

Hayes, Dennis. *"Love Makes the Air Light."* *The Scholastic* (University of Notre Dame), January 21, 1966, 25.

Hayes, Dennis. "Magic and the Magician. A Conversation with Father Raymond Roseliep on the Poet, His Method and his Art." *Today* 19:1 (October 1963), 20.

Heinrichs, Vincent. "Quiet Intensity" [review of *Walk in Love*]. *Chicory* 1 (1978), 4–6.

Higginson, William J. *"Swish of Cow Tail."* *Modern Haiku* 13:2 (Summer 1982), 31–32.

———. "The Joy of Erotic Haiku." *Modern Haiku* 14:3 (Autumn 1983), 40.

Inez, Colette. "Huzzah for the Kosmos. *Listen to Light.* *Parnassus* (Fall/Winter 1981), 244–46.

———. *"Swish of Cow Tail."* "Poetry in Review." *Parnassus* (issue and date not recorded).

Isbell, Harold. "The Small Rain." *The Catholic Worker* 30:4 (November 1963), 4–7.

Keith, Joseph Joel. "Spotlighting Excellence. An Appraisal of Eight Original Poets. Raymond Roseliep." *Mutiny* 4:1 (1961–62), 58–59.

"*The Earth We Swing On,* by Raymond Roseliep." *Frogpond* 8:1 (February 1985), 38.

———. "*The Earth We Swing On,* by Raymond Roseliep." *Frogpond* 8:2 (May 1, 1985), 34–36.

———. "*Light Footsteps.*" *Modern Haiku* 7:4 (November 1976), 45.

———. "Light Will Wheel to a Point Sharper than Rain: Commentary on *A Roseliep Retrospective. Delta Epsilon Sigma Bulletin* 25:4 (December 1980), 113–16.

———. "*Listen to Light.*" *Choice* (July–August 1981), 180.

———. "*Listen to Light.*" *Frogpond* 4:3 (1981).

———. "*Listen to Light.*" *Frogpond* 4:4 (1981), 34–36

———. "A Rich Harvest: Haiku Books of 1982–1983." *Haiku Review '84.* Battle Ground, Ind.: High/Coo Press, 1984, 2–15.

———. "*Step on the Rain: Haiku.*" *Modern Haiku* 9:2 (Summer 1978), 14–15.

Logan, John. "Priest and Poet." *Mutiny* 3:2 (spring 1961), 125–29.

"*Love Makes the Air Light.*" *Virginia Kirkus Bulletin*, September 15, 1965.

Mannere, Louis. "A Rare Brew" [review of *Light Footsteps: Haiku*]. *Chicory* 1 (1978), 10–14.

Martin, Dick. "Professor at Loras College Leads Three Lives." *The Telegraph Herald* (Dubuque, Iowa). No date listed on the clipping.

McDonnell, Thomas P. "Three Unpublished Poets." *America* 105:5 (April 29, 1961), 212–13.

Mullen, John. "Poetry, the Poet and Father Roseliep." *Sketchbook* (Spring 1964), 33–34.

Nusbaum, Willene H. "*Light Footsteps.*" *Modern Haiku* 8:1 (Winter–Spring 1977), 45.

Orlovitz, Gil. "Four Poets Take Note," *Mutiny* 4:1 (1961), 19–26.

Pauly, Bill. "*Step on the Rain.*" *Uzzano* 9/10 (Spring–Summer 1978), 14.

———. "The Various Light." *Lower Stumpf Lake Review* (St. John's University, Collegeville, Minn., 1967), 8.

Philbrick, Charles. "Four Poets Take Note," *Mutiny* 4:1 (1961), 19–26.

———. "Poems for Our Time" in *The Louisville Courier-Journal*, 1959.

Rader, R. W. Grandinetti. "*Rabbit in the Moon*: Book Review with Personal Note." *Frogpond* 7:1 (1984), 28–29.

———. "*Listen to Light.*" *Muse-Pie* 1:1 (1981).

Rielly, Edward. "Raymond Roseliep: First Poet." *Wind Chimes* 12 (1984), 44–46.

"Raymond Roseliep, *Rabbit in the Moon.*" *Wind Chimes* 10 (1983), 64.

Roberts, Hortense Roberta. "He Carves Heads on Cherrystones" [review of *Sun in His Belly*]. *Chicory* 1 (1978), 13–15.

———. "*Listen to Light.*" *Delta Epsilon Sigma Bulletin* 26:2 (1981), 58–60.

———. "*Sailing Bones: Haiku* by Raymond Roseliep." *High/Coo* 4:13 (August 1979).

Roffman, Rosaly DeMaios. "*Listen to Light.*" *Library Journal*, May 15, 1981, 1982.

"Roseliep, Raymond, *Listen to Light.*" *Wind Chimes* 2 (1981), 63.

Rooney, James P. "*Flute Over Walden.*" *Modern Haiku* 7:3 (Fall 1976), 44.

Rotella, Alexis. "Living Haiku, *Listen to Light*, by Raymond Roseliep." *Frogpond* 7:1 (1984), 21–22.

———. "*Rabbit in the Moon*, by Raymond Roseliep." *Frogpond* 7:1 (1984), 36–37.

———. "*Listen to Light.*" *East-West Journal* 13:7 (1983), 77–78.

"*Sailing Bones & A Day in the Life of Sobi-Shi,* both by Raymond Roseliep." *HSA Frogpond* 2:1 (February 1, 1979), 3.

Sato, Hiroaki. "*Aware—A Haiku Primer,* by Betty Drevniok; *American Haiku,* by Ross Figgins and Frank Higgins; *Listen to Light: Haiku,* by Raymond Roseliep; *Dengonban Messages,* by James Kirkup." *Frogpond* 4:3 (1981), 33–35.

"Sky in My Legs, by Raymond Roseliep." *HSA Frogpond* 2:3, 4 (November 1, 1979), 8.

Spiess, Robert. *"Sailing Bones, Sky in My Legs, and A Day in the Life of Sobi-Shi."* *Modern Haiku* 10:1 (Winter–Spring 1979), 50–52.

———. *"Rabbit in the Moon."* *Modern Haiku* 15:1 (Winter–Spring 1984), 35–37.

———. *"The Earth We Swing On: Haiku."* *Modern Haiku* 16:1 (Winter–Spring 1985), 67–68.

———. *"'Downpour': Author and Reader."* *Modern Haiku* 14:2 (Summer 1983), 34–35

Stefanile, Selma. *"Step on the Rain,* Haiku by Raymond Roseliep." *High/Coo* 2:6 (November 1977), 2.

———. *"Step on the Rain: Haiku."* *Modern Haiku* 8:4 (Autumn 1977), 47.

———. *"Step on the Rain: Haiku."* *Modern Haiku* 9:3 (Fall 1978), 34.

———. *"Step on the Rain: Haiku."* *Modern Haiku* 10:1 (Winter-Spring 1979), 42.

Swede, George. "Roseliep's Past Tense Haiku." *Frogpond* 7:1 (1984), 55.

———. *"Swish of Cow Tail."* *Inkstone* 1:1 (Summer 1982).

———. *"Swish of Cow Tail,* by Raymond Roseliep." *Wind Chimes* 4 (Spring 1982), 68.

———. *"The Earth We Swing On."* *Frogpond* 8:1 (February 1985), 38.

———. "The Roseliep Library." *Wind Chimes* 12 (1984), 68.

Vakar, Anna. "On Poetic Devices and Raymond Roseliep, The Forum—Comment/ Commentary." *Wind Chimes* 4 (1982), 62.

Van Dore, Wade. "Book Review" [*Flute Over Walden*]. *Thoreau Journal Quarterly* 8:4 (1976), 4.

Weil, James Weil. "Poetry Through the Spectrometer," in "Four Poets Take Note," *Mutiny* 4:1 (1961), 24–26.

Willmot, Rod. "The Woodcock's Beak: Book Reviews" (including *Listen to Light*). *Cicada* (Toronto) 5:3 (1981), 25–26.

———. "The Woodcock's Beak: Book Reviews" (including *The Still Point*). *Cicada* (Toronto) 4:2 (1980), 29–30.

Zderad, Josef. "Poems That Urge, Beckon, Invite and Dare" [review of *A Beautiful Woman Moves with Grace*]. *Chicory* 1 (1978), 7–9.

———. "Walk in Love." *Encore* 11 (Spring 1977).

Commemorative and memorial works

Chicory Number One, 1978: Raymond Roseliep Issue (Ernest and Cis Stefanik, ed.). Contains the following tributes: Raymond Roseliep, 6-haiku sequence "From a Rookery," 3; Vincent Heinrichs, review of *Walk in Love* "Quiet Intensity," 4–6; Josef Zderad, "Poems That Urge, Beckon, Invite and Dare," Review of *A Beautiful Woman Moves with* Grace, 7–9; Louis Mannere, "A Rare Brew," 10–12; Hortense Roberta Roberts, "He Carves Heads on Cherrystones," 13–15; Raymond Roseliep, 3-haiku sequence "Night Piece," 16.

Frogpond 7:1 (1984; Alexis K. Rotella, ed.) memorial section: Alexis Rotella, dedicatory editorial, 3; A. K. Wilson, one haiku, 4; Ruth Eshbaugh, 3 haiku, 4; Marco Fraticelli, "for R. R." (4 haiku), 5; Elizabeth Searle Lamb, "for R.R." (one haiku), 5; Bob Boldman, "for RR" (5 haiku), 6; LeRoy Gorman, 2 haiku, 6; David LeCount, one haiku, 7; Tim Jamieson, one haiku, 7; Lequita Watkins, 2 haiku, 7; Steve Dalachinsky, 3 haiku, 8; Stephen Hobson, 3 haiku, 8; Charles D. Nethaway, 5 haiku, 9; Ann Newell, "Sequence for R. R." (5 haiku), 10; Elizabeth Marshall, 2 haiku, 10; Hal Roth, "for raymond" (2 haiku), 11; Geraldine C. Little, one haiku with headnote: "Raymond Roseliep had a collection of antique Christmas cards which he loved (specifically Santa Clauses)," 11. Geraldine Clinton Little, 4-haiku sequence "Theme and Variations for Raymond Roseliep, Dec. 6, 1983," 16.

Frogpond 15:2 (Fall–Winter 1992): Sr. Mary Thomas Eulberg, essay "Father Raymond Roseliep, Poet, Priest, Professor, Friend," 60–71.

Modern Haiku 15:1 (Winter–Spring 1984; Robert Spiess, ed.): "This issue of *Modern Haiku* is dedicated to the Memory of Raymond Roseliep August 11, 1917–December 6, 1983." One Roseliep haiku appears on page 3 and "11 haiku by Raymond Roseliep" on pp. 4–5.

Modern Haiku 15:2 (Summer 1984; Robert Spiess, ed.). Contains editorial by Robert Spiess, "In Tribute to Raymond Roseliep," 4–5, and haiku by the following: Geraldine C. Little, 6, 10; Gloria H. Procsal, 6; Elizabeth Searle Lamb, 6; Frederick Gasser (2), 6; Evelyn Tooley Hunt, 6; Lenard D. Moore, 7; Sr. Mary Thomas Eulberg, 7, 10; L. A. Davidson (2) 10; Alexis Rotella, 4-haiku linked sequence "Christmas Rose," 7; LeRoy Gorman, acrostic haiku, spelling R A Y M O N D R O S E L I E P, 8; M. R. Doty, quote from "'The Soul's Buried Light': A Conversation with Roseliep," 8; H. Ronan, 8; Frederick Gasser, eyeku with "sobi*shi" arranged in the pattern of a kite, 9; David Locher, 10; C. S. Wainwright, 10; Barbara McCoy, haiku "after reading Raymond Roseliep's *Rabbit in the Moon*, 11; Virginia Brady Young (2), 11; Emily Romano, 11; Robert Spiess, 11.

Outch 8:1 (Spring 1984; Nobuo Hirasawa, ed.). Dedicated to the memory of Raymond Roseliep. Contains these tributes: Nobuo Hirasawa, 6-stanza linked sequence "A Dirge," inside front cover; Raymond Roseliep, 6 haiku.

A Roseliep Retrospective: Poems & Other Words By & About Raymond Roseliep. David Dayton, ed. Ithaca, N.Y.: Alembic Press, 1980. Contains the following: Raymond Roseliep, poem "for Katherine Anne Porter, loving friend of many years;" 7; Colette Inez, poem "From His Life in Iowa Father Raymond Roseliep Takes a Morning Out for Poems," 10; Sr. Mary Thomas Eulberg, from "Poet of Finespun Filaments: Raymond Roseliep," 11–15; John Judson, haiku sequence "For Raymond, By Early Sun," 15; Raymond Roseliep, essay from "Devilish Wine." 16–17; Dennis Schmitz, poem "To Raymond Roseliep," 18; Raymond Roseliep, essay from "This Haiku of Ours," 19–22; M. R. Doty, "'The Soul's Buried Light': A Conversation with Roseliep." 23–27; Raymond Roseliep, haiku sequence titled "M. R. Doty," 28 (note from Roseliep: "in appreciation for M. R's response to another morning-glory sequence we discussed in December 1979"); Donna Bauerly, essay "Raymond Roseliep: 'Where Are You Going? Where Have You Been?'" 29–34; Bill Pauly, essay "A Joyous Dance in Timelessness," 45–51; Thomas Reiter, poem "Returnings," 52–53. William Stafford, poem "Austere Hope, Daily Faith," 53; and Raymond Roseliep, haiku "a little love," 54. A second section, "A Roseliep Anthology," selected by David Dayton, includes: "from *The Linen Bands*," 56–64; "from *The Small Rain*," 65–70; "from *Love Makes the Air Light*," 71–81; from *A Beautiful Woman Moves with Grace*," 82; "from *Walk in Love*," 83–85; from *Tip the Earth*," 86–99; Some Early Steps in Haiku, 100–1; "A Selection of 'Thoreauhaiku'," 102–3; "In Full Stride: A Haiku Sampler," 104–5; "New Haiku: As the Swift Seasons Roll," 106–9; "Books of Poems by Raymond Roseliep," 110; "Books Edited by Raymond Roseliep," 111; Roseliep's entry from *Who's Who in America*. the back cover has Roseliep's haiku "Eschatology."

Studia Mystica 7:2 (Summer 1984, Mary Giles, ed.): "Dedicated to Raymond Roseliep 1917–1983." Contains the following tributes: Donna Bauerly, "One More Roseliep," 3–12; David Locher, poem "For Raymond Roseliep: Final Words," 13; Raymond

Roseliep, 12-haiku series "From a Haiku Diary....," 14–15; Elizabeth Searle Lamb, essay "Words for Raymond Roseliep," 16–17, and poem "Mission Ruins of San Gregorio de Abó (central New Mexico)," 18–19; Thomas Reiter, poem "Letter to Raymond Roseliep," 20–21; Dennis Schmitz, essay "Ray Roseliep," 22–24.

Wind Chimes 12 (1994; Hal Roth, editor). "In Memoriam. Raymond Roseliep. Priest/ Professor/Poet. August 11, 1917–December 16, 1983, "Against the Night." Glen Burnie, Md. Wind Chimes Press, 1984. Contains the following tributes: Elizabeth Searle Lamb, one haiku, 1; Donna Bauerly, one haiku, 1; Father Robert Vogl, "Funeral Homily for Father Roseliep, December 9, 1983," 2–4; James Minor, one haiku, 4; Bill Pauly, 7-haiku sequence "Father My Heart," 5; David Locher, "Peter's Poem for Raymond," 6; Ty Hadman, 8-haiku sequence "A Day With Sobi-Shi," 7; "Two Reviews: LeRoy Gorman, "*Rabbit in the Moon*, 8–10, and Donna Bauerly, "*Rabbit in the Moon*," 10–15. Jerry Kilbride, 3-haiku sequence "a carol for raymond," 16; LeRoy Gorman, 2 haiku, one titled "Christmas 1983, 17; Daniel Rogers, poem "In Memoriam: Raymond Roseliep — Feast of St. Nicholas, 1983," 18; Bob Boldman, 21-haiku sequence "The Moon of Li-Po (In remembrance of Sobi-Shi)," 19–21; Geraldine C. Little, 7-haiku sequence "Horae Canonicae for Raymond Roseliep, December 6, 1983," 22; Sr. Mary Thomas Eulberg, haiku "Breakfast, December 6, 1983," 23; Dennis Schmitz, "Ray Roseliep," 22–24; Sr. Mary Thomas Eulberg, essay "Month's Mind for Raymond Roseliep," 23–25, 3 haiku, 26, and 3-haiku sequence "Trilogy," 27; Bernard Kennedy OFW, 8 haiku, 28–29, and essay "The Nazareth Man: Musings on Roseliep," 30–31; L. A. Davidson, 8 haiku, 32; Patricia Wild, poem "To the Minstrel Roseliep," 33; Steve Dalachinsky, "all by myself: from a solo renga for raymond roseliep," 34; Guy R. Beining, poem "silence," 35; Loke Hilikimani, 7-haiku sequence "In the spirit of ...," 36; C. S. Wainwright, 5 haiku, 37; Lenard D. Moore, 3 haiku, 38; Steve Dalachinsky, 2 haiku, 38; George Swede, 2 haiku, 39; Leatrice Lifshitz, one haiku, 39; Rev. Thomas J. Carpenter, essay "Ever the Gentleman," 40; Barbara McCoy, one haiku, 41; John Pfaff, one haiku, 41; Gloria H. Procsal, one haiku, 41; Ty Hadman, 3-haiku sequence "A Trinity for Raymond Roseliep," 42; Bob Spiess, "Untitled — excerpt from Raymond Roseliep's last letter," 42; James Minor, 3-haiku sequence "Cor ad Cor Loquitur," 43; Edward J. Rielly, essay including haiku "Raymond Roseliep: First Poet," 44–46; Margaret Saunders, one haiku, 46; Marlene Mountain, 4 one-line haiku "rr sequence," 47; Zolo, one haiku, 47; Bob Spiess, excerpt from a letter to Roseliep dated February 1983, 49; and Anne McKay, "From a Letter," 49.

3. OTHER WORKS CITED IN TEXT

Anonymous. "O Western Wind" (1500). http://pinkmonkey.com/dl/library1/west_w .pdf; accessed March 15, 2014.

Belleau, Janick. "Anna Vakar." "Haiku: Women Pioneers in Canada (1928–1985)." Haiku Canada website; http://www.haikucanada.org/resources/articles/3.pdf; accessed March 15, 2014.

Bogan, Louise. *Achievement in American Poetry, 1900–1950*. Chicago: H. Regnery Co., 1951.

Campbell, Joseph. *The Hero with a Thousand Faces*. Princeton, N.J.: Princeton University Press, 1972.

Crane, Hart. "My Grandmother's Love Letters." *Hart Crane: Complete Poems and Selected Letters and Prose*. New York: Liveright Publishing Corporation, 1966.

Dickinson, Emily. Poem 636, "The way I read a letter," and Poem 1129, "Tell all the truth but tell it slant." *The Poems of Emily Dickinson*, edited by Thomas H. Johnson. Cambridge, Mass.: The Belknap Press of Harvard University Press, Copyright © 1951, 1955 by the President and Fellows of Harvard College. Copyright © renewed 1979, 1983 by the President and Fellows of Harvard College. Copyright ©1914, 1918, 1919, 1924, 1929, 1930, 1932, 1935, 1937, 1942, by Martha Dickinson Bianchi. Copyright © 1952, 1957, 1958, 1963, 1965, by Mary L. Hampson.

Eliot, T. S. "The Love Song of J. Alfred Prufrock." *Prufrock and Other Observations*. London: The Egoist, 1917.

Givner, Joan. *Katherine Anne Porter: A Life*. New York: Simon and Schuster, 1982.

Henderson, Harold G. *Introduction to Haiku* (New York: Doubleday, 1958).

Higginson, William J. *Haiku Compass: Directions in the Poetical Map of the United States of America*. Tokyo: Haiku International Association, 1994.

Hiroaki Sato, "HSA definition reconsidered," *Frogpond* 22:3 (1999), 73. http://thehaiku foundation.org/montage/Halloween2009_10_25.pdf.

Kullberg, Mary. *Morning Mist: Through the Seasons with Matsuo Basho and Henry David Thoreau* (New York: Weatherhill Press, 1993).

Lamb, Elizabeth Searle. "A History of Western Haiku" (I) *Cicada* 3:1 (1979), 3–9; (II) "Growth In the 1960's." *Cicada* 3:2 (1979), 3–9; (III) "Period of Expansion." *Cicada* 3:3 (1979), 3–10; (IV) *Cicada* 4:1 (1980).

———. *Across the Windharp, Collected and New Haiku* (Albuquerque, N.M.: La Alameda Press, 1999). Introduction by Miriam Sagan.

Lynch, Thomas Paul. *An Original Relation to the Universe: Emersonian Poetics of Immanence and Contemporary American Haiku* (PhD dissertation, University of Oregon, 1989).

Mankin, Monica. "Thomas Reiter—Poetry." *Connotation Press* website. http://connotation press.com /poetry/802-thomas-reiter-poetry26. Accessed March 15, 2014.

Marshall, Ian. *Walden by Haiku*. Athens, Ga.: University of Georgia Press, 2009.

Mormino, Kay Titus. "Across the Editor's Desk." *Modern Haiku*. 1:4 (autumn 1970), 3.

———, ed. *Haiku Anthology: 1968*. Danbury, Conn.: T.N.P.C. [The Nutmegger Poetry Club], no date [1968].

O'Donohue, John. *Anam Cara* (New York: HarperCollins, 1997).

"Official Definitions of Haiku and Related Terms." Haiku Society of America website; http://www.hsa-haiku.org/archives/HSA_Definitions_2004.html.

Pauly, Bill. *Wind the Clock by Bittersweet*. (Battle Ground, Ind.: High/Coo Press, 1977).

Reichhold, Jane. "Haiku Magazines in USA." *These Women Writing Haiku, Chapter Three*, ©1986–1998.

Russo, Dave. "Comparative Haiku," selected by Allan Burns," *Montage* 34 (week of October 25, 2009). http://www.thehaikufoundation.org/2009/10/25/montage-34/.

———. "Haiku Definitions" North Carolina Haiku Society website, http://nc-haiku .org/haiku-definitions. Accessed March 15, 2014.

Shakespeare, William. *King Lear*. Act III, Scene 4. *The Complete Plays and Poems of William Shakespeare*. Boston: Houghton Mifflin Co., 1942.

Shirane, Haruo. "Beyond the Haiku Moment: Bashō, Buson, and Modern Haiku Myths," *Modern Haiku*, 31:1 (Winter–Spring 2000): 48–63. Also available online at http:// www.haikupoet.com/definitions/beyond_the_haiku_moment.html.

Spiess, Robert. "The Problem of the Expression of Suchness in Haiku." *Modern Haiku* 7:4 (November 1976), 26–28.

———, ed. *A Haiku Poet's Thoreau: Passages from the Writings of Henry David Thoreau.* Madison, Wis.: self-published [mimeographed], 1974.

"Submission Guidelines and Policies." Modern Haiku website, http//www.modernhaiku .org /submissions .html.

Thoreau, Henry David. *Walden; or Life in the Woods.* Boston: Ticknor and Fields, 1854.

Tranströmer, Tomas. *The Great Enigma: New Collected Poems.* Translated from the Swedish by Robin Fulton. New York: New Directions, 2006.

Trumbull, Charles, "The American Haiku Movement, Part I. Haiku in English" and "Part II. The Internet and World Haiku," *Modern Haiku* 36:3 (Autumn 2005) and 37:1 (Spring 2006).

Van Dore, Wade. "Thoreauhaiku." *Thoreau Journal Quarterly* 5:4 (October 1973), 11–13.

Whitman, Walt. "Out of the Cradle Endlessly Rocking." *Leaves of Grass,* "Death-Bed Edition." New York: Modern Library, 1892.

4. Archival Materials

Raymond Roseliep's publications and papers are located in two rooms at the Loras College Academic Resources Center (LCARC), Dubuque, Iowa. A description and searchable database of the Roseliep collection is available online at libguides.loras .edu/roseliep.

5. Principal Correspondents and Persons Interviewed

Bauerly, Donna (1934–). Correspondence and personal interviews, 1978–1983. Author of this biography.

Beck, Rev. Robert (1940–). Bauerly interview, September 22, 2009, Loras College. Beck is a faculty member in Religious Studies at Loras College.

Becker, Marcella Anderson Becker (1911–2008). Three interviews by Bauerly, 2003, 2004, and 2005, at Sunset Park Retirement Village, Dubuque, Iowa, and at her daughter Margy's home. Becker's father, Albert Anderson was Raymond Roseliep's maternal uncle. Marcella maintained a genealogy of the Anderson and Roseliep families, including "Ancestors of Raymond Roseliep (1917–1983)" and generously made available these records as well as oral family history.

Boldman, Bob (1950–). Correspondence, 1980–1981. Haiku poet.

Brockway, George P. (1916–2001). Correspondence with Roseliep. He was president of W. W. Norton & Company.

Brooks, Randy M. (1954–). Correspondence, 1978–1983. Haiku poet, critic, editor, publisher, and college professor.

Bull, Gayle (1936–). E-mail correspondence, 2013. She was editor with her husband James Bull of the journal *American Haiku.*

Burden, Jean (1914–2008). Correspondence, 1974–1980. Poetry editor at *Yankee* magazine.

Carpenter, Margaret. Correspondence, 1966–1983. Friend who commissioned a reading of Roseliep's astrological sign and a color chart.

Chenoweth, Helen Stiles (1890–1987). Correspondence, 1970. Associate Editor, *Modern Haiku,* 1970.

Christensen, Vera. Correspondence, 1966–1983. Owner of Christensen's Greenhouse who sent flowers to Roseliep's mother Anna as well as to Roseliep on multiple occasions in multiple years.

Dammacco, Kelly. Correspondence, 1965. Member of the W. W. Norton editorial staff.

Dayton, David, and Ruth Dayton. Correspondence, 1977–1983. David was editor and publisher of Alembic Press, which began in Ithaca, N.Y. Ruth Dayton, his mother, managed the day-to-day business from 1982 to 1986 while David was living in Mexico and Puerto Rico.

Doty, Mark (1953–). Correspondence, 1978–1982. Poet and editor of *Blue Buildings*, 1978–1980.

Eberhart, Richard (1904–2005). Correspondence, 1970–1980. Poet.

Friedl, Msgr. Francis. Bauerly interview, summer 2007. Friend and classmate of Roseliep, priest of the Dubuque Archdiocese and President of Loras College, 1971–1977.

Frost, Robert (1874–1963). Correspondence, 1959? Poet.

Givner, Joan (1936–). Correspondence, 1978–1981. Biographer of Katherine Anne Porter.

Gorman, Anne. Correspondence, 1967. Editor at W. W. Norton.

Gorman, LeRoy (1949–). Correspondence, 1980–1983. Poet and editor of *Haiku Canada Review* and many other haiku publications.

Hadman, Ty (1948–). Correspondence, 1979–1983. Haiku poet.

Harr, Lorraine Ellis (1912–2006). Correspondence. Editor of *Dragonfly.*

Hayes, Dennis. Interviewed Roseliep in 1963 and 1964. Poet, playwright, and television scriptwriter.

Heinrichs, Vincent (1937–1988). Correspondence, 1967?–1983. Student of Roseliep's, and he and his wife Denise remained lifelong friends. He was also one of the pallbearers at Roseliep's funeral and an alternate literary executor until his death.

Hirasawa, Nobuo (1935–1985). Correspondence, 1977–1983. Editor of the Japan-based English-language haiku journal *Outch.*

Isbell, Harold M. Student and reviewer of Roseliep's *The Small Rain.* Isbell joined the faculty of the University of Notre Dame in 1963.

Jacobsen, Josephine. Correspondence, 1962–1982. American poet, short story writer, and critic. She was appointed the twenty-first Poet Laureate Consultant in Poetry to the Library of Congress in 1971. She wrote a tribute for a poster-sized broadside advertisement for two books, *A Roseliep Retrospective* and *Listen to Light.*

Jacobsohn, Peter. Correspondence with Roseliep, 1965. Editor for W. W. Norton.

Judson, John (1930–), Correspondence. Poet and editor of Juniper Press and editor of the Center for Contemporary Poetry, University of Wisconsin, La Crosse. Professor Emeritus of English (American Literature) and Creative Writing at the University of Wisconsin, La Crosse.

Kilbride, Jerry (1930–2005). Correspondence with Roseliep, 1981–1983; Bauerly interview, April 2003, Sacramento, Calif. Haiku poet and a founder of the American Haiku Archive.

Klein, Robert (–1983). Correspondence, 1979–1983. Director of the Loras College Library, 1969–2004.

Lamb, Elizabeth Searle (1917–2005). Bauerly interview, May 2004, Santa Fe, N.M. Voluminous correspondence, 1976–1983. Lamb was an early president of the Haiku Society of America, editor of *Frogpond* for eight years, and first honorary curator of the American Haiku Archive (1998–1999).

LeCount, David (1944–). Correspondence, 1981–1983. Haiku poet.

Lehner, Francis (1921–2001). Roseliep correspondence, 1964–1983. Poet, professor of English at Loras College (1955–1985) and colleague of Roseliep's. Editor of the *Delta Epsilon Sigma Bulletin*, 1964–1979.

Levertov, Denise (1923–1997). Correspondence with Roseliep, 1964. Poet.

Locher, David A. (1923–2010). Interviews, September 9, 2002, and February 27, 2003. Student and friend of Roseliep's.

Logan, John (1923–1987). Correspondence, 1960–1982. Poet, critic, and teacher.

Mannere, Louis. Reviewer of Roseliep's work for *Chicory*, 1978.

McHale, John J. Extensive correspondence with Roseliep, 1960–1996. Editor of Newman Press.

Merton, Thomas (1915–1968). Correspondence, 1965. Catholic writer and mystic.

Minor, James. Correspondence, 1978–1983. Poet from Loras College.

Moore, Marianne (1887–1972). Correspondence, 1960–1968. Poet.

Mormino, Kay Titus (1905–1983). Correspondence, 1970–1977. Founder of *Modern Haiku* and its editor 1969–1977.

Mountain, Marlene (Marlene Morelock Wills, 1939–). Correspondence, 1977?–1983.

Otting, Rev. Loras (1936–). Bauerly interview, 2007. Archivist of the Archdiocese of Dubuque.

Palmer, Mary. Interview, 2005. Historian of the town of Farley, Iowa.

Pauly, Bill (1942–). Bauerly interview, June 2003. Poet, especially haiku. Student and friend as well as a correspondent of Roseliep's.

Perkins, Maxwell (1884–1947). Editor at Scribner's.

Porter, Katherine Anne (1890–1980). Correspondence, 1964–1980. Roseliep kept his typed notes of their telephone conversations, 1979–1980.

Rabe, David (1940–). Bauerly telephone interview, October 2005. Obie-winning playwright and former student of Roseliep's.

Rayher, Ed (1953–). Correspondence, 1980–1983. Editor of Swamp Press.

Reilly, Cyril A., (1920-2008) and Renée Travis Reilly. Correspondence, 1980–1983. Cyril had been a priest with Roseliep at Loras College. He and his wife Renée were photographers who collaborated with Roseliep on *The Earth We Swing On*.

Reiter, Thomas (1940–). Bauerly e-mail interviews, March/April, 2011. Correspondence with Roseliep, 1962–1983. Poet, a student of Roseliep's, and lifelong friend. Professor Emeritus, Monmouth University.

Rogers, Rev. Daniel (1927–). Bauerly interview, November 2007. Priest and close friend of Roseliep and his literary executor, 1983–2015.

Rotella, Alexis (1947–). Correspondence, 1983. Poet, artist, founding editor of *Brussels Sprout* (1980), and editor of *Frogpond* (1983–1984)

Roth, Hal (1931–). Correspondence, 1981–1983. Haiku poet and editor of *Wind Chimes*.

Schmitt, Sr. Gracia (1930–). Bauerly interview, July 2002. Dubuque Franciscan nun who often visited Roseliep at Holy Family Hall when Roseliep was chaplain there.

Schmitz, Dennis. (1937–). Bauerly interview, Sacramento, Calif., September 9, 2007. Student of Roseliep's and poet.

Schultz, Charles (1922–2000). Correspondence, 1967–1993. Cartoonist.

Stafford, William (1914–1993). Correspondence, 1965–1974). Poet.

Starr, Kevin (1940–). Bauerly interview, Sacramento, Calif., April 2003. Historian and university professor; California State Librarian, 1994–2004.

Stefanik, Ernest (1944–2008), and Cis Stefanik. Correspondence with Roseliep. Editors of the Rook Press.

Stefanile, Felix (1920–2009) and Selma (1922–). Correspondence with Roseliep. Editors of the poetry journal *Sparrow* and Vagrom Chap Books.

Streif, Jan and Mary. Editors of the haiku journal *Bonsai*, 1976–1978. Correspondence with Roseliep.

Triem, Eve (1902–1992). Correspondence, 1960–1983. Poet.

Trumbull, Charles (1943–). Correspondence and editorial assistance, 2009–2015. Haiku poet and critic; biographer of Elizabeth Searle Lamb; president of the Haiku Society of America, 2004–2005; and editor and publisher of *Modern Haiku*, 2006–2013.

Van Dore, Wade (1899–1989). Correspondence, 1969–1980s. Poetry editor of the *Thoreau Journal Quarterly.*

Vlakos, Jon. Correspondence 1982–1983. Artist and book illustrator.

Vogl, Msgr. Robert (1920–2014). Interviews, June 2003, June 2004, October 2007 and October 2014. Priest of the Archdiocese of Dubuque. Friend and executor of Roseliep's estate.

Wilwert, Joanie (1936–). Genealogical and historical information. Researcher from Bankston, Iowa.

Young, Virginia Brady (1918–2012). Correspondence, 1974–1983. Haiku poet.

Appendix

This curriculum vitae was compiled by Raymond Roseliep and updated frequently, last in 1983. LCARC 325, D:2, 30.

VITA

Raymond Roseliep
Holy Family Hall, 3340 Windsor Ave.
Dubuque, Iowa 52001

BIRTH: Farley, Iowa. 11 August 1917.

EDUCATION:
B.A. (English), Loras College, 1939.
Postgraduate (theological) studies, The Catholic University of America, 1939-1943.
M.A. (English), The Catholic University of America, 1948.
Ph.D. (English), University of Notre Dame, 1954.

ORDINATION:
Roman Catholic priest, St. Raphael's Cathedral, Dubuque, 1943.

APPOINTMENTS:
Assistant Pastor, Immaculate Conception Church, Gilbertville, Iowa, 1943-45.
Managing Editor, *The Witness*, Dubuque, 1945-46.
Loras College, Department of English, 1946-66. Highest rank: Associate professor.
Conducted Creative Writing Workshop, served as moderator of student magazine, The Spokesman.
Poetry Editor, *Sponsa Regis* [now *Sisters Today*], published at St. John's University, Collegeville, Minn., 1959—66.
Poet-in-residence, Georgetown University, summer 1964.
Director of Poetry Workshop at Georgetown's 5th annual

Writers' Conference, summer 1964.
Resident Chaplain, Holy Family Hall (infirmary for Franciscan nuns], 1966—

SOCIETIES, MEMBERSHIPS:
Gallery of Living Catholic Authors
Delta Epsilon Sigma, Alpha Chapter
The State Historical Society of Iowa
The Academy of American Poets
The Marquis Biographical Library Society
The Thoreau Fellowship
The Haiku Society of America (Honorary Member)
Yuki Teikei Haiku Society of the United States and Canada

AWARDS, HONORS:
Magazines & Societies:
Carolina Quarterly
Writers' Digest
Yankee
Modern Haiku
Cicada (Canada)
Poetry Society of Virginia
Yuki Teikei Haiku Society of America and Canada
Thoreau Journal Quarterly
Bonsai
Haiku Appreciation Club
Hawaii Education Association Haiku Contest
The Kenneth F. Montgomery Poetry Award, 1968, Society of Midland Authors, Chicago
The Harold G. Henderson Haiku Award, 1977, Haiku Society, of America
Grand Prize—Shugyo Takaha Award, 1980, Yuki Teikei Haiku Society of the United States and Canada.
Poetry in Public Places Award, 1980. Poem placard placed on more than 2,000 buses in New York State.

BOOKS:
Light Footsteps. Juniper Press, 1976; Second Edition, 1978.
A Beautiful Woman Moves with Grace. The Rook Press, 1976.
Sun in His Belly. High/Coo Press, 1977.
Step on the Rain. The Rook Press, 1977.
Wake to the Bell. The Rook Press, 1977.
A Day in the Life of Sobi-Shi. The Rook Press, 1978.
Sailing Bones. The Rook Press, 1978.
Sky in My Legs. Juniper Press, 1979.

Firefly in My Eyecup. High/Coo Press, 1979.
The Still Point. Uzzano Press, 1979.
A Roseliep Retrospective: Poems & Other Words By and About Raymond Roseliep. Edited by David Dayton. Alembic Press, 1980.
Listen to Light. Alembic Press, 1980.
Swish of Cow Tail. Swamp Press, 1981.
Untitled Collection of Haiku. With photographs by Cyril A. Reilly. In preparation.
Untitled Collection of Haiku. In preparation for 1982 publication.

ANTHOLOGIES (Selected List):
Joyce Kilmer's Anthology of Catholic Poets. Rev. Edition. James Edward Tobin, ed. Image Books, Doubleday & Company, Inc., 1955.
Sealed Unto the Day. The Catholic Poetry Society of America, 1955.
The Second America Book of Verse, 1930-55. James Edward Tobin, ed. The America Press, 1956.
Invitation to the City. The Catholic Poetry Society of America, 1960.
Fire and Sleet and Candlelight: New Poems of the Macabre. August Derleth, ed. Arkham House, 1961.
A Selection of Contemporary Religious Poetry. Samuel Hazo, ed. Deus Books, Paulist Press, 1963.
Of Poetry and Power: Poems Occasioned by the Presidency and by the Death of John F. Kennedy. Basic Books, 1964.
Of Poem. James L. Weil, ed. Elizabeth Press, 1966.
Poets of the Midwest. J. R. LeMaster, ed. Young Publications, 1966.
Heartland: Poets of the Midwest. Lucien Stryk, ed. Northern Illinois Press, *1967.*
American Christmas. Second Edition. Webster Schott & Robert J. Myers, ed. Hallmark Cards, Inc., 1967.
War Resisters' League Engagement Calendar--Out of War Shadow. Denise Levertov, ed. 1967.
Emily Dickinson: Letters from the World. Marguerite Harris, ed. Corinth Books, 1970.
Inside Outer Space. Robert Vas Dias, ed. Anchor Books, Doubleday & Company, Inc., 1970.
My Music Bent. James L. Weil, ed. Elizabeth Press, 1973.
A Celebration of Cats. Jean Burden, ed. Paul S. Eriksson, Inc., 1974.
Ipso Facto: An International Poetry Society Anthology. Robin Gregory, ed. Hub Publications Ltd., Derbyshire, England, 1975.
Out of This World: Poems from the Hawkeye State. Gary

Gildner and Judith Gildner, ed. The Iowa State University Press, 1975.

A Tumult for John Berryman. Marguerite Harris, ed. Dryad Press, 1976.

Encore! Encore! Alice Briley, ed. Allegheny Press, 1976.

Cathedral Poets II: New Poetry. Lawrence Lee & Mildred Durham, ed. The Boxwood Press, 1976.

Once in a Sycamore: A Garland for John Berryman. Ernest & Cis Stefanik, ed. The Rook Press, 1976.

The Sound of a Few Leaves. Ernest & Cis Stefanik, ed. The Rook Press, 1977.

An Introduction to Poetry. Fourth Edition. X. J. Kennedy, ed. Little, Brown and Company, 1978.

Haiku from the Windless Orchard. Robert Novak, ed. IU-PU University, 1977.

Religion Teacher's Class Record & Planner: 1978-79 School Year. Winston Press, 1978.

A Celebration of Cats. Jean Burden, ed. Softcover ed. Popular Library, 1976.

The Windflower Almanac of Poetry. Ted Kooser, ed. Windflower Press, 1980.

Aware—A Haiku Primer. Betty Drevniok, ed. Portals Publications, 1980.

70 on the 70's: A Decade's History in Verse. Robert McGovern & Richard Snyder, ed. The Ashland Poetry Press, 1981.

Beowulf to Beatles & Beyond: The Varieties of Poetry. David R. Pichaske, ed. Macmillan, 1981.

From A to Z: 200 Contemporary American Poets. David Ray, ed. Swallow Press, Ohio University Press, 1981.

An Introduction to Poetry. Fifth Ed. X.J. Kennedy, ed. Little, Brown and Company, 1982.

Literature: An Introduction to Fiction, Poetry, and Drama. 2nd Ed. X.J. Kennedy, ed., Little, Brown and Company, 1978, 3rd Edition, 1

PERIODICALS: Selected List (from over 200 which have published, in various issues, poems, reviews, articles, interviews)

Poetry (Chicago)
The Nation
Shenandoah
The New York Times
The New York Herald Tribune
Prairie Schooner
The Minnesota Review
Chicago Review
Choice

Modern Age
Chicago section of the *Chicago Tribune*
Tribune Magazine
The Colorado Quarterly
The University of Kansas City Review
New Letters
Time
Esquire
The Massachusetts Review
Poetry Northwest
Northeast
The Georgia Review
The Beloit Poetry Journal
Arts in Society
Yankee
The Carolina Quarterly
Sparrow
Elizabeth
The Wormwood Review
The English Journal
College English
Art Journal
Transatlantic Review
South Dakota Review
Thoreau Journal Quarterly
Shaman
Annals of Iowa
Hawk & Whippoorwill
Hawk & Whippoorwill Recalled
Counter/Measures
Poetry Now
The Hollins Critic
Bits
John Berryman Studies
The Journal of Freshwater
Alembic
West Hills Review: A Walt Whitman Journal
Blue Buildings
The Blue Hotel
Studia Mystica
Images
Slow Loris Reader
Voyages
Mutiny
The New Orleans Poetry Journal
Manhattan Review
The Literary Review
Approach

Hartwick Review
Modern Haiku
Gallery Series
Catfancy
Spectrum: The Richmond Tri-Annual Review
Charlatan
Michigan's Voices
The Hartford Courant
The Lake Superior Review
Poetry Venture
North Country Anvil
New World Haiku
Encore
The New Salt Creek Reader
The Echo
Fragments
Wind Magazine
Green's Magazine
Gravida
Bonsai
The Spoon
River Quarterly
Blue Cloud Quarterly
High/Coo
Unaka Range
The Windless Orchard
Green Revolution
Blue Unicorn
Third Coast Archives
Uzzano
Pikestaff Forum
Pikestaff Review
Pilgrimage
Frogpond
Haiku Journal
Portals
The Blue Canary
Muse-Pie
Guts & Grace
Milkweed Chronicle
August Derleth Society Newsletter
Midwest Poetry Review
The Honolulu Advertiser
The Southborough Villager
The New Jersey Poetry Journal
Wind Chimes
Brussels Sprout
The Christian Century

Delta Epsilon Sigma Bulletin
Monks Pond (Thomas Merton, ed.)
Ramparts
Commonweal
America
Catholic World
New Catholic World
The American Ecclesiastical Review
The Catholic Worker
The Critic
The Tablet (London)
The Waterloo Review (Canada)
The Antigonish Review (Canada)
The Dubliner (Ireland)
The Indian P. E. N. (Bombay)
Haiku Spotlight (Japan)
Haiku Magazine (Canada)
Cicada (Canada)
Blackfriars (Cambridge, England)
Outch (Japan)
Poet (India)
Yukuharu (Japan)
Landfall (New Zealand)
The Gorey Detail (Ireland)
Poetry Nippon (Japan)
Haiku Byways (England)
Tweed (Australia)
Hai Hakkosho (Japan)

RECORDINGS:
Lamont Library, Harvard University, 1961.
In preparation: The Library of Congress.

READINGS, LECTURES: High schools, colleges, universities
(before 1966).

BIOGRAPHY: Selected List
Who's Who in the World
Who's Who in America
Who's Who in the Midwest
Contemporary Authors
Who's Who in Religion
Who's Who in American Education
The American Catholic Who's Who
Community Leaders and Noteworthy Americans
Contemporary Poets of the English Language
Dictionary of International Biography
A Directory of American Poets
Directory of American Scholars

International Scholars Directory
International Who's Who in Poetry
Leaders in the Humanities in America
Mondo Cattolico (Italy)
Personalities of the West and Midwest
The Writers Directory
The International Authors and Writers Who's Who